The
Archival
Enterprise

The Archival Enterprise

Modern Archival Principles, Practices, and Management Techniques

BRUCE W. DEARSTYNE

American Library Association
Chicago and London 1993

Cover and text designed by
  Charles Bozett
Composed by Alexander Typesetting
  in Caslon on a Datalogics Pagination System

Printed on 50-pound Glatfelter,
  a pH-neutral stock, and bound
  in Roxite cloth by Braun-Brumfield

The paper used in this publication meets the minimum requirements of American National Standard for Information Sciences—Permanence of Paper for Printed Library Materials, ANSI Z39.48–1984. ∞

Library of Congress Cataloging-in-Publication Data

Dearstyne, Bruce W. (Bruce William), 1944–
    The archival enterprise : modern archival principles, practices,
  and management techniques / Bruce W. Dearstyne.
      p.   cm.
    Includes bibliographical references and index.
    ISBN 0-8389-0602-8
    1. Archives—Administration.   I. Title.
  CD950.D4   1992   92-24279
  025.1—dc20

Printed in the United States of America.

96 95 94 93   5 4 3 2 1

Contents

Acknowledgments

Many people contributed directly or indirectly to the development of THE ARCHIVAL ENTERPRISE. Theodore R. Schellenberg, the most influential teacher and writer on archival matters of his generation, first introduced me to archives and the rewards of archival work through a course he taught at Syracuse University in 1967. Kenneth L. Brock provided an opportunity to work with records by hiring me as a public records analyst with New York Office of State History a few years later. The book draws on many years of working with archivists and historical records programs throughout New York State. It reflects the experience of working with Larry J. Hackman and talented and energetic colleagues at the New York State Archives and Records Administration who have built a program distinguished by its excellence and achievements. It draws on my professional work and on the best writing by the profession's leaders during the past two decades. Teaching an archives course at the State University of New York at Albany and working with students for a number of years convinced me of the need for a single book to present both archival theory and practice. Dr. William Saffady of the State University of New York at Albany encouraged me to pursue the development of a book on archives.

Herbert Bloom, Senior Editor at ALA Books, was exceptionally helpful during the period that the book was under development. His counsel to provide more extensive narrative, more examples, and tighter focus made the book much better that it would otherwise have been.

Of course, I am solely responsible for the contents and interpretations in the book.

My family also deserves major credit for this book. My wife Susan encouraged me to write it, read and commented on all the chapters, and made suggestions for improving it. My daughters, Annmarie and Emily, were patient and supportive during the many months that the book was being written. This book reflects a belief that through study and understanding of the past, we can shape a better future. I hope that in some small way it will help lead to a better world for my daughters.

Preface

THE ARCHIVAL ENTERPRISE is intended for history, library and information science, and archival studies students, people working in historical records programs, their supervisors, and other people interested in the identification, care, and use of historical records. It introduces archival theory and principles, describes the elements of historical records programs, explains archival techniques and procedures, and analyzes some of the problems and issues archivists face as a profession. As the title implies, the book maintains that professional archival work is an *enterprise*—a big, bold, and sometimes difficult undertaking requiring energy and initiative. Archivists deal with history, the transmittal of knowledge, and the management of information—broad, important responsibilities requiring dedication, imagination, and adaptability. The archival profession is dynamic, adaptive, and undergoing continual change. The book discusses some recent transformations and indicates where broadscale change is still under way. One chapter is devoted to explaining the essentially professional nature of archival work, and the others reflect its complex, challenging nature.

THE ARCHIVAL ENTERPRISE also reflects a belief that archival work is of fundamental importance to society, culture, and education, and that it even contributes to our economic progress. Inspiration for the book's title comes from the work of Dr. David B. Gracy II, who has the impressive and suitable academic title of Governor Bill Daniel Professor in Archival Enterprise at the University of Texas—and who has done much to energize and advance the archival enterprise in recent years.

THE ARCHIVAL ENTERPRISE covers historical records work in a sequential manner, from an orientation to the field on through emerging challenges.

The **Introduction** defines key terms and introduces several hypothetical historical records programs which are used as illustrations later in the book.

Chapter 1, **Archivists: Culture, History, Practicality,** introduces the archival profession, delineates the various roles archivists play, explores the relationship between theory and practice, and advances the case for the importance of the archival enterprise. It maintains that archivists blend theory and pragmatism and asserts that their work supports practical research of immediate importance as well as contributing to cultural continuity and historical understanding.

Chapter 2, **Historical Records Programs: Diverse Types, Common Elements,** introduces the concept of historical records programs, discusses the varieties of these programs, and spells out the core or basic elements that they must have in order to function effectively. It stresses that, while the nature and makeup of programs vary, they have shared traits that make them essentially similar.

Chapter 3, **The Age of Archival Analysis: Historical Records Conditions and Needs,** summarizes recent studies of archival issues and programs, generalizes about conditions and needs, and draws conclusions about the issues that confront the nation's historical records programs as a whole. This chapter maintains that recent studies have provided unprecedented insights into archival conditions and needs and provided a point of departure for new initiatives and approaches, some of which are described in chapter 4.

Chapter 4, **The Professional Nature of Archival Work,** characterizes new developments that have strengthened the archival profession: growing professional associations, supportive funding agencies, guidelines for archival work, professionwide planning, educational guidelines, and certification of archivists. As a result of these and other changes, the profession's ability to meet its responsibilities has been measurably strengthened.

Chapter 5, **Administering Historical Records Programs,** discusses historical records program administration and its components, including leadership, management, working with people, planning, and monitoring and reporting. Historical records programs, whatever their size, need sound administration to make the most effective use of available, often scarce resources; a central part of the challenge is to provide staff members opportunities to act on their own initiative and enterprise.

Chapter 6, **Identification and Selection of Historical Records,** discusses the primary challenge of archival work: identification and selection of that small percentage of records that are worthy of continuing retention because of their historical research or other value. The chapter explores issues and concerns in documenting society, discusses documentation strategies, advises on repository acquisitions policies, advances suggestions for anticipating the impact of new accessions, and concludes by discussing appraisal of records.

Chapter 7, **Arrangement and Description of Historical Records,** discusses how archivists arrange records and, more importantly, how they describe them. It includes traits of a descriptive program, a discussion of finding aids, and a review of the standard archival descriptive format. Systematic description is important to provide access to the records and to attract researchers to them and to encourage their use, a theme continued in chapters 9 and 10.

Chapter 8, **Preservation of Historical Records,** describes the physical problems of chemistry, environment, and human threats that afflict historical records, discusses preservation planning and administration, and goes into preservation techniques. It explains that preservation is a fundamental archival responsibility; if it is not handled well, historical records will not survive.

Chapter 9, **Researcher Services,** discusses outreach to researchers, the need to promote use of historical records, research room policies, and the archivist as mediator between the researcher and the records. It maintains that the archivist must actively encourage and assist the researcher and make researcher services a central part of historical records programs.

Chapter 10, **Promotional Marketing,** covers archivists' work to draw the attention of the general public to their holdings and to explain the archival function in society. Archivists need to make outreach and public programming efforts both to call attention to their immensely valuable holdings and indirectly to secure greater understanding of the value and importance of those materials.

Chapter 11, **Electronic Records: A Challenge for Archivists,** explores the archival implications of the information revolution wrought by computers. Electronic records, so unlike their paper counterparts, require new analysis and new directions from archivists, attention to technical considerations, and new approaches to identification of records and information with continuing value. This chapter maintains that archivists are developing strategies to cope with this information revolution but also observes that the information revolution may transform the nature of archival work in the years ahead.

Appendix A, a statement by the Society of American Archivists, delineates the roles that archivists play, the tasks they carry out, and the knowledge they need to do their work.

Appendix B contains a sample long-range plan and a sample annual workplan for a model historical records program.

Appendix C provides examples of records descriptions and finding aids.

Finally, the **Bibliography** at the end of THE ARCHIVAL ENTERPRISE discusses some of the best published material in the field. It is intended for readers who need additional information on any of the topics covered in the book.

Introduction
The Archival Enterprise and the World of Historical Records

Having at least a working definition of key terms is essential to understand the field of archival endeavor. There is no lexicon of archival terms; instead, the commonly understood usages explained here are used in this book.[1]

Record means any type of recorded information, regardless of physical form or characteristics, created, received, or maintained by a person, institution, or organization. The broad definition of records encompasses correspondence, reports, diaries, journals, ledgers, minutes, photographs, maps, drawings, blueprints, agreements, memoranda, deeds, case files, and other material. Records come in many physical formats—parchment, paper, microfilm, cassette tape, film videotape, and computer tapes and disks. Records are extensions of the human memory, purposefully created to record information, document transactions, communicate thoughts, substantiate claims, advance explanations, offer justifications, and provide lasting evidence of events. Their creation results from a fundamental human need to create and store information, to retrieve and transmit it, and to establish tangible connections with the past. Records are thus essential links with and evidence of the past.

Records generated by an organization or institution such as a government are often called *official records*. The speech files accumulated by a commissioner of education, for example, are official records of and belong to the Department of Education in that state government. *Records management* refers to administrative procedures for oversight of the creation, use, maintenance, and disposition of records. In many settings, archival work and records management are really two parts of a single, comprehensive approach to total control over records and the information they contain.

Most records are not needed for long. Their significance diminishes after the purpose of their creation has been satisfied. Archivists use the term *life cycle* to describe the evolutionary process that records go through: they are created; they are actively used for their intended purpose; they become less frequently used (a phase sometimes called *semi-active* or *noncurrent*); and they eventually are either destroyed or identified for continuing preservation because of their enduring value. In many archival programs, this process is effected through *appraisal*—the process of ascertaining the value and continuing importance of records, taking into account their administrative, legal, and fiscal use, their research value, and their relationship to other records.

For instance, the vast majority of the records of a bank have significance for documenting fiscal transactions and obligations and supporting audits, but later their significance wanes. Records of individual checking account customers will have little value a few years after the accounts close. Appraisal and analysis might lead to the decision that these records should be consigned to an inactive records center or facility a few years after the closing of the accounts, and that they should be destroyed a few years after that as part of a comprehensive records management program. This disposition process could be authorized through a *records retention and disposition schedule*—a document approved by the bank's officers that lists records and states how long they are to be retained.

The small percentage of records that have enduring value are called *historical records* or *historically valuable records*. They contain significant information about the past and are therefore worthy of long-term preservation and systematic management for historical and other research. The term *historical records,* as used in this book, includes those from the present as well as the past; the criteria are informational content and usefulness, not age. Common types of historical records are letters, diaries, photographs, journals, and maps but any records can and should be considered historical records if they have sufficient value and usefulness. For instance, a sketchy diary kept by Mary Smith, with irregular entries mostly devoted to the weather and television shows watched by Smith, is a record but probably not a historical record (in fairness, an appraisal would be needed to determine this status for sure.) On the other hand, a diary kept by Mary Jones, successful president of an innovative computer and information systems development firm, noted author, and U.S. senator, with detailed information on her career and contacts, is also a record but most likely a historical one because of the importance of the information it contains.

Historical records will be used here to include both archives and manuscripts. Historical records are sometimes equated with old files but that notion is too restrictive. For one thing, electronic records created by and stored in computers are also included in the definition. Historical records created today or tomorrow may be just as valuable as those created decades or centuries ago. A deliberate, organized effort to care for historical records is called a *historical records program*. The physical location for the historical records is referred to as a *historical records repository* or, more simply, a *repository*.

Though *archives* is obviously the profession's most important term, its use is not totally consistent, even among seasoned archivists. The historical records of an organization or institution are called *archives, archival records* or, sometimes, *archival materials*. The official records of a public library that have continuing value may be called the library's archival records. The American Library Association's records of enduring research value would appropriately be called the ALA's archives. *Archives* or *archival program* may also mean the agency responsible for selecting, preserving, managing, and making available archival records and also the repository where such materials are kept. An organized, continuing effort to systematically care for the ALA's archives would be called its archival program. People sometimes use the word archives to refer to all historical records. This book avoids that usage and instead uses historical records, as defined above, to include both archives and other types of historical records.

As noted earlier, many people carrying out archival functions may, because of their backgrounds, program settings, job requirements, or personal preferences, call themselves manuscripts librarians or curators, or use some other title. It is not unusual for a prominent leader of the archival profession or an officer in an archival association to have a home institution position title of curator of manuscripts or manuscripts librarian. This book uses the term *archivist* to encompass all people who, through training and experience, are qualified and competent to identify, acquire, manage, make available, and encourage and guide the use of, historical records. Their work must be part of or connected with a historical records program. The public records specialist in the state archives who accessions the state librarian's records into the state archives, the librarian at the bank who takes charge of establishing a bank archives, and the manuscripts curator at a local historical society who eventually appraises the Mary Smith and Mary Jones diaries to determine their disposition can all be considered archivists if their training and experience enable them to carry out their assigned responsibilities in an acceptable fashion. *Archival* is an adjective that refers broadly to the work and concerns of archivists.

The term *document* in this book means approximately the same thing as record, and *historical document* means roughly the same thing as historical record. Records created or received by individuals in the conduct of their personal, private, or professional endeavors are often called *papers, personal papers,* or *personal records*. For instance, the Susanna Vultaggio Papers held by a manuscripts library refers to the letters, diaries, photographs, and other records of continuing value and importance created or received by that person.

The term *manuscript* literally means a handwritten or typed record, but the terms *manuscript* and *historical manuscript* are often used to refer broadly to historical records.

Manuscripts and *historical manuscripts* are also often used to refer to records created or assembled by a person, group, or organization and collected by and transferred to a repository, such as a library or historical society, for preservation and research use. The term *manuscripts* also includes the situation where an individual collected and assembled historical records from a variety of sources over a long period of years and then donated them to a library or other repository. Thus, if Luke Evans collected letters and diaries from the Civil War era, the Luke Evans Manuscripts in a library's special collections division might include little on Evans himself but much on soldiers' views and battle conditions in that war.

Archival writings often distinguish between archives and manuscripts, with the former being the records of enduring value of an organization or institution and the latter referring to practically all other historical records. In most of these writings, and in most good finding aids in repositories, the terms are defined, or else it is obvious from context what they mean. THE ARCHIVAL ENTERPRISE attempts to deal with the inconsistency of terminology by relying on the term historical records, as broadly defined above, rather than manuscripts or papers.

The term *collection* means a body of historical records having a common source. For instance, all the historical records created by Susanna Vultaggio and collected by a library historical records program might be called the Susanna Vultaggio Collection, as well as the Susanna Vultaggio Manuscripts or the Susanna Vultaggio Papers. Collection also refers to historical records assembled by an individual; the Luke Evans Manuscripts might therefore be called the Luke Evans Collection. In yet one more variation, a library might group together all of its scattered photographs, for example, and call them its photographic collection. Finally, some people refer to a repository's historical records as a whole as its collections. A better term for all of a repository's historical records, one less susceptible to misinterpretation, is *holdings*.

Historical Records: Variations on a Theme

Chapters 1 through 3 in particular describe the varieties of historical records and programs to care for them. Inconsistent terminology, misperceptions in the public mind about the nature and importance of historical records and archival work, and changing information technology may all compound and perpetuate uncertainty about the archival endeavor. Some hypothetical but revealing and typical examples may help clearly set the stage for the rest of the book. (These examples use some fictitious names. Any resemblance to actual persons is purely coincidental.)

A research library in a west coast city—we'll call it Auburn Research Library—has built up an outstanding collection of books, newspapers, periodicals, and other published research materials in several fields of concentration. The trustees and director decide to expand the Research Library's capacity in several areas, including art history and the performing arts, to cater to and expand research traffic in those topics. Art history is of particular importance because of the presence nearby of a number of major art galleries and museums and two universities with strong art and art history majors. After discussion with the museums and universities, the Research Library staff determines to begin collecting the papers of artists and artistic performers. The general rationale is that these materials will help researchers understand the creative spirit, reveal how artists viewed their own art, document the source and development of ideas and artists' influence on each other, and show how artists and artistic performers related to galleries, museums, and theatres. The collecting focus is on correspondence, notebooks, diaries, photographs, videotapes, and other first-hand materials created during the course of people's careers, replete with information, frankly created because they were not intended for publication, and systematically maintained over the years.

The new program gets off to a good start by acquiring the papers of Reginald Seymour, a painter renown for his landscape work, who in his later years chaired the art history department at one of the two major universities in the city; Jane Stapleton, a prominent choreographer who influenced dance styles nationally; and Malcolm Hayden, supporter of the arts and the founder and moving force behind a local art history museum. Other acquisitions follow, and the Research Library makes provision for the adequate preservation and management of its growing holdings and for encouraging their use. In this example, historical records pertaining to a particular theme in a particular region are saved for the future.

In another example, a modest sized midwestern university—we'll call it Madison University—was founded as a land-grant college more than a century ago and has graduated thousands of people, many of whom rose to distinction in their chosen professional fields. Two of the state's twentieth-century governors were Madison graduates, as were many members of the state legislature and other leaders in state government. The university's research programs contributed significantly to progress in several fields, but particularly agricultural economics, industrial and labor relations, and state and local government public administration. A major economic and cultural presence in its town, Madison has also been distinguished in attracting, admitting, and supporting minority students. In short, it has been important, influential, and successful.

Recognizing its long and proud history and desiring to ensure that their university has a corporate memory in an era of rapid turnover of administrators, the trustees direct the university president to establish a university archival program. The president delegates the responsibility to the university librarian, in part because she assumes the librarian has expertise and interest, and in part because the new university library has storage space. The librarian proceeds to establish an archival program that gathers the university's older official records of continuing importance and also makes provision for the continuing identification and retention of those of the present and the future. Later, the university begins to collect outside historical records in fields related to its major interests, agricultural economics, industrial-labor relations, and public administration. The University Archives and the Historical Records Program are combined into the Division of Archives and Manuscripts, and this division, along with the library's Rare Books Program, comes to constitute the library's Department of Special Collections. Thus, a university archival program is born, and a related collecting effort is launched, both solidly based in a library setting.

In another illustration, the new head librarian of a public library in a small mythical mid-Atlantic city, called Salem Public Library, is cognizant of the library's historical roots (it was established during the colonial period and its founders were influenced by Benjamin Franklin's notions about libraries) and its cultural and educational influence on the community. With the support of the library's board of directors, he establishes a small but effective library archival program to identify and save the library's own archival records, a few of which date from the era of its founding. Later, the librarian is contacted by the daughter of a recently deceased business and civic leader, Donald Shultes, whose family owned one of the city's major companies which provided sustained employment and economic stability to the community for more than a century. Would Salem Public Library wish to accept Shultes' papers, his daughter asks?

The library's decision is not easy, for it carries with it selection decisions (to appraise the papers with a view to preserving only the materials that merit it), custodial obligations (to arrange, describe, and care for the papers), storage implications (the papers are bulky), service responsibilities (researchers presumably will want to use the papers, so access provisions and reference services will have to be provided for), and questions about future collecting (will the library seek or accept the papers of other community leaders, for instance?). The head librarian asks for time to make an informed decision. He consults with the library's directors, assesses the library's resources, consults with other potential collecting agencies including the local historical society, and writes an initial collecting policy for the library that would include the Shultes Papers. He works out terms of donation with Shultes' daughter to define access, and he also arranges for a donation from the family and the Shultes Company to help process and care for the records. (He then takes a short vacation to contemplate the implications of his actions!) This illustration shows how important historical records have been saved, and how a new historical records program with two elements—the library's own archives and outside historical records—has been launched.

In a fourth example, a city in the southwest called Westlake initiates a total record management program, including an archival component. Consultation with the state archives, attendance at a workshop sponsored by a regional archival association, and reading several publications of the National Association of Government Archives and Records Administrators, the Society of American Archivists, and the American Association for State and Local History, provide the city clerk with enough information to get started. She recognizes that there are generally accepted approaches to setting up an archival program; that appraisal and identification of archival records are crucial challenges; that people and financial resources will be needed and that secure storage space must be found; but also that a well-administered program should result in the availability of important records both for city officials and for historians and other researchers.

The program is launched after development of a careful plan and assurance from the city council of space and appropriate support, including a position for a professional archivist. The mayor of Westlake dedicates the "Archives Room" in a ceremony where he extols the value of archives for documenting public policy. Beginning with identification of the city's earliest minutes, the program eventually encompasses all key series of city records. Council minutes, hearing transcripts, mayor's correspondence, maps, budget documents, and selected records from city agencies are transferred to the custody of the City Archives after a specified period of time in their originating offices and, in most cases, a stay in the city inactive records storage center, according to approved schedules. City officials interested in precedents and policy development, counsel's staff preparing for litigation, and historians from several colleges and universities soon form a steady stream of researcher traffic. Most heartening of all to the city clerk, herself a historian at heart, is the use of the archives by

Westlake's school teachers for document packets and teaching lessons on Westlake history and a popular document exhibit during the city's centennial. In this example, local government archives—an important species of historical records—are appreciated and used by government, community, and scholarly researchers.

These four examples illustrate the variety of historical records, the diversity of programs to care for them, and the diversity of opportunities and circumstances that can give rise to a historical records program.

NOTE

1. The standard glossary is William L. Rofes, ed., "A Basic Glossary for Archivists, Manuscript Curators, and Records Managers," *American Archivist* 37 (July 1974):415–433. A forthcoming publication by the Society of American Archivists, Lewis Bellardo and Lynn Lady Bellardo, *A Glossary for Archivists, Manuscript Curators, and Basic Managers* (Chicago: Society of American Archivists, 1992), will supersede Rofes's glossary. Several of the definitions in this book are adapted from New York State Historical Records Advisory Board, *Toward a Usable Past: Historical Records in the Empire State* (Albany: New York State Education Department, 1984), 71–72.

1 Archivists: Culture, History, Practicality

Archivists identify, select, manage, preserve, and make available records with enduring value. They work in governments, banks, corporations, churches, nonprofit institutions and associations, libraries, historical agencies, museums, and various other settings. Though archivists have a distinct professional identification, their work combines aspects of the work of historians, librarians, records managers, information resource specialists, research consultants, program managers, and public relations experts. The archival enterprise perpetuates an essential component of our collective social memory, transmits part of our cultural heritage from generation to generation, and contributes to the process of people learning from and building on the experiences of their predecessors.

Government, businesses, and other institutions and organizations also value archival work for less grand but more practical and immediate reasons. Archivists maintain and furnish documentation for institutional continuity, legal rights and responsibilities, precedents, and the origin and development of policies; this role is sometimes described as corporate or institutional memory. Archival work is characterized by an accent on service—to the institutions where archivists work, to the records they save and maintain, and to the researchers who seek their help. It is marked by a sense of pride and mission derived from archivists' sense of the importance of the archival function to the continuity and welfare of society.

A Profession in Transition

The archival function has deep historical roots back to Greek and Roman times. The earliest archivists were designated societal, religious, or official government records keepers, and their fundamental role was to preserve documents needed to sustain legal and personal rights and institutional authority. The tenure of the organized archival profession is much shorter; the establishment of the National Archives in 1934 and the founding of the Society of American Archivists in 1936 mark its beginning in the United States. Almost six decades later, the profession is still evolving and not fully defined. It retains a degree of freewheeling flexibility at the same time it is moving toward greater predictability and uniformity. It blends a tradition of pragmatism with adherence to theory. Its recent past has been characterized by adherence to fundamental precepts but also clarification of purpose, revamping of techniques, and reconsideration of relationships with allied professions, such as librarianship and history.

The Society of American Archivists (SAA), the nation's largest archival association, recently launched a program to certify archivists, but there are no prescriptive standards for practicing archival work or even an exclusive definition of "professional archivist." There may be as many as 10,000 people engaged in archival work in the United States, but many would style themselves manuscripts librarians, curators, records managers, or local historians, rather than archivists.[1] The SAA has published guidelines for graduate archival training but not definite standards. National and regional archival organizations are considered to be professional associations but most accept as members anyone who works with historical records and is willing to pay dues. These associations provide training and development opportunities and forums for analyzing issues and problems and for developing common approaches. They offer cohesiveness and focus for archival work. Yet archivists often show a proclivity for independence, disinterest in concerted cooperative efforts, and traits of "singularity, autonomy, and nonsystematic growth."[2]

The National Historical Publications and Records Commission estimates there are more than 4,500 historical records repositories in the United States.[3] Reaching an exact count is impossible since there are no hard and fast standards or central registry. Many historical records programs are situated in library, historical agency, or other settings that obscure their identity as discrete programs. There are few standards for historical records programs and no mechanism for enforcing them. However, most programs carry out the same general functions and have similar core program elements. Archivists have been moving toward more consistent and uniform approaches and guidelines and agreeing on canons of good practice that are increasingly regarded as the norm. It is now possible to establish reasonable expectations for responsible historical records program administration and performance. Those expectations are described in this book.

Roles Archivists Play

Institutional archivists—in governments, banks, companies, associations, churches, and many other settings—are responsible for the care and management of the archival institutional memory of their employers. Archivists are also at work in libraries (often in special collections departments), historical societies, museums, and other agencies that collect and preserve historical records from the outside. Whatever the setting, archivists' work is seldom routine or repetitious.

Dealing with a constantly changing array of historical records and using a variety of analytical, interpretive, physical, and interpersonal skills make the work engrossing. For example, the manuscripts librarian for a city library's manuscripts collection may process (arrange and describe) the records of a novelist and discover that the novelist occasionally corresponded with a United States president on literature and politics. In the course of a single day, a state government archivist may draft a workplan, appraise a cache of records, work on a descriptive finding aid, and guide a notable researcher to the material needed to finish a study. A corporate archivist might retrieve and make available records that determine whether the company wins or loses a patent case in court and also open an exhibit of old advertising material. The archivist in a city historical society might evaluate the records of the community's leading civic leader to decide whether the society should accept and maintain those records. Of course, many archivists, particularly in larger programs, specialize in a particular area of the work, such as appraisal or researcher services, but even within these subfields there is daily variety, constant challenge, and even exciting discovery.

Archivists may play any or all of several roles, sometimes simultaneously.[4]

1. *Archivists are the arbiters in decisions of whether to keep or discard records.* Archivists are concerned with documentation of people, groups, events, developments, localities, and subjects. Operating within frameworks of documentation objectives and program collection policies, they carefully evaluate records to measure their significance against two criteria. First, how extensive, important, and revealing is the information the records contain, especially in comparison to other types of information on the same topic? Second, what is the likelihood that researchers will use the records if they are saved? Balancing the answers to these questions with realistic assessments of institutional resources, archivists identify a small percentage that merit continuing preservation. The identification process at best is far from perfect. The archivist seldom has an opportunity to study the total universe of

documentation on a given topic and must make a selection from the available records. In the example on page 6, the Salem Public Library head librarian probably did not know for sure where the Donald Shultes Papers fit in with the total available universe of documentation either on Salem or on regional business and industry, but he made an informed decision based on available information and within the very practical constraints of the time available for a decision. The selection process is sometimes rushed and imperfect, but the results are enduring. If the archivist selects well, an adequate record will be saved for the future; if not well, the record will be incomplete or skewed. Records not identified as having continuing value are, in most cases, destined for eventual destruction, an inevitable—and desirable—consequence of the appraisal process.

2. *Archivists assert control and bring order.* Archivists value order. They either try to describe it (where it exists) or to impose it (for instance, when historical records are received in disorder from a donor or originating entity). They are responsible for the systematic and logical arrangement and description of historical records to make them accessible to researchers. Archivists deal with records as collective entities rather than as individual documents. They are concerned with relationships and connections among records and realize that the organic nature of records gives them part of their meaning and significance. A single Jane Stapleton letter at the Auburn Research Library, discussed in the introduction, may tell us something about a single choreographed performance, for instance, but a series of Stapleton's letters will be revealing about choreography as a movement, Stapleton as an impresario, and the evolution of dance as a form of artistic expression. The single letter is interesting but limited and isolated; the series of letters presents sustained information and is revealing and instructive. Records arrangement requires understanding the functions and processes that produced the records; how they were originally created, filed, and stored; and how researchers are likely to access them. Description entails understanding informational content, likely research use, and standard descriptive formats.

3. *Archivists encourage use of historical records and serve researchers.* Archivists do not (or at least should not) wait for researchers to seek out their holdings. Quite the opposite—a fundamental archival tenet is service to people with an information need that can be met through the use of historical records. To meet this obligation, the archivist calls attention to the records and tries to draw potential researchers to them by preparing guides and other finding aids, making presentations, and using other approaches. The

archivist actively assists researchers who inquire about the holdings or who visit the repository. In another example in the Introduction, the city clerk of Westlake probably did not retire into her office after the city council voted to support an archival program and the mayor dedicated the Archives Room in city hall. Instead, she recognized her obligation both to let city offices know what the City Archives held and how the materials could be useful for the business of government and to contact local historians and teachers to inform and perhaps even excite them about the new and growing treasure trove of historical information.

4. *Archivists preserve and protect historical records.* Archivists have an important curatorial and custodial responsibility to safeguard the records under their charge. Because the records are unique, irreplaceable, and important, this responsibility is a significant one that should not be taken lightly. If the Auburn Research Library discussed in the Introduction announces the acquisition of the local Arts Council's records but later misplaces or loses the records, a piece of history is lost, posterity is cheated and researchers are frustrated. The library is embarrassed, its reputation is tarnished, and its ability to attract new accessions is compromised. The custodial and curatorial responsibility includes physically protecting records, such as storing them in fireproof facilities that are secure from unauthorized intrusion and theft and monitoring their use in the research room to make sure they are properly handled and not stolen. The archivist also has a responsibility to ensure the continuing physical survival and availability of the records and the information they contain (for example, through making microfilm or other copies.)

5. *Archivists promote and advocate.* Archivists cannot afford to assume a passive stance in acquiring support, recognition, or, for that matter, researchers. The archival function is insufficiently appreciated by the public as a whole. Most historical records programs lack sufficient support and visibility. All of the examples in the Introduction need substantial and growing financial support. Many of the nation's programs described in chapter 3 simply do not have enough wherewithal to get the work done. The archivist must be part salesperson, part public relations expert, and part promoter. Some of the archivist's time and energy must go to drawing attention to the program's functions and accomplishments; to pointing out its choicest records; and to educating people on the importance of historical records for understanding the past.

6. *Archivists prepare for and help shape the emerging information universe.* The world of records and archives is changing as a result of new and emerging information technology. "Electronic records" created by and stored in computers may contain no less important

information than their paper-based counterparts, but the archival challenges of dealing with this intangible new form of information is daunting. Archivists are searching for ways to help shape the information universe so that information with lasting value, no matter its form, is identified, preserved, and accessible to researchers both now and in the future. This challenge requires archivists to step beyond their customary custodial roles and become ombudsmen for information of continuing value. This role also requires a new perspective on the nature of information, new approaches to handling it, and new emphases on advocacy and persuasion in dealing with automation experts and information systems specialists. New technology is the frontier or cutting edge of archival work, and it has the potential for significantly transforming the profession in the future.

7. *Archivists are program managers*. Archivists do not just handle historical records. Even in a small program, an archivist is a manager, though the resources that are managed may be only one or two people's time and talents. The librarian in charge of the archives and other historical records at the hypothetical Madison University in the Introduction, for instance, must set priorities for herself and her staff members, including some part-time and some student workers. Archivists plan, allocate available resources for maximum impact, set priorities, organize the work, assess results, prepare reports, and carry out other managerial functions. Frequently they deal with the dilemma of low resource levels and high service demand levels, making sound management crucial to the archival enterprise. Without sound planning and management, work is likely to outweigh or outdistance resources and the archival program will stagnate, falling further and further behind reasonable expectations for service and performance.

Theory and Practice

Archivists tend to emphasize the practical over the hypothetical. The archival field includes little in the way of formal theory or abstract notions and concepts. Writings on archival theory are rare, and nowhere in the literature is there a distillation of theory. Archivists have developed a theoretical basis for some work and operate on some important general principles and pragmatic approaches, mostly modified from European archival practices or derived from practical American experience. But they lack a more fundamental philosophical underpinning that addresses such basic questions as the ultimate purposes of archival work, the role of the archivist in documenting society, or how to gauge archival achievements. This lack of a significant body of theory troubles some archivists, who view theory as a prerequisite to full standing as a profession. It is sometimes disconcerting for archivists to explain and justify archival work without being able to refer to fundamental purposes. Furthermore, lack of an extensive theoretical base has sometimes made it difficult for the profession to maintain consistent directions while, at the same time, adjusting to changing needs.

The practical, nontheoretical bent of the archival discipline is at least in part the result of its historical development. The modern American archival profession, launched in the mid-1930s, was for many years guided by people with historical or library backgrounds and a pragmatic, "get-the-job-done" approach to archival work. Archival practice was initially shaped in response to practical needs to organize sizeable quantities of archival records, especially at the National Archives, and was refined, but not basically modified, in the ensuing decades. As one pioneering archivist later recalled, this was "the self-taught generation. . . . At the commencement of our employment, we were apprenticed to no one and began work immediately. . . . Our first years were spent in learning."[5]

A National Archives administrator and teacher, Theodore R. Schellenberg, distilled early principles and practices in the two most influential books in the profession's history: *Modern Archives: Principles and Techniques* (1956) and *The Management of Archives* (1965). While young archivists today may not read Schellenberg, they are nonetheless affected by the ideas he articulated. Both books reflect his strong views that "archival principles and techniques should be systematized and, to a very large extent, standardized, if work with records, whether public or private, is to become truly professional."[6] Schellenberg drew on French, Prussian, British, and other European archival traditions but went beyond them and added a practical slant to suit American conditions. He cared little about articulating the fundamental mission of archival work, encouraging planning and priority setting for the profession, promoting research use of archival materials, or advancing strategies to secure sufficient recognition and support.

In Schellenberg's view, archivists drew on historical training and on library techniques, modified both (substantially, in the case of library descriptive approaches), and developed a pragmatic, service-oriented thrust to their work. He concentrated on archival appraisal, arrangement, and description and on the relationship between archival work and records management and librarianship. Schellenberg wrote systematically and conveyed a sense of competence and authority; to a large degree, his writings exemplified what archivists were and what they did.

Leaders of the archival profession have, of course, contributed to its growth and direction in the years since the pioneering archival generation. Until the 1970s, however, there was little inclination to push the profession beyond the bounds and premises of Schellenberg and the pioneering generation of archivists. Even then, revision, not revolution, was the order of the day. Archival publications and sessions at professional meetings tended to address practical concerns or to discuss current practices at historical records programs. Even the *Basic Manuals* series launched by the Society of American Archivists in the 1970s as a comprehensive guide to archival practice broke little new ground, although these volumes did present a fresh roundup of the best approaches and techniques. The SAA's *Archival Fundamentals* series, published in the 1990s, will present the field's freshest thinking and approaches but probably will not strike out in any radical new directions.

Busy archivists have been so engrossed in their work that they seem to have lacked the time for theoretical speculations. Because there have been only a few full-time archival education programs, little in the way of challenges to tradition or new theory emerged from academic settings. These training programs lacked full-time professors "looking for rationales, for basic concepts, for means of fitting the archivist into the warp and woof of society, for the *theory* behind the practice," and therefore archival training has produced "a large corps of parish priests when no one has bothered to devise a theology under whose standard they can act."[7]

"American archival theory does not exist as a systematically formulated body of ideas," notes one expert. "It is essentially an aggregation of ideas drawn from well-tested and widely accepted European archival principles and of pragmatic concepts developed to meet special needs of American archival administration and democratic traditions."[8] This writer and others interpret American archival practice as having the broader tendencies historically perceived as American: pragmatic, flexible, adaptable, and results-oriented. In fact, there are probably only five types of bedrock archival theory, and even here the "theory" has strains of pragmatism and expediency:

> *Archival work is integrally tied to broader records management work through adherence to the "life cycle" concept.* As noted above, the notion that records move through cycles roughly comparable to human existence (birth, intensive activity, declining activity, and either death or redemption—presumably the spiritual analog of going to an archives!). The archivist's intervention to save the small percentage of choicest records provides some theoretical underpinning for the work of appraisal and selection of historical records.
>
> *The appraisal of records is essentially an exercise to identify and measure important values.* The two most important values are *evidential*

value, meaning the extent to which the records document the operations and accomplishments of the records-creating entity, and *informational value,* the extent to which the records contain unique, useful information on people, places, subjects, and events.

Historical records should be maintained together according to their source. Usually referred to as the principle of provenance, this is of central importance as a principle for gathering and organizing historical records in repositories.

Historical records should be maintained in the order originally imposed on them. This principle of "original order" is also a central tenet in organizing historical records.

Arrangement of historical records should correspond to the natural hierarchical arrangement of the records themselves. The arrangement begins at the topmost or most summary approach (the entire repository), then proceeds downward with increasing detail (record groups, subgroups, series, file units, and, finally, individual documents, as discussed in chapter 7).

The Archival Contribution

Archival work is important because historical records are important. "The wide variety of documentary material preserved in our archives constitutes the recorded memory of the nation. . . . Like any memory, it can be drawn upon in many ways, from studying a casual reference, to analyzing some past event, to providing a base for future planning. . . . [Archives] constitute one of our basic national cultural resources."[9] The terms archives and historical records may to some people imply aged records of interest only to antiquarians or historians or useful only for narrowly defined historical research purposes. Actually, historical records are important to society as a whole for understanding the past and providing guidance for the future. In a broader sense, historical records constitute an important part of the collective memory of our society and of our cultural heritage. They present firsthand, direct, unprocessed information about people, places, and developments. Records were deliberately created to embody and hold information, and so they may be very useful in yielding that information to the inquiring researcher. Sometimes, historical records are the only reliable evidence that has survived from the past and are therefore essential to recovery and reconstruction of historical developments and to historical analysis.

For instance, institutional and organizational archives constitute an institutional memory that can be invaluable to administrators.

They may use letters, minutes, directives, administrators' files, and other archival records to study the origins of programs and policies, analyze program development and performance, and ensure administrative continuity. The new insurance company president who is interested in the history of the company's investments, the bishop who needs historical background information on church finances, the trustee of a fraternal group who wants to know how his predecessors came to a key decision—all may find answers in their institutions' archives. Archives are thus an important, practical tool for sound administration.

Government archives may have information on development of legislation and on legislative intent that make them important for understanding and interpreting laws. As shown in the Introduction, hearing minutes, minutes of governing bodies, memos written by government counsels and other advisors, and other records in the Westlake City Archives all help provide context and offer clues to meaning and intention. Some archival records document agreements and obligations, substantiate legal claims, and protect individuals' rights. Vital statistics records, official maps, and wills and deeds filed in local government offices are essential legal documents. The citizen who visits city hall to verify his property boundary, the worker who needs proof of birth and age to obtain Social Security or other benefits, the attorney who checks a will in the county court house to advance her client's claim to an inheritance—all, whether they realize it or not, are drawing on archives.

Government archival records may be scrutinized by the press and citizens concerned with open, responsive government because they constitute evidence of the care and faithfulness of government administrators. For instance, minutes of city council meetings indicate the views and votes of city leaders, document decisions, and give evidence of program direction and administration. Budget documents reveal priorities and reveal the administration of public funds. Coupled with a records management program, an archival program ensures the orderly periodic destruction of materials with transitory significance while at the same time ensuring the survival of those with continuing importance. An archival program thus contributes to efficient, economical, and open government.

In recent years, Indian tribes have used archival records to establish legal rights to lands and claims to privileges from the state and federal governments. Texas attorneys used 300-year-old Spanish boundary maps to establish state ownership of submerged oil-laden lands in the Gulf of Mexico, with great fiscal benefit to the state. Oil company planners who wanted to know whether long-term icing patterns would make it unfeasible to move oil from Alaska to the

Are Historical Records Important? Some Examples
from the Madison University Library

How important are historical records in providing insights into the past, keys to unlock historical mysteries, and information to deal with present-day concerns? Here are a few examples from the hypothetical university that made its debut in the Introduction.

- A Madison political science professor writing a book on reapportionment used the records of a former Madison president who chaired a citizens' committee on reapportionment in the 1960s, the most recent time it was done. The professor found evidence that the committee's main concern was to preserve the rural flavor of the state through ensuring rural dominance in the state legislature, even if this had to be done at the expense of the state's growing cities. Particularly revealing was the correspondence between the Madison president and the leaders of the state's Rural Alliance and Farm Bureau on the importance of traditional rural values and state aid for rural schools. The professor's findings, published in an article and later in a book, helped influence the contemporary reapportionment debate and, in the view of several political commentators, helped ensure significantly increased urban representation.

- Several graduate students in the university's new public history program used the university archives and historical records collections for their master's theses. A paper on the 1946 strike at the local tractor factory drew heavily on labor union records held by the university. The minutes of the strike committee and diaries maintained by several of the strikers chronicled strike activities and also noted the economic hardship of the strike and its impact on their families. One of the research papers was accepted for publication in the national public history association's journal.

- The university's original charter, which was granted by the territorial legislature, was included in a mobile exhibit that toured the region. The document's striking appearance—engravings depicting the values of higher learning, multiple colors, striking design, and bold signatures at the bottom—attracted exhibit-goers' attention. The exhibit caption noted that concern for higher education actually predated state government.

- An automobile accident that caused an injury to the driver resulted in a lawsuit and court proceedings. At issue was responsibility for maintenance of the short road between a city avenue and the campus's main gate, where the crash occurred when the driver swerved to avoid a large pothole. For years the university had voluntarily maintained the road but the superintendent of buildings and grounds claimed after the accident that it really belonged to the city. The original charter and map and early correspondence in the university archives documented that the university, not the city, was responsible.

- The university's holdings of state Grange (Patrons of Husbandry) records were used extensively in a public television special presentation on changes in rural living conditions during the past century. Grange minutes, membership and meeting attendance rosters, photos of Grange picnics and other social functions, and operating records provided evidence that the automobile, television, and other modern conveniences gradually transformed life in the countryside.

lower United States via a water route found an important part of their answer in the Public Archives of Manitoba, which had records of sailing vessels that entered Hudson Bay for the Hudson's Bay Company many years ago. Barbara Tuchman's discovery in the National Archives of the original copy of the Zimmermann Telegram contributed to our understanding of the origins of World War I. Research at the National Archives undermined the claims of military necessity for relocation of Japanese-Americans during World War II and helped lead to reparation legislation. Studies based on Freedman's Bureau records have changed our interpretation of Reconstruction.[10]

Of course, not all archival uses have such broad or far-reaching results, but every day people make use of historical records for practical purposes and with notable beneficial results. Engineers have used land-use permits, maps, photographs, and other archival records to document the location of toxic dump sites and prepare environmental studies. Engineers and public works specialists study old maps, plans, reports, and other records for information on the age and physical characteristics of bridges, buildings, and other elements of the infrastructure. Building owners, engineers, and architects use building files, original blueprints, engineering drawings, and old photographs for historical restoration projects designed to restore aging structures to their original appearance. Historical records can also aid health care. For instance, medical researchers use patient records to trace genetic and familial diseases that are transmitted from generation to generation and to study the spread of contagious diseases.[11]

Historical records can help educate. Students in elementary and secondary schools may study them for information on historical developments. Historical materials, when used in this way to supplement social studies and history courses, stimulate development of analytical skills and challenge students to reach conclusions about historical evidence that may be inconclusive and even contradictory. College and university students carry out research in historical records to derive firsthand evidence about topics in history and other courses. Scholarly researchers mine historical records collections every day for insights and explanations of historical events. The example of the Donald Shultes Papers at Salem Public Library reveals the possibilities: a family history expert might use Shultes' diary for information on marital relations and childrearing; a student of philanthropy might use his files on donations as part of a study on individual giving; and a history professor writing a book on Republican politics in the 1930s and 1940s would be fascinated by Shultes' letters to and from prominent party leaders and officeholders.

Historical records can stimulate the historical imagination, illustrate, and even entertain. Letters and diaries helped Alex Haley write the book and television production of "Roots" and yielded information for more recent productions such as the movie *Glory* and the public television special "The Civil War." Businesses such as Coca-Cola, Kraft Foods, and Wells Fargo use historical records in advertising, public relations, and promotional efforts. Newspaper writers draw on historical records for background to provide perspectives on current news stories and bases of comparison with the past. A feature article on pollution, for instance, can be enhanced by a quotation from a turn-of-the century letter showing how clean the streams were then (or, by contrast, that pollution was already a problem). Historical photographs are particularly useful because they provide striking visual images of the past, allowing people to actually see what contemporaries of the photographs saw.[12]

Historical records can also bring a sense of excitement and discovery, transporting the viewer into the presence of the record's creator through exposure to the materials he or she created. Historian David McCullough described his sense of historical discovery and direct personal contact with historical records at the National Archives:

> [Handling an actual document] can be an experience you never forget. [The National Archives holds] an incredible documentary record of everyday affairs and of people who never ever imagined themselves as Historical. . . . Each new fragment of information leads to something more, almost always, and the personal satisfaction, the education, that comes with the search only increases the farther you go. What may have seemed at first a lot of mountainous dusty old paper—deadly stuff from the dead past—becomes vital evidence. You are caught up, carried forward by all the elements of surprise and fascination in detective work. You find things you were not looking for and these trigger new ideas that never would have occurred to you otherwise.[13]

Archivists' Professional Cousins

Some people regard archivists as displaced librarians or adjunct historians. This mistaken impression detracts from a distinct image of archival work. Archivists strive for recognition as a profession that is separate from closely related fields, such as history and library science. There are both similarities and differences in training, materials, and programs that are worth noting in comparing archivists to their "professional cousins," historians and librarians.

RECORDS MANAGERS

Records management, as noted above, pertains to creation, use, maintenance, and disposition of records. Modern-day records management includes such things as overseeing the creation and use of forms, correspondence, and other records; developing filing and indexing systems to ensure rapid access to records and the information they contain; segregating and managing inactive records; reproducing records, including microfilming; and adopting and using computers, optical media, and other aspects of modern information management technology. Largely a phenomenon of the post–World War II period and in part a spin-off from archival work, records management is today a separate and distinct field with its own national organization and its own program for certifying practitioners. In some settings, the archival program is a subset of the records management program, and the archivist's work of identifying and preserving the records of continuing value is tied closely to broader records management activities. At the very least, archivists and records managers need to work closely together on the development of records retention and disposition schedules, which indicate how long records must be retained and identify archival records by giving them a permanent retention period. Moreover, records that are well managed through systematic filing and indexing are easier to appraise (and, if determined to have lasting value, to accession and control in the archives) than records that are not well managed. Therefore, archivists and records managers should be natural allies and team players.

HISTORIANS

The modern archival profession counts the historical profession as one progenitor. They continue to have a close connection: archivists identify and preserve records that historians (among others) use for research. If the archival appraisal function is not carried out effectively, the basis for sound history is appreciably diminished. However, there is an essential difference between archivists and historians. Archivists identify, preserve, and make available records, while historians do research in them, analyze and interpret their evidence, and present narratives and conclusions based on the research. Some training in history is highly advantageous for any archivist and practically indispensable for those engaged in appraising records and in providing reference services. The appraisal archivist needs historical perspective, awareness of current and emerging research trends, and understanding of how historical records can be used to recover and reconstruct history. The reference archivist can profit from following research trends and understanding how researchers identify and use their sources.

Several archival training courses are offered by history departments. Historical training "gives, or should give, [archivists] a knowledge of what scholarship is, what research is, how research is conducted—the relationship of the scholar to his sources, and the uses and limitations of various kinds of sources—the whole story of man, and, as part of that story, how man has used the record in writing his own story."[14] Some archivists, concerned that the profession is drifting toward the large and undifferentiated field of information management, assert that "the historian still makes the best archivist. . . . The archivist must be a historian, at least by inclination, and preferably by calling" and that archivists and historians together are "keepers of the well" of culture and history.[15] Even with changes resulting from new information technologies, an ability to understand and interpret history will continue to be essential to archival work.

The relationship between historians and archivists can be more fruitful than it has been in the past. In fact, an emerging field of history, called public history, advocates the use of historical training for a wide range of cultural resources management and for bringing a historical perspective to institutional policy analysis and development. Some leaders of this new and expansive field argue that archival work is, or should be, just a subset of public history. This view finds few adherents within the archival community, but public history practitioners have helped illuminate areas where archivists and historians of all types can and should collaborate.

For instance, historians and archivists can consult in such complicated areas as the systematic documentation of modern society where both professions have an interest and neither has the solutions to the problems. There could be collaboration on advocacy efforts, for instance for more resources so that archival programs can better serve historians and other researchers. The public history field, which has had successes in demonstrating the relevance of history for policy making and other areas beyond teaching, could instruct archivists in how to promote themselves and their programs. Not all issues invite a united front between historians and archivists, however. Historians may differ with archivists over access to sensitive or confidential records and may bridle at what archivists regard as prudent and reasonable searchroom security requirements or restrictions designed to protect fragile material.[16]

LIBRARIANS

Many historical records programs are located in library settings, and many archivists have been trained in library schools. The library and the archival professions both handle information resources, carry out broadly defined service responsibilities, and make accumulated knowledge available for the benefit of present and future generations.

Some experts—a minority within the profession—assert that the master in library science degree provides the best preparation for archival work. Through library training, future archivists can learn fundamentals of cataloging and classification (though library techniques need modification to fit archival needs), security, preservation, and the basics of reference services. They also learn how to serve seekers of information, ranging from narrow specialists to the general public. In addition, so the argument goes, training in the library field will help cement the professional status of the archivist and garner recognition for archival work.[17] Most archival educators, while recognizing the value of library science training, will advise the archivist to supplement it with information science, history, and possibly other disciplines to derive the well-rounded education that is needed for modern archival work.

Librarians and archivists both preserve information—librarians through acquisition of mass-produced materials, such as books, and archivists though careful selection of unique, one-of-a-kind materials. In building collections, librarians usually tend to be user-oriented; the objective is to anticipate and meet the needs of researchers. Archivists also support this objective, but they have a transcending interest in adequacy of documentation and the richness and extent of the information in a given set of records. Libraries, for the most part, collect books and other printed and published materials that are deliberately created by authors with an external readership in mind. Most library materials are published and therefore available in multiple copies. By contrast, archivists acquire materials that were created in single copies by people whose objective was to document an event or set down information for some other immediate, practical purpose. Unlike the producers of library material, records creators did not conscientiously intend to produce material for research by posterity.

While librarians build collections around defined themes and research needs and are concerned with what has been published on a particular topic, archivists conduct records surveys, develop records retention and disposition schedules, and carefully analyze and appraise the informational content of materials before selecting what seems most worthy. Indeed, the *appraisal* function, which requires significant understanding of subject matter, documentation context, and individual document content, sharply distinguishes the archivist's work from the librarian's. Moreover, if the librarian misjudges, there are likely to be other opportunities to obtain the material. If the appraisal archivist misjudges, the material is gone forever.

Libraries may respond to changing research needs by shifting the emphasis of their purchasing and collecting policies. Historical records programs find shifts in research interests and trends more difficult to accommodate. By the time the trends are apparent, it may be too late to collect needed material simply because it is gone. Archivists, for apparent reasons, take a great interest in the sources of their material, to understand it, to schedule it, and in some cases to get donors to donate it to the repository. Librarians take a much different view of the main suppliers of their materials, mostly book and serial publishers.

Most books and many other library materials are meant to circulate; in fact, one of the missions of a library is to carry the lamp of learning beyond its doors. Historical records, by contrast, are used only in their repository, under the watchful eye of the custodial archivist, and often with access restrictions based on the records' content or condition.

Librarians adhere to a universal classification scheme, a comprehensive system for organizing knowledge, tested through historical development and embodied in long-standing standards. In effect, these standards prescribe both arrangement and description of library material. Historical records are more unpatterned and do not fit a classification scheme; in fact, the only organizational scheme that counts is the filing system and order of the creating person or institution. Archivists have developed pragmatic approaches to arrangement and description. They treat their material organically, are concerned with how items relate to each other, and in fact assert that records have meaning only if maintained together by source, preferably in their original order. The card catalog, in paper or modern automated version, is central to information retrieval in a library, which treats each item as a discrete entity or unit warranting separate consideration. A historical records program must depend on looser, less standardized finding aids and describes its holdings in summary form rather than item by item. While library items on similar topics reside side by side on library shelves, an archival collection may be located in several locations for convenience of storage. The archivist treats "all records as a unity, describes them in their proper organic relationships, and only notes in passing that they are physically separated."[18]

Librarians and archivists differ in their approach to dealing with patrons (the common library term) and researchers (the preferable archival term). Patrons are used to browsing in library stacks; researchers are barred from archival storage areas. The librarian's main challenge may be to explain the institution's access tools to the patron, who can then proceed to identify the material that is needed. By contrast, archival finding aids are much less standardized, and the reference archivist may have to spend considerable time orienting the researcher to the repository's holdings and explaining their potential usefulness. As discussed in chapter 9, archivists must mediate among researchers, finding aids, and the archival materials themselves, a complex challenge that requires well-developed communications and interpretation skills. In serving researchers, as in other areas, there are similarities between library and archival approaches, but there are also important differences.

NOTES

1. Telephone conversation with Donn Neal, Executive Director, Society of American Archivists, March 12, 1990.

2. Margaret S. Child, "Reflections on Cooperation among Professions," *American Archivist* 46 (Summer 1983):287.

3. National Historical Publications and Records Commission, *Directory of Archives and Manuscript Repositories in the United States,* 2nd ed. (New York: Oryx Press, 1988), Introduction.

4. A summary of archival roles is provided in "SAA Role Delineation," Society of American Archivists *Newsletter* (January 1989):6–8. The summary is reproduced here in Appendix A.

5. Herman Kahn, "Documenting American Culture through Three Generations: Change and Continuity," *American Archivist* 38 (April 1975):148.

6. Theodore R. Schellenberg, *The Management of Archives* (New York: Columbia University Press, 1965), ix.

7. Frank G. Burke, "The Future Course of Archival Theory in the United States," *American Archivist* 44 (Winter 1981):40–46.

8. Harold T. Pinkett, "American Archival Theory: The State of the Art," *American Archivist* 44 (Summer 1981):222.

9. Consultative Group on Canadian Archives, *Canadian Archives: Report to the Social Sciences and Humanities Research Council of Canada* (Ottawa: Social Sciences and Humanities Research Council of Canada, 1980), 6, 8.

10. Society of American Archivists, "Who Is the 'I' in Archives?" (Chicago: Society of American Archivists, n.d.), pamphlet; National Coordinating Committee for the Promotion of History, *Developing a Premier National Institution: A Report from the User Community to the National Archives* (Washington: National Coordinating Committee for the Promotion of History, 1989), 9.

11. New York State Historical Records Advisory Board, *Toward a Usable Past: Historical Records in the Empire State* (Albany: New York State Education Department, 1984), 21–23; "Archives: What They Are, Why They Matter," Society of American Archivists *Newsletter* (May 1984):6–7.

12. New York State Historical Records Advisory Board, *Toward a Usable Past*, 21–23.

13. David McCullough, "Introduction," in Herman J. Viola, *The National Archives of the United States* (New York: Harry N. Abrams, 1984), 12–13.

14. Herman Kahn, "Some Comments on the Archival Vocation," *American Archivist* 34 (January, 1971):7, quoted in Mattie U. Russell, "The Influence of Historians on the Archival Profession in the United States," *American Archivist* 46 (Summer 1983):282.

15. George Bolotenko, "Archivists and Historians: Keepers of the Well," *Archivaria* 16 (Summer 1983):5–25.

16. Richard J. Cox, "Archivists and Public Historians in the United States," in Bruce W. Dearstyne, ed., "Archivists and Public History: Issues, Problems, and Prospects," special issue of *Public Historian* 8 (Summer 1986):29–45.

17. Nancy E. Peace and Nancy Fisher Chudacoff, "Archivists and Librarians: A Common Mission, a Common Education," *American Archivist* 42 (October 1979):456–472.

18. Frank G. Burke, "Materials and Methodology," in Robert L. Clark, ed., *Archive–Library Relations* (New York: R.R. Bowker, 1976), 35.

2 Historical Records Programs: Diverse Types, Common Elements

This chapter describes the basic elements of historical records programs and discusses the variations in those programs. Some of the themes it introduces are covered in more detail in later chapters.

The term *historical records program,* as discussed in the Introduction, includes any deliberate, organized effort to acquire, hold, care for, and make available historical records. This broad definition encompasses two general types of programs. *Institutional and organizational archival programs* appraise, accession, and care for the archival records created by their parent institutions. The hypothetical examples of the Madison University Archives and the city of Westlake Archives fit this category. These programs are often regarded as mainline administrative services because they furnish documentation for operational, legal, and other purposes.

The second type includes *collecting programs in libraries, historical societies, museums, and other settings* that acquire historical records from beyond their own institution. Auburn Research Library and Salem Public Library, examples from the Introduction, fit the classification of collecting programs. Sometimes the two types of programs are combined; for instance, an art museum may have an office that cares for its own archival records and also collects records of artists and arts organizations. A university may maintain a special collections section in its library that encompasses both university archives and a program for collecting and servicing manuscripts from the outside. The Madison University example would fit this category.

Whether it is a manuscripts program in a city library, an archival program in a bank, or a university archives, any historical records program should have at least the following characteristics:

It acquires and maintains significant historical records.
It has a discernible sponsorship by some organization or institution and a definite program setting within that organization or institution.

It approaches its work in a deliberate, organized, concerted manner rather than in an casual, offhand way.

Its work is continuous rather than onetime or intermittent.

It has a facility, staff, and other resources to do its work.

It makes its holdings available for research, sometimes with appropriate restrictions on their use.

Varieties of Historical Records Programs

A number of studies and reports completed during recent years makes it possible to categorize historical records programs as well as to generalize about their conditions and needs, as covered in chapter 3. The Society of American Archivists conducted a census of historical records programs in the mid-1980s. The National Historical Publications and Records Commission issued an updated national directory of historical records programs in 1988. During the same decade, most of the states carried out historical records needs assessment studies. Based on these and other studies, it is possible to categorize historical records programs into ten groupings.

1. *Federal government archival programs.* This category includes the National Archives and Records Administration's main office in Washington, D.C., and its network of presidential libraries and regional archives and records centers throughout the country. NARA carries out the federal government's archival functions, the most important of which is identifying and caring for the government's archival records. Its records centers provide efficient, low-cost storage and retrieval service for inactive government records. NARA also conducts research and development activities to address government records management and archives issues. The National Historical Publications and Records Commission, an agency that provides grants for historical records projects and publication of papers and documents important for American history, is located at NARA and chaired by the Archivist of the United States. Some federal agencies, such as the Department of Energy, Department of Defense, and the Environmental Protection Agency, have their own records programs, which coordinate with NARA's work.

2. *State archival programs.* Every state has an agency that is charged by statute with identifying, collecting, maintaining, and making available the records of state government with continuing historical or other research value. Alabama was the first state to establish an archival program (1904); New York, the last (1978). State archival agencies are found in secretary of states' offices, state historical societies, divisions of archives and history, state

libraries, and other settings. Taken together, they hold over a million cubic feet of archival records. In the older states, holdings include colonial government records as well as those reflective of the development and services of state government. Because state governments have been such an enduring and influential institution, their archival records document environmental, social, economic, and political changes. The best place to study land policy and settlement may be the original maps and land grant records at the state archives; changes in water pollution may be documented in the records from the state conservation department; records from the labor department reveal the unemployment impact of the Great Depression; files of the department of education demonstrate that concern over dropouts, crime in the schools, and academic achievement is really not new. Often, the archival program is combined with the state government records management program. In many states, the director of the state archival program also provides leadership to address statewide historical records issues.

3. *Local government archival programs.* Some of the nation's largest counties and cities—New York City, Philadelphia, and Los Angeles, for instance—have developed formal archival programs, situated in mayors' offices, city administrators' offices, and other settings, but most local governments have not organized archival programs. However, important archival records, such as minutes, deeds, maps, and other documents with obvious legal significance, are filed and maintained by county, city, town, and other municipal clerks. Most municipal clerks would not regard themselves as archivists. They carry out a partial archival function, however, in their role as official keepers and custodians of records with enduring value. In other cases, municipal libraries or local historical societies take care of local government archival records, sometimes as the result of informal arrangements resulting from the library or society's interest in preserving sources of community history and the local government's disinterest in mounting its own archival programs. Because local government is so close to the people, its taxation, education, police, court, welfare, and other records often contain incredibly rich detail on individuals.

4. *Institutional archives.* These are the internal archival programs of businesses, banks, insurance companies, other corporations, and other types of institutions and organizations. Coca-Cola, Chase Manhattan Bank, Wells Fargo Corporation, Corning Glass, and Kraft General Foods are among the archival elite—companies with prominent programs. These programs are usually established and maintained primarily to serve the parent institution by saving records of its activities for administrative, legal,

commemorative, and advertising purposes. In some institutional archives, access to holdings is restricted on account of the confidential nature of the information or the need to safeguard trade and commercial information from potential competitors. The holdings of institutional archives may yield information about economic conditions, business ethics, relationships between businesses and their home communities, labor policies, advertising and promotional strategies, and administrative techniques.

5. *College and university programs.* Colleges and universities often combine two types of programs: maintenance of the college or university's own archival records, and collections of historical records to support student or faculty research interests or to meet other educational objectives. College and university archival records document educational policies, student life, and "town-and-gown" relations. Major research universities, for example Cornell, New York University, the University of California at Berkeley, and the University of Michigan, maintain historical records programs that collect on a national and even an international scale. The Bentley Historical Library at the University of Michigan, for instance, houses one of the nation's foremost collections of labor history records. Cornell University has for years collected materials pertaining to rural, upstate New York. These and other university programs hold some of the nation's most important historical records.

6. *Religious archives.* These are the archival records of individual parish churches, dioceses or other regional configurations, and sects or denominations. Within church archives are found important operational records, materials that provide enlightenment on theological and religious tenets, and registries of parishioners, births, deaths, marriages, and other records pertaining to church participants. Diocesan and denominational archives include broader policy documents that reflect the relationship between regional or central church authorities and individual parishes or churches. Religious archives also present broad religious and ethical issues and trends.

7. *Museum archives.* These usually consist of the museum's own archival records but may also include external materials, such as documentation on exhibits and the records of artists or other individuals connected with the museum or its work. The Smithsonian Institution in Washington sets the pace for museum archives through its work in maintaining its own archives and actively collecting in anthropology and other topics directly related to its mission. Often, the archival program is tied to the museum's exhibits program, making possible exhibits that include both two-dimensional and three-dimensional historical items.

8. *Public libraries.* Libraries range in size from one- or two-room village libraries through significant urban libraries to the New York Public Library. State libraries and even the Library of Congress fit under this heading. Collecting policies are often vague and general, especially for smaller libraries, which may collect almost any types of historical records from within their localities or regions. Typical holdings include letters, files, photographs, scrapbooks, account books, and maps. It is common for these materials to be regarded as a species of special collection and to be held with newspapers, rare books, and other nonbook items in a special collections division. Because large numbers of citizens visit public libraries for research, historical records collections in these settings tend to be extensively used.

9. *Historical societies.* There are thousands of historical societies ranging from small, informal outfits with only a few members to large, prestigious societies such as the Massachusetts Historical Society and the New-York Historical Society. In some areas, particularly the Midwest, state historical societies function as quasigovernmental agencies and maintain the state government's archival records and also collect and hold nongovernment historical records pertaining to the state's past. The numbers of community historical societies increased rapidly in modern times, particularly during the bicentennial of the American Revolution. Often, they collect records of local social, political, and business leaders, local business records, and other materials documenting the locality. Small to modest-sized societies tend to operate within a pattern of low budgets, heavy reliance on volunteers, and restricted hours, but they play an important role in preserving the nation's documentary heritage. The local historical society is often the best place to go for grassroots historical documentation.

10. *Subject-oriented programs.* This category includes dozens of programs that are subject or theme oriented, such as labor history, transportation, the arts, literature, music, and science. In most cases, these programs are supported by institutions or groups that are interested in preserving the records of particular topics, groups, or localities.

Of course, not all programs fit these neat and seemingly mutually exclusive categories. The SAA survey found that "widely diverse institutions call themselves archives" and that their holdings may include "an incredible mishmash of documents, books, audiovisual items, and all manner of artifacts" as well as archival material. Far from a simple, uniform pattern, historical records programs in the United States are more like a diverse mosaic. "Most archives are part repositories of historical documents, part museum, and part library," the SAA's report concluded.[1]

Basic Elements of Historical Records Programs

Historical records programs vary so greatly in origin, scope, purpose, and support that it would be impossible to devise a single set of standards that would fit them all. In fact, these programs may be organized and function without meeting any standards except for charter or incorporation provisions, legal requirements, or other directives that apply to a particular program or set of programs. In the examples in the Introduction, the collections at Auburn Research Library accumulated around a defined theme, arts and performing arts, but otherwise there were no particular requirements or constraints, at least at the outset. Madison University put its own archives in order and set out to collect in certain topical areas, but there were no definite requirements or standards that its program had to meet. Salem Public Library acknowledged a definite obligation to the Donald Shultes family and a less definite one to potential researchers (to make the materials available), but beyond that the head librarian might have proceeded as he chose. The city of Westlake, by contrast, was bound by its state's statutes that governed retention and disposition of its archival records, and public access to them, but the city clerk was free to organize, arrange, and describe them as she wished.

There are, however, patterns and commonly acknowledged approaches that the four example programs and all viable historical records programs follow. This commonality sets historical records *programs* apart from casual, unorganized collecting efforts. Historical records programs need several fundamental components if they are to function in a minimally acceptable fashion. In recent years, the archival field has developed guidelines, canons of good practice and descriptions of how historical records programs should operate and what they should aim to accomplish. These descriptions are found in journals articles, manuals, and other publications and have not been drawn together into a single publication.[2] Nor do the statements, taken together, add up to program standards; they are more modest, flexible, and broad enough to fit any one program. But they are also precise enough to impart a sense of common purpose and to establish reasonable expectations for responsible program administration and performance.

From this body of literature, it is possible to characterize what might be called the basic elements that every viable historical records program needs to function in a satisfactory way. They are summarized below under four headings: program foundations, structural elements, service elements, and program promotion and enhancement elements. They are discussed in more detail in later chapters. They are also illustrated in figure 1.

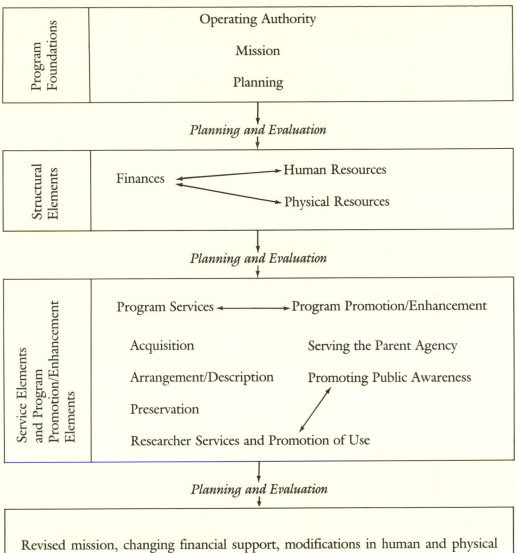

Figure 1. An operational diagram of historical records programs.

This diagram shows graphically the relationship among historical records program elements. The only constant is operating authority—the charter, law, resolution, or other legal basis for the program's operations. The other elements change over time to meet diversifying and growing needs of a dynamic program. Planning is shown as an essential foundation for the entire program, but a continuing planning and evaluation process is essential to keep the program moving. Horizontal arrows indicate close mutual interdependence. For instance, finances obviously help determine the level of human and physical resources; program services and program promotion and enhancement are interrelated.

PROGRAM FOUNDATIONS

Two program elements—an operating authority and mission statement, and a continuous planning process—are essential prerequisites to program administration and delivery of services. They define the nature, purposes, and direction of the program, which is essential for the parent institution, the program's employees, and researchers and others it serves. Programs that spring up and proceed without these foundation elements are much less likely to have a clear sense of purpose and to succeed in their work than programs that have them.

Operating Authority and Mission Statement

It is highly desirable for a historical records program to have a law, charter, administrative directive, or other document that defines its operational authority, general purposes, and responsibilities and that establishes its place in the organizational setting of its parent institution. This authority-bestowing foundation statement gives the program standing and recognition as an operational entity, an important prerequisite to sustained operation. The operating authoritystatement also attests to the program's importance to the parent agency, establishes its claim to resources, and may be helpful in defending it against reductions or dissolution in difficult financial times.

Connected to and derived from this foundation document should be a mission statement that describes the program's fundamental purposes and sets expectations in more detail. The mission statement is usually developed in consultation and discussions involving administrators of the parent institution, the manager of the historical records program, and the program's employees. Once derived and published, it should not be changed unless the fundamental nature or direction of the program changes. The mission statement explains the program's deepest and most important purposes. It should spell out why the program was initiated and how it relates and contributes to the parent agency's work. It provides the basis for the program's service elements by discussing what geographical region, groups, experiences, or other topical areas the program aims to document; what types of records or information it intends to collect; and what types of research groups or interests it supports or serves. The mission statement is the program's fundamental departure point for setting goals and objectives, seeking resources, explaining and justifying its work, and gauging its long-term success.

An Effective Planning and Evaluation Process

Successful historical records programs require at least a general planning process that proceeds from the mission statement and addresses, on a continuing basis, the questions of the business of the program, what the program is expected to accomplish, the program's priorities, and how available resources should be marshalled and applied. Sound programs require both strategic planning, which entails setting long-term objectives and gearing the program to meet them, and operational planning, which is short-term (for instance, annual) and concrete.

In most planning efforts, the first step is to develop goals based on the mission statement. Goals are broad statements of outcomes expected to be reached by a designated point in the future. For each goal, a set of objectives should be developed: concrete, achievable targets of attainment that, if all achieved, would put the program at or near the goal. Under the objectives are activities: smaller, more discrete work benchmarks that must be achieved in order to reach the objectives. In general, activities are sufficiently concrete and well defined that individual staff workplans can be tied to them. Many program plans also identify priorities—activities or objectives that the program is most determined to carry out because of their central importance to the program's mission, because they are important to the program's standing and well-being, or because they are mandated services.

A planning effort need not be elaborate or unduly time consuming, but it should be taken seriously and regarded as important program work. Planning enables the institution's trustees and administrators in charge of historical records programs to establish direction and assert and maintain control. It imparts a sense of purpose and consistency, makes the most effective use of resources and facilities, establishes a unifying vision of anticipated products and goals, and provides a yardstick against which to monitor and report on progress. Where planning is disregarded or slighted, programs may be characterized by drift, erratic changes in course in response to changing circumstances, and general lack of development.

Continual program evaluation is a natural implication of a well planned and soundly managed program. Evaluation tells the archivist how well the program is progressing and how effective it is in serving its home institution and its service clientele. Evaluation also leads to renewed planning and program development by providing a realistic basis for charting future program direction.

STRUCTURAL ELEMENTS

Structural elements—finances, human resources (people), and facilities—are the essential structural components that make historical records programs operate.

Adequate, Continuing Financial Support

Historical records programs need an established presence in their parent programs' budgets. "Financial resources dependably available to the archives must be adequate to carry out its stated purpose," says the SAA's assessment manual. [3] Adequate implies a level of resources that can reasonably be expected to support the service elements summarized below and discussed throughout this book. This means steady, reliable funding that is derived from the parent agency's regular budget, or from some other continuing source. Inclusion in the budget connotes recognition that the program is an important part of the parent agency's work. The person in charge of the historical records program should participate in the budget-making process and have an opportunity to represent the program's needs in hearings, discussions, and other review processes that lead to final budget decisions. In order to do so effectively, he or she needs convincing measurement systems and statistics both on program accomplishments, particularly work that supports the parent institution's mission and that provides services to researchers, and on program needs. An adequate financial system for a historical records program includes means to acquire, use, track, and report on funds.[4]

The historical records program manager may need to remind institutional resource allocators of the value and importance of the historical records program, of its contributions to the institution's own objectives, and of the fact that quality programming requires at least a modest investment of resources. In the case of libraries, the program should have its own section in the budget and the resources allocated should be sufficient to enable the program to do its work. While frugality is a virtue, slighting the program, cutting corners, and postponing basic work such as arranging and describing a backlog of holdings are not sound cost-saving strategies in the long run.

Sufficient, Qualified Staff ("Human Resources")

Archival work is demanding and exacting and should be carried out by trained, experienced personnel. Therefore, every program "must include on its staff at least one person who possesses, through training and experience, professional competence in archives management."[5] This person is not simply a librarian or a historian. The person must know how to administer historical records in line with commonly accepted archival approaches and guidelines, and how to direct others in doing so. Depending on the size of the program, additional qualified professional and support staff and volunteers will be needed to carry out the service elements of the program. A historical society might do well with a half-time librarian with archival training and experience for its modest historical records program. A corporation might need a program director, a professional staff of two or three archivists, and clerical and other support personnel. A program with larger scale responsibilities and growing holdings and service expectations will need a larger staff commensurate with its needs. A sizeable manuscripts section in a library could require a dozen or more staff members, depending on the size of its holdings, the rate of their growth, and the level and intensity of the service demands.

Secure, Adequate Physical Facilities

Historical records are invaluable cultural resources. Collecting them imposes an important custodial responsibility to preserve and protect, as well as to make available. Therefore, historical records programs need secure, fireproof facilities, with fire detection and extinguishment systems if possible. Temperature and humidity controls are essential and air conditioning is highly desirable. Storage space should be adequate in size to accommodate existing holdings and anticipated growth for the immediate future. There should also be enough room, equipment, and facilities for staff to arrange, describe, preserve, and carry out other work on records. The ultimate objective of the program is to serve researchers. The program therefore needs secure research room space of sufficient size to meet the needs of all researchers who visit the program, laid out in such a way that staff can maintain surveillance and therefore deter theft of the records.

SERVICE ELEMENTS

Historical records programs stress service—to the people who create records of enduring value and to the people who have an information need that can be satisfied through the use of those records. The service elements—identifying and collecting records, arranging, describing, and preserving them, and promoting their use—constitute the essential work of a viable historical records program.

A Systematic Approach to Records Acquisition

Historical records programs should follow a systematic approach to the selection of records for acquisition and preservation. Programs must be anticipatory as well as curatorial; they must make provision for saving records that will be needed by future generations of researchers. Archivists always operate with an eye to the future as well as concern for the records of the present and the past. Organizational and institutional archives should have authority and responsibility to identify and receive the records of continuing value that are produced by the institution of which they are a part. Collecting programs should have the general scope of their collecting mission set forth in their mission statements. Acquisition efforts should be based on at least three interrelated considerations, each of which is discussed in detail in chapter 6.

The first consideration might be called the program's *documentation objectives*. This term refers to what the program aims to document, in cooperation with and under arrangements worked out with other programs that collect in the same or related geographical or subject areas. Documentation planning involves more than just collecting records from the past. It assumes an interest in documenting the present and the future as well and is therefore future-oriented more than past-oriented. It provides for continuing the systematic creation, collecting, maintenance, and availability of adequate documentation in the future. Acquisition planning that begins with definition of documentation objectives has as a starting point a clear view of the future.

The second consideration is a *collection policy*, which defines what sorts of records the program is most interested in acquiring. It is based on the program's mission statement and documentation objectives. The collection policy serves as a public notice of what the program wishes to collect, alerts potential donors about its interests, offers potential researchers information on the scope of collecting efforts and holdings, and provides the basis for the program's own appraisal and acquisitions work.

The third consideration is *appraisal*. Appraisal is the process of systematically analyzing each set of potentially valuable records to determine if they have sufficient continuing research value to warrant making them part of the program's holdings. Appraisal requires an understanding of the operation of the person or institution that produced the records and familiarity with research interests and trends. It typically involves direct examination of the records and may require consultation with outside experts. As discussed in chapter 6, the appraisal process concentrates on determining how much important information the records contain and how much evidence they provide about the person, organization, or institution that produced them. Sound appraisal is essential to make sure that only records appropriate to the program's documentation objectives and collection policy are preserved. Appraisal is the key to ensuring that holdings are built systematically and that the records best suited for continuing retention are identified and preserved.

Arrangement and Description

Arrangement is the process of organizing historical records to reflect their original order and to facilitate use. Records should be arranged in line with the two basic principles of *provenance* and *original order*. These two principles hold that records from different sources or offices should not be intermingled and that records should be retained in their original order whenever possible. If the original order has been lost, records should be arranged in some logical order that will facilitate research use. Description refers to the process of asserting intellectual control over the records and developing descriptions so that they may be accessed and used by researchers. There should be a system of finding aids that facilitates easy access to holdings by researchers and by members of the program's staff. In general, the system should provide for at least preliminary description of all records soon after they arrive at the repository and at least summary description of all records before any of them are described in detail.

Preservation of the Records and Their Information

Every program has a basic custodial responsibility to preserve the records it acquires and holds, including appropriate environmental and antifire provisions, as noted above. The program should guard against damage from mishandling by staff or researchers and against theft by providing secure storage and appropriate surveillance in the research room while materials are being used. Records should be kept in acidfree folders and boxes. There should be a basic conservation program that includes minimal treatment, such as unfolding and cleaning, by program staff, and referral of more complicated conservation challenges to professional conservators. There should be a disaster recovery plan to enable the program to respond to natural or man-made disasters such as fires and floods.

Promotion of Use

Historical records programs make their holdings available at convenient hours on a reasonable basis to people whose information needs can be met in whole or in part through the use of the records.

Reference personnel should be available to guide the researchers to finding aids, suggest records, retrieve and make available those records, and answer questions. Just standing ready to serve researchers is not enough. A historical records program should actively encourage and promote research by providing information directly to researchers on the holdings and their potential research use and on program services. Production and distribution of materials that describe the records and explain their research potential; talks to researcher groups; and providing material for researchers' newsletters, journals, and other publications are all ways to promote the holdings. Programs also need access policies to govern the availability of their holdings to researchers.

PROGRAM PROMOTION AND ENHANCEMENT ELEMENTS

Few programs are at the level of resources and attainment where they can rest on their laurels; most acknowledge a need for more resources, better facilities, and enhanced services. People in charge of historical records programs need to put their programs in the best possible light, emphasize services and achievements, and search for means of promoting and strengthening the programs. There are two closely related elements—promotion and enhancement with the sponsoring institution or organization, and promoting broader public awareness of individual historical records programs and of the archival function in society in general.

Serving the Sponsoring or Parent Agency

Though not often isolated as a discrete element, service to the agency that provides a setting and resources to historical records programs should in fact be regarded as a central concern. Work in this area may include involving supervisors, administrators, and resource allocators in planning activities; ensuring that the historical records program's mission and goals are, to the degree possible, compatible with and reinforce the parent program's mission and goals; devising a reporting system that keeps higher level administrators apprised of the program's work; and involving them in program activities, for instance, participating in public events and opening exhibits.

Promoting Public Awareness

A historical records program has obligations beyond acquisition, conscientious stewardship, and promoting and facilitating use. There is a need to reach out to the concerned public with information on the program and its holdings, and on the work of archivists in general. Such efforts are discussed in chapter 10, characterized there as "promotional marketing." This work promotes public awareness of the holdings, engendering appreciation and possibly research use. It also leads to increased public appreciation, which indirectly heightens awareness of program need and may eventually increase program support. The program "should identify its various constituencies in terms of its purpose [and] plan and implement methods to assess the needs of these groups in relation to the resources of the institution, and devise outreach programs that will fit their needs."[6] For many programs, approaching schools is desirable to demonstrate to young people the usefulness of historical records. Public education or outreach programs may include publications, courses, exhibits, open houses, and other events aimed at reaching beyond the traditional research communities.

Historical Records Programs in Library Settings

Historical records collecting programs are compatible with other library purposes even though the approaches and methodologies of archivists and librarians are different. Archivists are concerned with documentation, with collection and preservation of coherent bodies of materials, with collective ordering of materials, and with specialized services. The discussion in chapter 1 notes, however, the divergences between library and archival practices. As Paul McCarthy of the University of Alaska has pointed out, the "corporate culture" may also be different, leading to potential misunderstandings. Librarians, part of a long-recognized and highly respected profession, may feel that the archival profession is not fully organized or developed. While acknowledging that great strides have been made during the past two decades—the development of archival certification, tighter educational guidelines, more definite program expectations—librarians may feel that archivists have some distance to go to achieve full professional status. Librarians may see historical records as a species of special collections, and may classify and catalog them as books. They may underestimate the magnitude and cost of the work of caring for archival materials and for addressing the arrangement, description, preservation, and reference demands associated with them.[7]

The archivist in a library setting may feel unappreciated—and underfinanced. In the competition for already scarce library resources, the historical records program may not be regarded as a priority. In such cases, the historical records program may feel like an unsuccessful and disillusioned Cinderella. Brought into a family already living in desperate circumstances, her unique gifts and talents went unappreciated. Typically, she is assigned less desirable quarters and expected to accomplish her work without reasonable assistance. She comes to the attention of those in power who apparently appreciate her virtues, however momentarily, only through the good offices of her fairy Godmother, Celebration, when there is a need for material for exhibits or commemorative activities.[8]

Historical Records Programs in Library Settings: Ten Keys to Success

Historical records programs can prosper in library settings. Following are some characteristics of successful programs that operate in libraries:

- The historical records program has a distinct, written mission, a clearly defined organizational presence, and reasonably high visibility within the library.

- The program's documentation mission and collecting policies are well articulated and reinforce broader library collecting and service priorities.

- The program's performance, and its status in and contributions to the library's overall program, are reviewed periodically and renewed and refined through a regular planning process.

- The program is accorded a distinct budget and develops, defends, manages, and spends it on the same basis, and under the same controls but no more controls, as other library departments and offices. Within the limits of the library's overall budget situation, the resources are sufficient to support an acceptable approach to the program's responsibilities.

- The professionals associated with the program, whatever their formal titles, are accorded the same status as their professional colleagues in the other parts of the library's program.

- Appropriate archival techniques and approaches, suitable for the historical records materials, are applied.

- Whenever possible, exhibits, public programs, and other collaborative efforts are developed to combine the talents and resources of the historical records program with the talents and resources of other parts of the library.

- The historical records program makes a particular effort to measure and report on its activities and services, as part of the library's overall monitoring and reporting approaches.

- Library administrators familiarize themselves with the historical records program's holdings and services; reciprocally, the historical records program manager makes a special effort to keep administrators and resource allocators fully informed about the program and its particular needs and accomplishments.

- Library reference services and historical records program researcher services are coordinated (or even combined), finding aids are integrated or proximate to each other, and researchers seeking information on a given topic are directed to historical records as well as books and other library materials.

In a well-planned and well-administered program, of course, the relationship will be better (see the above box for some suggestions). Some of the largest and best historical records programs are in research libraries, such as Clements, Newberry, Bancroft, Library of Congress, and New York Public Library. University libraries, including the Bentley Library at the University of Michigan, Cornell, Duke, and the University of California at Berkeley, also have historical records programs. Hundreds of other college and university libraries and thousands of county, city, town, and other community libraries maintain small historical records holdings. In successful programs, the historical records program is an integral part of the library's mission, but the distinctiveness of archival work is recognized and preserved. Librarians, often the most proficient information professionals in a particular community or on a college or university campus, are in a good position to plan and develop historical records programs that accord with and reinforce larger library objectives.

NOTES

1. Paul Conway, "Perspectives on Archival Resources: The 1985 Census of Archival Institutions," *American Archivist* 50 (Spring 1987):177, 184.
2. The most helpful publication is Paul H. McCarthy, ed., *Archives Assessment and Planning Workbook* (Chicago: Society of American Archivists, 1989). Also useful are New York State Archives and Records Administration, *Strengthening New York's Historical Records Programs: A Self-Study Guide* (Albany: New York State Education Department, 1989), written primarily by Richard J. Cox, and *Basic Elements of Historical Records Programs* (brochure) (Albany: New York State Education Department, 1989). This chapter follows the framework outlined in that brochure.
3. McCarthy, ed., *Archives Assessment and Planning Workbook*, 22.
4. New York State Archives and Records Administration, *Strengthening New York's Historical Records Programs*, 13.
5. McCarthy, ed., *Archives Assessment and Planning Workbook*, 25.
6. Ibid., 50.
7. Paul H. McCarthy, "Archives under Library Administration: Points of Convergence and Conflict," in Lawrence J. McCrank, ed., *Archives and Library Administration: Divergent Traditions and Common Concerns* (New York: Haworth Press, 1986), 17–34. McCarthy's article contains very helpful insights on the operation of historical records programs in library settings.
8. Ibid., 18.

3

The Age of Archival Analysis: Historical Records Conditions and Needs

The four decades between the organization of the American archival profession and the mid-1970s were characterized by relative quiet, continuity, and even complacency in the archival community. Much archival talent and energy during the 1950s and 1960s were given over to consolidating, elucidating, and explaining what had originally been conceived in the 1930s and 1940s.[1] Refinements and incremental change were common; rallying cries for new directions were unusual at archival meetings, iconoclastic articles a rarity in the journals. By contrast, the period since the mid-1970s might well be called "The Age of Archival Analysis" owing to the dozens of surveys, analytical studies, profiles, and reports on historical records programs and archival issues. These sweeping studies constituted the first full reckoning on archival work and gave rise to many of the transformational changes described in chapter 4. The studies themselves and the problems they found are described in this chapter.

The 1960s' campaigns for civil rights, women's rights, and social justice and the antiwar movement may have helped precipitate change in archivists' outlooks. These crusades occasioned review of many hoary institutions and the place of various groups in American society. Urban historians challenged archivists to do a better job of documenting city life. Researcher interest in "history from the bottom up" and the historical experiences of women, ethnic and racial minorities, and the disadvantaged exposed the unevenness and imbalance of the nation's historical record. Many archivists began scurrying to collect in new areas such as black history and women's history. They were drawn to oral history and other new techniques to fill gaps that had been revealed in the nation's historical documentation. New "special collections" programs were launched to locate and preserve sources of black history so that the historical story of blacks could be told at least in part from firsthand materials, including some created by blacks themselves.

By the early 1970s, forces for change were clearly on the move in the archival community.

But it was the dramatic 1974 Society of American Archivists' presidential address that marks the beginning of Age of Archival Analysis. F. Gerald Ham, State Archivist of Wisconsin, raised fundamental questions about how archivists go about their most important work of selecting information to provide future generations with a representative record of human experience. "Why must we do it so badly?" he asked rhetorically. "Is there any other field of information gathering that has such a broad mandate with a selection process so random, so fragmented, so uncoordinated, and even so accidental?" Warning his colleagues that "far too much effort and money go to document the well documented" whose abundant records fill the stacks of university and government archives, he called on archivists to turn away from the old ways of serving the elite. "The archivist must realize that he can no longer abdicate his role in the demanding intellectual process of documenting culture." Ham closed with an exhortation to his fellow archivists to move out to the "archival edge" and take on "big, undreamed-of things" in reconceptualizing their work and remaking their profession.[2] Ham's flair for dramatizing issues, his ability to turn a phrase, and the thrust and logic of his arguments called attention to the speech and helped make it a turning point for the American archival enterprise.

While Ham and other leaders spurred the profession on to new frontiers, two other forces were also stimulating change. Professional growth was a major catalyst. In the mid-1970s, the Society of American Archivists opened its first permanent office and hired its first full-time executive director; a second national group, the National Association of State (later expanded to Government) Archives and Records Administrators, was born; and dozens of regional archival associations came into existence. These associations recognized the need for more detailed information on conditions and needs to develop services to assist their members. Federal government support and interest also helped inspire change. In 1974, at the behest of the historical and archival communities, Congress changed the name of the National Historical Publications Commission to the National Historical Publications *and Records* Commission and expanded the Commission's mandate to include grants for historical records programs. The new NHPRC became a major supporter of projects that dealt with fundamental archival issues. Another federal funding agency, the National Endowment for the Humanities, also played an important supporting role, particularly in the areas of preservation and archival education. The role of these federal agencies is described in chapter 4.

Dozens of Studies

The nation's historical records programs, from the largest in Washington, D.C., to the smallest in outlying towns and villages, all came under scrutiny. The National Archives received intense attention from the executive branch and Congress during several years of public debate, which resulted in legislation separating it from the General Services Administration in 1985. A blue-ribbon committee of distinguished citizens, sponsored by several scholarly groups and supported by foundation grants, issued a report on the Archives' program that emphasized the need to deal with computer-generated records. The National Academy of Public Administration carried out a study of NARA's role in managing electronic records of the Federal Government. The National Coordinating Committee for the Promotion of History, a consortium of archival, history, and library organizations, issued a report on NARA's services to researchers. These diverse studies played on three themes: NARA's ability to care for its voluminous holdings, its capacity to deal with emerging challenges such as electronic records, and its potential for leading and supporting work in the broader arenas of government records and archives in general.[3]

A 1982 SAA study of college and university archives provided unprecedented detail on programs in that sector of the archival arena. The National Association of Government Archives and Records Administrators (NAGARA) gathered and published important statistics on state archival programs as part of a study of state archival preservation needs. NAGARA also issued a report on how archivists and related professionals secure and exchange technical information. The NHPRC published a national directory of historical records programs in 1978 and a revised and expanded version in 1988 that summarized holdings and also included collecting areas, hours of operation, and other information. The states of New York, Kentucky, and Washington developed more detailed computer-generated listings of repositories and their holdings. Along the way, there were ground-breaking studies in such areas as business, science, and technology.[4]

The Society of American Archivists carried out the first national census of historical records programs in 1985; though the response was not complete, the census provided descriptive and statistical information on a cross-section of programs.[5] The SAA census revealed how great was the variety and diversity of historical records programs. Over half of the nation's repositories were located in the mid-Atlantic and Midwest regions of the country, with most of the remainder in the South. The survey factored out the National Archives Washington-based programs because of their magnitude, and it compiled statistics for the remainder of the respondents—the first time such figures had been compiled and presented. More than 90 percent of the programs were created in the twentieth century, many since 1960, and a quarter since 1975. The average age of the parent institution at the time the historical records program began was 68 years, ensuring that new programs had a great deal of "catching up" to do.

Only 60 percent of those that responded had separate, identifiable budget lines at their home institutions, and newer programs tended to report particularly slim budgets. While state archives budgets were modest, the public sector archival programs were mostly larger and better funded than those in the private sector, which tended to be starved for resources. Staffs ranged from one to 156 people, but half of the programs had fewer than two full-time equivalent professional staff. Salaries were low to modest. Many programs depended heavily on volunteers. Holdings ranged from six to 137,000 linear feet, but half had less than 2,200 feet. Researcher traffic ranged from two visitors to over 37,000 annually; fully half of the programs averaged one visitor per day or less. Many programs did no analysis of reference traffic; some did not even count their researchers.

Even more sweeping and revealing were the state assessment and reporting project reports funded by the NHPRC. In 1980 and 1981, the commission, threatened with possible extinction from federal budget cuts, decided to leave a legacy of assessment reports that the states could use as a basis for planning and action. Grants were offered to the states to study historical records conditions, problems, and needs. The studies, eventually completed in almost all states, probed the condition of state archival records, local government records, libraries and other historical records repositories, and statewide issues and needs. The studies, conducted under the sponsorship of state historical records advisory boards, involved the use of detailed questionnaires and resulted in published reports that were widely distributed and received considerable attention. Taken together, these state reports constitute the most thorough analysis of historical records programming ever carried out in the United States.

The "Cycle of Poverty" in State Archival Programs

The state assessment reports provide the basis for generalizing about state archival programs. Many need more resources to manage their present holdings and increased capacity to care for more. Kansas called support for its program "grossly insufficient," Hawaii referred to "chronic understaffing," and Massachusetts mentioned "too many [state government] agencies, too few hands."[6] Many state programs are hampered by obsolete legal authority and thwarted by lack of prominence in state government structure. The North Carolina program, for instance, one of the nation's oldest and strongest, reported being "critically handicapped by lack of space" and noted that "most state agencies do not know of the archival program . . . even if their records are in the archives." Another well-established program lamented its "lack of identity and visibility," which put it in a weak position to demand the additional staff and other resources needed to take care of the growing volume of archival records.[7]

In other states, the problems were lack of coordination between the state's records management and archival programs and inadequate development of records retention and disposition schedules. The state archives received mostly records that agencies offered to them or took records on short notice as agency storage space ran out or agencies packed up to move. Old, crowded archival storage facilities and poor storage conditions meant a less than hospitable home for transferred archival records. Several states reported a backlog of archival records that were not arranged or described due to lack of staff, while more material poured in. Lagging production of finding aids and limited outreach efforts meant that even the choicest holdings were often underutilized. "The public is unlikely to use materials well if they do not know the materials exist," the California report observed, with a touch of irony.[8]

A summary of most of the reports concluded that state archival programs face "a cycle of poverty . . . inadequate resources which prevent state archives from mounting effective programs while the lack of [such] programs renders the archives vulnerable to disregard by departmental administrators and state budget officials."[9] The reports called for stronger, more comprehensive statutes, increased support from state government, better integration of records management and archival programming, and increased staffing.

Most of the state archival programs—and many other historical records programs as well—reported severe and growing preservation problems. Records were being lost or were threatened with eventual loss due to deterioration of the paper and other preservation problems. The survey of state archival preservation needs conducted by NAGARA documented preservation needs and concluded that:

> Serious danger threatens the nation's archival records. The paper on which most of our documentary heritage is written is deteriorating at an alarming rate while some newer recording media are even more transitory. Most government records set down during the past century, and those created today, cannot withstand the rigors of use and time without significant losses in image quality, physical strength, and chemical stability. Unless archivists

successfully meet this preservation challenge, a significant portion of the historical records contained in our archives will literally crumble to dust by the mid 21st century.[10]

Problems in Local Governments

If conditions in the fifty state archives seem less than optimal, the archival situation of the nation's more than 80,000 local governments is alarming. The archival significance of local government records is often overlooked, and the archival profession has until comparatively recently given them little attention. In fact, local government archives include important foundation documents of government itself, such as minutes, local laws, resolutions, and ordinances. They provide legal documentation and protection of rights; for instance, deeds define property ownership, maps define boundaries. From a research standpoint, they provide rich information for historical studies of the government and the community, social history and genealogy and family history.

Despite their value, local government archival records "have been frequently neglected, leading, in some cases, to severe deterioration or unwarranted destruction," in the words of one state report.[11] The Minnesota historical records assessment report indicated that "most local records are kept in environments that ensure their swift deterioration. . . . Rats, mice, bats, and pigeons inhabit countless attics and basements of courthouses and school buildings where valuable records are stored. The records of one rural school district in central Minnesota had been stored in a barn, where cattle trod. The list of ruinous storage areas is long indeed."[12]

Few local governments have archival programs. The reasons are apparent to anyone familiar with local governments' priorities. Busy clerks and other local officials lack the training and time to identify and care for archival records. Local legislators see them as a drain on the budget rather than as a productive cultural and informational asset. Secure storage space is almost always at a premium in crowded local government buildings. Other activities that provide direct service to the taxpayers have a higher priority.

In some states, statutes relating to local government records management are obsolete, state retention and disposition requirements and schedules are difficult to apply, and state oversight and advisory services are virtually nonexistent. To many jurisdictions, records management means nothing more than finding additional storage space for accumulating records. Archival records are lost in the mass of unimportant records or are simply discarded when storage space runs out. Many jurisdictions have arranged with local libraries or historical societies to take and care for the archival records. Such arrangements may work well when they are defined by written agreements that spell out both the local government's and the receiving repository's responsibilities, including commitment of resources to adequately care for the materials, and provide for continual transfer of archival records over the years. More often, the records are transferred without concomitant financial support, and they become a burden on the library or historical agency. This burden may mean, in turn, that these repositories cannot mount programs to collect and preserve other types of historical records.

The state assessment reports suggested several remedies, including modernizing local records statutes and clarifying retention and disposition requirements. Local government officials and legislative bodies need to recognize the advantage of sound records management and the value of archival records and provide resources for their care. The state archival program or some other state office must be assigned clear responsibility to oversee retention and disposition and to advise local governments on records management and archival administration.

Institutional Archives and Historical Records Programs: The Need for More Support

Most nongovernment institutions, including businesses, banks, and insurance companies, have not established archival programs. For the most part, corporate America has been archivally irresponsible. The studies showed that these archival records are either ignored and lost or are transferred to collecting repositories, usually with little provision for continuing support. Severe restrictions on researcher access may diminish the value of many of the programs that have been organized. In other cases, institutions have archival programs but they are appendages to the records management office or small units in the institution's library and lack the resources and support to be effective. Churches may maintain records on administrative and spiritual matters and membership information, but they do not always make these materials accessible to researchers. Associations, which create and hold some of the most interesting archival documentation in the nation, have for the most part been disinterested in preserving their archival records.

Lack of extensive institutional archival programs puts an added burden on the nation's libraries and other collecting programs. The state studies identified a relatively small number of strong, well-supported programs in universities and other settings that hold a sizeable percentage of the nation's historical records and have trained professional staff who are equal to the task. These programs carry out their functions well year after year and support some of the most significant research based on historical records. The programs also furnish many of the leaders of the archival profession and serve as models for other, less well off programs. Their approach to their archival responsibilities exemplifies sound techniques and procedures. Because of these factors, their significance and impact are greater than their modest numbers suggest.

There is a significant gap, however, between these programs and the numerical majority:

> There is a stark contrast between the few major archival institutions—the "haves"—and the many minor ones—the "have nots." Not only do the "haves" hold most of the records, but they have most of the expertise and practically all the trained staff. These larger repositories have adequate procedures for accessioning and initial control of records as well as for the security and storage of material. In the scores of smaller repositories and institutional archives, records preservation functions are at best minimal and rudimentary; often they are nonexistent.[13]

In the words of another state report, many small programs in libraries and other settings proceed with "little or nothing in the way of institutional commitment to the enterprise in the way of paid and trained staff, proper facilities, and integration into the institution's program."[14] Many libraries have collected small caches of letters, diaries, account books, and clipping scrapbooks, often in response to offers from local people to donate such materials. Their rationale seems to be that someone might find the materials useful someday for some research purpose, but the collection is unsystematic, resources inadequate, services to researchers insubstantial, and a backlog of unprocessed materials continues to increase.

A separate study of college and university archives, most in library settings, found that more than a third of those responding had no professional staff, and another third had only one professional. Most reported having no records management programs on their campuses, confounding the archivists' work in locating and identifying the archival records. Many reported lack of space and a backlog of unarranged and undescribed records, factors that were matched by low visitation and researcher figures. The average number of researchers was reported to be 18 per week, with half reporting eight or fewer per week.[15]

The majority of the nation's historical records programs—in libraries, historical societies, museums, and other settings—are small, isolated, and underdeveloped, according to the state reports. They may be proud of their role in saving history and resist suggestions that their custodianship is less than perfect, but clearly they struggle with the responsibility and burden of historical records. The Arizona report complained that most of that state's collecting programs were "underfunded, understaffed, underequipped, underutilized, underappreciated, and often unknown to the public." North Carolina reported that most of its programs were "experiencing serious problems. Most are crowded for space and are hampered by large backlogs of unprocessed holdings, insufficient personnel, inadequate equipment, major conservation as well as security problems, and responsibilities that exceed their resources."[16]

Many programs lack a clear collecting focus. As the Wisconsin report observed, "few institutions, large or small, public or private, have a written statement delineating collecting policy, and those statements which do exist are often so vague as to be meaningless." In Massachusetts, home to some of the most preeminent programs in the nation, smaller programs "are unlikely to have firmly defined collecting policies and, while the broad outlines of such a policy can often be found in the minds of [historical] society or library officials, variation from that policy can easily result. Acquisition actions are likely to be sporadic if not passive."[17] Crowded, less-than-secure storage space was a common lament in the reports. Programs operating in cramped space with less than reliable funding sources and dependent on the energies of volunteers quite understandably were not always up to high performance standards.

Many collecting programs concentrate on important political or literary figures or other leading citizens to the exclusion of women, ethnic minorities, the disadvantaged, and even ordinary people. For instance, repositories tend not to coordinate collecting efforts and often are unaware of what other programs in their geographical or subject area are collecting. The situation is changing as historical records programs take a more enlightened view of their collecting obligations, but there is much catching up to do. The modern era is apparently not *historical* in the minds of many program managers, so recent materials—sometimes the entire twentieth century—are not collected. The result is unevenness and inconsistency in collecting and serious gaps in the nation's historical record considered as a whole. Many programs reported sizeable—and growing—backlogs of unprocessed records and inadequate or nonexistent finding aids, meaning that the records are difficult or impossible for researchers to use.

Some repositories lacked even an accurate estimate of their holdings. In Connecticut, for instance, about half the repositories responding to the assessment report's questionnaire could not estimate the quantity of their holdings. Libraries that could report precisely the number of books they held had only a general notion of the volume of historical records they had collected. Several of state reports provided statistics that explain the state of affairs. In California, nearly 75 percent of the programs responding to the questionnaire reported that historical records were not the major function of their organization or institution; 61 percent said that they spend less than $5,000 per year on historical records work; 64 percent have no written collecting policies; 26 percent have no finding aids; and more than 80 percent do not report new accessions to scholarly journals or other sources where they are likely to be seen by researchers.[18] Some programs exhibit a narrow, proprietary attitude, seeing their collections akin to priceless antiques to be locked up out of harm's way rather as resources to be used for research. Others catered primarily to local historians and genealogists and, in part due to lack of staff, made little attempt to attract other researchers. Many repositories responding to the questionnaires revealed that they did not even keep counts of researchers.

Underlying the pattern of need is a general lack of public recognition and support that makes it difficult for programs to advance. "Lack of public understanding and regard leads to underfunding of historical records repositories and underutilization of their holdings," noted a summary of the state reports. "This process has a circular effect in that low use perpetuates low funding which prevents repositories from upgrading the management of their collections which might in turn increase their use."[19]

Patterns of Need

"At times, the American archival profession seems to resemble nothing so much as Sisyphus endlessly rolling his rock up the mountainside," one summary of the assessment reports concluded, because the reports reflect "a wide range of problems which were often intractable in nature."[20] The state assessment reports and other recent studies show a significant gap between "what is" and "what ought to be" in American archival enterprise. One state report concluded that most of its programs "are crowded for space and are hampered by large backlogs of unprocessed holdings, insufficient personnel, inadequate equipment, major conservation as well as security problems, and responsibilities that exceed their resources."[21] They were revealing and instructive—even mildly shocking—for the archival community that, since getting organized in the 1930s, had not undertaken a fundamental scrutiny of how well the nation's archival legacy was being cared for.

One common thread in the reports is lack of public understanding of the value and importance of historical records and limited appreciation of the need for strong programs for their management.

The Age of Archival Analysis: Insights for the Library Community

The reports and studies of historical records issues during the past decade helped inform librarians about conditions and needs and provided insights for them to shape historical records programs in their own institutions. Many librarians served on advisory or study committees, participated in meetings where studies and reports were discussed, and read widely distributed reports. Insights and messages for librarians in particular include:

- For the first time, the reports provided empirical information on the number, condition, collections, and other characteristics of historical records programs. The nature, purposes, holdings, researcher traffic, and other issues, were summarized and presented in reports that were widely available within the library community.

- Similarities between some archival and library issues—for instance, preservation needs—were made clear. On the other hand, differences in approaches—for instance, to the description of holdings and development of finding aids—were also clarified.

- Librarians, as the leading information professionals in their communities and their institutions, need to play a leadership role in shaping and acting as advocates for developing programs.

- The collecting policies of many library-based historical records programs need to be sharpened, revised, or updated to ensure that collecting efforts accord with broader library priorities and are compatible with the collecting policies of other institutions.

- More institutional and local government archival programs are needed so that the records of these entities are not transferred to libraries that are already overcrowded and overextended.

- Researchers would like to locate and access books, other library holdings, and historical records through common databases; provisions must be made for getting data on historical records into library databases.

- Archival preservation needs, particularly those arising from the deterioration of high-acid paper, are very similar to library preservation needs; common approaches should be considered.

- The archival profession is increasingly concerned with program performance, work measurement, educational guidelines, and program standards. In many ways, these emerging concerns parallel or resemble concerns of the library community.

- Archival training and education needs may be addressed at least in part through programs in library schools.

"It is easy to ignore [historical records]," said one report. "They do not crowd the streets, nor do they complain, write letters, lobby, or vote. . . . They are known to only a few."[22] Historical records programs need a higher institutional priority, parent institutions' administrators lack an appreciation of archival work, and the managers of the historical records programs face stiff competition for limited resources. One solution is to build public support, which will require imaginative approaches to dramatize seemingly obscure issues pertaining to old records.

Many of the reports concluded that increased visibility and public support are essential preconditions to stronger historical records programs and called on archivists to become champions for their profession. Several reports themselves advanced the basic case for historical records, as an example and inspiration to historical records programs. Historical records "document the activities of people and the institutions they create, serving as a collective recorded memory of civilization," said the Ohio report. "As such, they are a vital civic and cultural resource."[23] Carrying this message to the world beyond archivists themselves constitutes a long-term investment in strengthening the capacity of the archival community to meet expectations and needs.

A related need is archival leadership. The reports, directly and by implication, attested to the need for clearer objectives for the profession. The absence of clearcut archival objectives undermined programs' credibility and made it difficult to achieve and hold support for them. The evidence showed the need for a clearer, better defined leadership role for the National Archives and Records Administration and its grants agency, the National Historical Publications and Records Commission. Professional associations at both the national and regional level need to redouble their training, advocacy, and public education efforts. To combat the lack of central focus at the state level, the reports showed the need for the state archival agency or some other program to take the lead and coordinate statewide program development.

Leadership is needed to raise public consciousness, to encourage coordinated collecting, to deal with difficult issues such as documentation strategies, and generally to advance the archival cause. It is needed to define the future nature and objectives of archival work in an era of rapidly changing information technology, and to help organize the archival community to move in a concerted manner toward those objectives. The leaders need to be more than highly proficient archivists who are thoroughly familiar with their profession's approach to its work. They must be visionaries, able to articulate a clear view of a desired future for the archival endeavor. They must be inspirational, with an ability to convince archivists to move together toward a brighter future and to persuade other people of the importance of archival work. They must be political in the sense of forging alliances with other professionals and groups whose influence and resources are essential.

Too many programs collect records without written policies or guidelines. As a result, collecting is haphazard and incomplete. The lack of cooperation sometimes results in competition for collections, or even in dividing collections among two or more repositories. This is part of the general need for cooperation among programs. Decentralization and fragmentation were shown to be major traits—major weaknesses—of the archival community. Many reports noted the propensity of archival programs to go it alone rather than cooperating with each other in key areas such as collection development. Lack of cooperation means that large gaps are left in the nation's archival record (by neglecting certain groups, topics, or geographical areas). In the words of the perceptive Wisconsin report, "if institutions can integrate collecting efforts, such an approach will provide a statewide program that will make most effective use of limited collecting resources, fill major gaps in the record, and allow the fortuitous accession to become part of a comprehensive and coherent acquisitions program."[24] Programs also miss opportunities for cooperative purchase of materials and services that would make the best use of limited financial resources. Programs seldom share staff—for instance, experts in appraisal or preservation—as a way of obtaining expertise that none of the programs can afford by itself. With technology creating an increasingly complicated and fluid information world, archival programs need to work more closely together than ever before. The reports also show the need for cooperation across state lines and urge archivists to throw over a "single state context" perspective. The reports hit on the themes of communication, coordination, and cooperation in almost monotonous fashion.

Another common recommendation was for the development of a statewide database or guide to historical records in all repositories. Such a tool, the reports maintained, would aid programs in developing or refining collecting policies and lead to more coherent collecting in the future. They would also substantially assist researchers in locating needed material.

The need for improved archival education was identified as an important issue in many of the reports. As long as archivists come to their work without understanding a well-defined body of theory and techniques, their work is bound to lack some measure of consistency and unity of purpose. Opportunities for graduate training in archival work are still confined to a limited number of universities. Post-appointment professional development possibilities, while increasing through professional conferences, seminars, and workshops, are still not widely available. The reports advocate a more thorough approach to archival education than has been the case in the past, including developing standards, launching more university-based training programs, and providing for workshops in archival techniques and procedures.

Another thread running through the reports is the absence of documentation programs in critical and sensitive areas. Few programs are collecting in the broad area of ordinary people and everyday events, and the historical contributions of large segments of the population, such as women and ethnic minorities, are underrepresented. Many businesses and corporations lack archival programs and do not have arrangements to transfer their archival records to an established repository, which means that their important role in American society and the economy will not be reflected in the archival record. Many collecting programs concentrate on older material and ignore more recent items.

One final dominant theme was the need for preservation action. Here, the state reports—and other reports carried out during the same time period—sound the theme of archives in danger. Many archivists came to realize for the first time that the physical preservation of their records is a vast challenge because of the rate at which paper, the medium for most records, deteriorates. Preservation was identified as the highest and most pressing priority in several of the reports.

From Analysis to Action

It would be an exaggeration to say that the Age of Archival Analysis has been followed by the Age of Archival Renaissance. The studies did, however, initiate change. The reports helped dramatize the issues, raise awareness, and galvanize archivists into unprecedented action as planners, public relations experts, and proponents for their programs. They presented concrete statistics and narrative information on the nature and dimensions of archival problems, giving archivists reliable empirical evidence as a basis for generalizing and developing action strategies. Armed with the evidence in the studies, they could and did seek out allies to help remedy the problems that were revealed. Several of the major new initiatives discussed in chapter 4—stronger professional associations, a planning framework for the profession, certification of archivists, guidelines for archival training, and more publications and training opportunities—are the direct or indirect result of the consciousness-raising impact of these studies. The new emphasis on marketing and promotion, summarized in chapter 10, resulted in part from the awareness that archivists need to be more aggressive in "selling" themselves and their services.

The state reports in particular, by turning attention to the state archival agencies and the state historical records advisory boards that sponsored them, provided renewed incentive for focused statewide leadership and for action on identified statewide priorities. The reports provided a rallying point for people interested in improving historical records programs, securing more resources, and creating programs where needs had been documented. The reports, which were printed in relatively large quantities and widely distributed beyond the archival community in many states, reached an audience of concerned citizens with a message about conditions, opportunities, and needs. The reports thus played a publicity and advocacy role on a broader scale than previous archival publications. The studies of the 1970s and 1980s also led to revised funding priorities for the National Historical Publications and Records Commission, the National Endowment for the Humanities, and other funding agencies. The state assessment reports in particular advanced state priorities, which served as important criteria for judging applications to the NHPRC and encouraged applications in areas identified as priority needs.

The intensive examination of archival affairs during the past decade and a half has also led to subtle but real transformation in the attitudes and outlooks of archivists themselves. The reports increased their sense of being part of a community and a profession that is doing important work. They showed the commonality of problems from program to program and therefore encouraged a heightened sense of community. They helped stimulate work through professional associations to meet defined training and professional development needs. They helped demonstrate the need for archivists to act as advocates for their own programs and for their profession. In short, the reports helped stimulate an archival rejuvenation, rededication, and redirection.

NOTES

1. Trudy H. Peterson, "The National Archives and the Archival Theorist Revisited, 1954–1984," *American Archivist* 49 (Spring 1986):125–133.

2. F. Gerald Ham, "The Archival Edge," *American Archivist* 38 (January 1975): 5–13.

3. Committee on the Records of Government, *Report* (Washington: Committee on the Records of Government, 1985); National Academy of Public Administration, *The Effects of Electronic Recordkeeping on the Historical Record of the U.S. Government* (Washington: National Academy of Public Administration, 1989); National Coordinating Committee for the Promotion of History, *Developing a Premier National Institution: A Report from the User Community to the National Archives* (Washington: National Coordinating Committee for the Promotion of History, 1989).

4. Nicholas C. Burckel and J. Frank Cook, "A Profile of College and University Archives in the United States," *American Archivist* 45 (Fall 1982):410–428; National Association of Government Archives and Records Administrators, *Preservation Needs in State Archives* (Albany: National Association of Government Archives and Records Administrators, 1986); Victoria Irons Walch, *Information Resources for Archivists and Records Administrators: A Report and Recommendations* (Albany: National Association of Government Archives and Records Administrators, 1987); National Historical Publications and Records

Commission, *Directory of Archives and Manuscript Repositories in the United States,* 2nd ed. (New York: Oryx Press, 1988); Joint Committee on Archives of Science and Technology, *Understanding Progress as Process: Documentation of the History of Post-War Science and Technology in the United States* (Chicago: Society of American Archivists, 1983).

5. Paul Conway, "Perspectives on Archival Resources: The 1985 Census of Archival Institutions," *American Archivist* 50 (Spring 1987):174–191.

6. Bruce W. Dearstyne, "The Records Wasteland," *History News* 40 (June 1985): 19.

7. *Archives and Records Programs and Historical Records Repositories in North Carolina: An Analysis of Present Problems and Future Needs* (Raleigh: North Carolina Division of Archives and History, 1983), 10–20; *Public and Private Record Repositories in Virginia: A Needs Assessment Report* (Richmond: Virginia State Library, 1983), 15.

8. *Final Report of the California State Archives Assessment Project* (Sacramento: Office of the Secretary of State, 1983), 7.

9. Edwin C. Bridges, "Consultant Report: State Government Records Programs," in Lisa Weber, ed., *Documenting America: Assessing the Condition of Historical Records in the States* (Albany: National Association of State Archives and Records Administrators, 1984), 8. *Documenting America* includes a summary of the findings and recommendations in approximately half of the state historical records assessment and reporting projects.

10. National Association of Government Archives and Records Administrators, *Preservation Needs in State Archives* (Albany: National Association of Government Archives and Records Administrators, 1986), 1.

11. *Final Report of the California State Archives Assessment Project,* 11.

12. *Historical Records in Minnesota* (St. Paul: Minnesota State Historical Society, 1983), 12.

13. Wisconsin State Historical Records Advisory Board, *Planning to Preserve Wisconsin's History: The Archival Perspective* (Madison, 1983), 17.

14. Jay M. Hammond, ed., *Utah Records Needs Assessment Project: A Report to the People on the Management of Historical Records* (Salt Lake City: Utah State Archives and Records Service, 1985), 19.

15. Nicholas C. Burkel and J. Frank Cook, "A Profile of College and University Archives in the United States," *American Archivist* 45 (Fall 1983):410–428.

16. *Preserving Arizona's Historical Records: The Final Report of the Arizona Records Needs and Assessment Project* (Phoenix: Department of Library, Archives, and Public Records, 1983),12–13; *Archives and Records Programs and Historical Records Repositories in North Carolina,* 63.

17. Wisconsin State Historical Records Advisory Board, *Planning to Preserve Wisconsin's History,* 14; *Historical Records in Massachusetts: A Survey and Assessment* (Boston: State Historical Records Advisory Board, 1983), 16.

18. *Final Report of the California State Archives Assessment Project,* 22.

19. William L. Joyce, "Consultant Report: Historical Records Repositories," in Weber, *Documenting America,* 39.

20. Margaret Child, "Consultant Report: Statewide Functions and Services," in Weber, *Documenting America,* 47.

21. *Archives and Records Programs and Historical Records in North Carolina,* 40.

22. *Preserving Arizona's Historical Records,* i.

23. Dearstyne, "The Records Wasteland," 21.

24. Wisconsin State Historical Records Advisory Board, *Planning to Preserve Wisconsin's History,* 24.

4 The Professional Nature of Archival Work

"A consistent theme in the history of this Society has been the interest, perhaps even the obsession, with the idea of professionalism," noted an SAA President in the mid-1970s. "We are still not sure what a professional archivist is or what makes him so or how he is different from a nonprofessional or unprofessional archivist."[1] Now, that uncertainty has all but vanished. The archival field has acquired most of the major traits of a profession and archivists, with justification, consider themselves *professionals*.

There is a distinction between a profession and a craft, calling, occupation, or discipline. A profession is "an occupation based upon specialized intellectual study and training, the purpose of which is to supply skilled service or advice to others for a definite fee or salary."[2] Professions are characterized by their emphases on service, sound judgment based on professional knowledge, and relative freedom and autonomy in their work. They are marked by high skill levels; a coherent body of both theoretical and practical knowledge, learned by people entering the field under experienced professionals; high educational requirements; control over entry into and work within the field through certification, licensure, or some other device; a code of ethics; and appropriate prestige and status. Professionals may claim primary or exclusive right to practice the work of their field. They know that certain standards are expected of them because of the profession's need to justify and guarantee its work before society.[3]

Several factors slowed the development of the archival profession. Archivists have often been too busy with their everyday work to worry about broader, long-range professional concerns. Lack of a strong academic base limited development of professional training and standards. Professional associations have concentrated on membership development, information sharing, and training for entry-level or middle-level archivists. Until comparatively recently, they have been less concerned with clarifying the professional status of their members' work and with insisting on appropriate recognition. Archival literature has emphasized descriptions of programs, practices, and techniques rather than analyses of the mission and needs of the profession as a whole. Some archivists, content with pursuing rewarding work, have thought it pointless to debate whether their profession needs further development.

Most archivists, however, believe that the importance of their holdings, the complexity of appraisal and other aspects of their work, their proficiency and dedication, and their service to scholarship clearly qualify their field as a worthy profession. They realize that a recognized profession may find it easier to attract and hold dedicated, competent members than a nonprofessional group. Professionals are often accorded higher status—respect, recognition, prestige, and salaries—than nonprofessionals. The studies of the 1980s noted in chapter 3 suggested the need for a consistent professional approach to solving problems and advancing historical records work. A major study commissioned by the Society of American Archivists revealed that the "resource allocators" who control archival programs' budgets regarded them as carrying out a "comparatively subterranean activity," having "the impotence of virtue," and needing to "define more coherent objectives, and communicate greater freshness and distinctiveness by their training, programs, self-assertion, publicity, advertising, and relevance to modern life."[4]

Professions on an ascendant, developmental path typically stress their distinctiveness, develop training and selection procedures, form or strengthen professional associations, write codes of ethics, stress their separation from other professions, and agitate for public recognition and for control over entry to the profession.[5] Archivists fit this pattern. In recent years, through the development of principles and standard practices, initiation of professionwide planning, improved educational guidelines, and a program for certification of archivists, archivists have cemented their professional status.

The Archival Infrastructure

The profession has been strengthened by expansion of what might be called the "archival infrastructure"—the funding agencies and professional associations that support archival work or serve as forums for discussion of archival issues.[6] The National Historical Publications and Records Commission (NHPRC) has a statutory responsibility to make grants for historical records work, but its members and staff have interpreted their mandate broadly. Commission grants have played a major role in strengthening the capacity of the archival profession to carry out its mission. Many projects funded by the commission have involved arrangement, description, or other work directly with records. These grants thus assisted repositories to reduce backlogs and to tackle mainline work.

In other cases, the commission has supported consultative studies, planning, and start-up activities that led to permanently strengthened individual programs. Several grants have resulted in studies of issues and needs and the production of tools to assist archivists in their work. Indicative of its broad vision, the very first NHPRC records grant was made to the SAA to support a series of basic manuals on archival practices. Additional grants have supported the Society's work on goals and priorities for the profession, professional training workshops, additional publications, and other activities. The commission supported a NAGARA study of state archival preservation needs, a follow-up project to produce a self-study manual and software to assist programs in meeting those needs, a study of the information interchange needs of archivists and records managers, and several local government initiatives. It also fostered and provided support for meetings of experts to discuss the archival implications of increased use of computers.

Commission regulations require the appointment of a state historical records advisory board in each state to review applications. In several states, these boards have become important forums for archival planning and advocacy. As noted in chapter 3, the commission funded assessment and reporting projects in most of the states, which analyzed needs and advanced solutions. Without trying to replace or overshadow professional associations, the commission has been a major catalyst for change and improvement.

A second agency, the National Endowment for the Humanities, has also had an important influence. The NEH preservation grant program has assisted with the physical preservation and reproduction microfilming of key collections, encouraged cooperative solutions to the preservation problem, strengthened education in preservation techniques and administration, and raised public awareness about the seriousness of the preservation problem facing the nation's libraries and archival programs. NEH funding for the study of archival descriptive practices led to the development of a standard cataloging format for archives and manuscripts, a major advance in standardizing archival descriptive practices. The NEH and the NHPRC have both supported descriptive projects, finding aids to individual collections, statewide guide projects, and national databases with information on historical records holdings.

The Society of American Archivists has been the profession's leading organization since its founding in 1936. In the mid-1970s, pursuing the recommendations of a committee on the Society's future direction, it hired its first paid full-time executive director, opened its first permanent office, embarked on a major membership expansion campaign, and, often with the help of grant funding, became a major publisher of manuals, guidelines, reports, and studies. Its journal, the *American Archivist*, continues to be the most important outlet for articles on issues and techniques and its annual meeting the leading forum for presentations and discussions of issues. SAA is a major publisher itself and a distributor of items on archival affairs from other publishers. It sponsors workshops and other training opportunities. Through a series of committees, task forces, and round tables, its work in specialized areas has been extended. In recent years, with a new series of manuals on "Archival Fundamentals," new guidelines on archival education, and a new program to certify archivists, SAA has extended its leadership role. SAA has been an engine for change, carrying the profession to progressively higher attainment.

A younger organization, the National Association of Government Archives and Records Administrators, is also an important part of the archival infrastructure. Begun in 1974 as the National Association of State Archives and Records Administrators, the organization widened its scope and changed its name a decade later to encompass the records management and archival concerns of all governments. NAGARA carried out a key study of state archival preservation needs and developed a preservation program self-study and planning manual. It has taken important actions to improve the management of local government archival programs. Through its newsletter and annual meetings, it serves as a clearinghouse of information and a forum for discussion. Its attention has also focused on electronic records and government information policy issues. NAGARA was for several years affiliated with the Council of State Governments, an organization of state government officials. This connection enabled NAGARA to coordinate with state library directors and state information systems directors and to bring important records and archival issues to the attention top state policy makers.

The archival infrastructure also includes approximately three dozen local and regional archival associations, most founded during the past two decades. They range from small and sometimes informal associations in several cities, through more organized groups in New York and Boston, to large and influential regional associations drawing members from several states. The regionals, once regarded as potential rivals of SAA, are now viewed more as partners. More intimate than SAA, they provide forums for discussion of the local or regional dimensions of national issues and offer entry-level training for beginning archivists. Their newsletters provide a sense of regional identification. They serve as forums for discussion of new and emerging ideas and concepts which gradually are refined and percolate into the profession as a whole.[7] Several regionals have undertaken modest publications efforts, and two—the Midwest Archives Conference and the Society of Georgia Archivists—support publication of quality journals that provide outlets for archival writing in addition to the *American Archivist*.

Guidelines for Archival Work

Archival standards and requirements are still few in number, but there is an increasing number of authoritative statements about how archivists do their work. Often, the statements are prepared by professional association committees or acknowledged experts hired by those associations, sometimes with grant support. Archival guidelines appear in diverse brochures, manuals, articles, other publications and a growing array of audiovisual productions. They fall under three headings: archival practices and procedures, elements of historical records programs, and explanatory or advocacy items.

ARCHIVAL PRACTICES AND PROCEDURES GUIDELINES

Several books cover archival practices and procedures. Two of the best books are *Managing Archives and Archival Institutions*, edited by James G. Bradsher,[8] and *Keeping Archives*, edited by Ann Pederson.[9] Bradsher's book consists of nineteen essays on topics ranging from the history of archival administration through appraisal, arrangement, description, preservation, and public programs, to a closing chapter on archival effectiveness. It is an excellent summary of American archival practice and its chapters, taken together, approximate a textbook. The articles in Pederson's book, by contrast, are written by leading Australian archivists. The book provides details on archival techniques and procedures and, despite minor differences between Australian and American practices, provides an excellent source of guidance for everyday archival work. Its detail permits use as a manual of practices.

The Society of American Archivists' "Basic Manuals" series, developed from 1977 to the mid-1980s and partially supplanted by a new series in the 1990s, sum up and express a general archival consensus on how surveys, appraisal, arrangement and description, preservation, reference, microfilming, outreach, public and educational programming, and other aspects of archival work should be carried out. Another series of manuals deals with particular types of records, i.e., religious, business, and cartographic records. The manuals reflect existing practices rather than trying to break new ground, and they cover only the fundamentals. "Because American archivists have widely different educational backgrounds and experiences and are widely dispersed, and because institutions holding papers and records vary greatly in origin, function, and resources, there has been little standardization of techniques, procedures, or policies," noted one manual introduction. While intending to accommodate diversity, the manuals are based on the assumption that there are "obligations and goals common to all." [10] Their authors are respected and experienced practitioners, and because the manuals are issued by SAA, they are regarded as authoritative guides to archival practice. In the early 1990s, SAA is partially supplanting the "Basic Manuals" series with another series, "Archival Fundamentals." The new series is expected to cover the nature of archives and manuscripts, arrangement and description, appraisal, preservation, reference, and a glossary of terminology.

SAA and NAGARA have both developed guidelines for keeping track of and reporting on program activities. Some of the regional associations have developed their own publications. For instance, the Mid Atlantic Regional Archives Conference (MARAC) issued manuals on preservation and historical records program elements and a brochure on finding aids. MARAC and the Archivists Round Table of Metropolitan New York issued a brochure, *Selecting an Archivist* which discusses archivists' work, describes needed background and training, and advises on recruitment. The materials issued by the regional associations complement and supplement the SAA publications by filling gaps and, in some cases, providing information that is suited to their particular regions.

Professions typically have codes of ethics that define their purposes, deal with potential conflicts of interest, and help ensure that their members' expertise will be used in the public interest. The SAA's 1980 "Code of Ethics for Archivists" defines basic duties and areas of responsibility; discourages competition for collections; calls for appraisal, arrangement, and description in line with commonly accepted archival approaches; and advocates open access to records but with restrictions to protect confidentiality. "Archivists answer courteously and with a spirit of helpfulness all reasonable inquiries about their holdings, and encourage use of them to the greatest extent compatible with institutional policies, preservation of holdings, legal considerations, individual rights, donor agreements, and judicious use of archival resources." Archivists should "share knowledge and experience with other archivists through professional activities and assist the professional growth of others with less training and experience." The code is accompanied by a commentary which elaborates key points and explains applications and has suggestions for access to sensitive information in records.[11]

HISTORICAL RECORDS PROGRAMS GUIDELINES

A second category of guidelines publications describe the makeup of historical records programs. Foremost is the SAA's *Evaluation of Archival Institutions: Services, Principles, and Guide to Self-Study*, published in 1983, and its *Archives Assessment and Planning Workbook*, edited by Paul H. McCarthy, issued in 1989. Both are cast as self-study manuals for program analysis, but, to provide a background against which to gauge programs, they both describe recommended program elements. The *Assessment and Planning Workbook* presents the best succinct description of program elements anywhere in the literature. A few other publications, such as the New York State Archives and Records Administration's *Strengthening New York's Historical Records Programs: A Self-Study Guide*, also summarize program elements. NAGARA's *Principles for Management of Local Government Records* brochure and two books published by the American Association for State and Local History—H.G. Jones' *Local Government Records: An Introduction to Their Management, Preservation and Use* (1980) and Bruce W. Dearstyne's *The Management of Local Government Records: A Guide for Local Officials* (1988)—discuss local government archival programs.

The area where the profession has come closest to a standardized approach is in descriptive format. The MARC AMC (Machine Readable Cataloging for Archives and Manuscripts Control) format has become a *de facto* standard for recording and exchanging descriptive information on historical records. As explained in chapter 7, this development occurred in part because of the need for standardized handling of information by computers and the need for consistency in automated databases. The SAA issued a looseleaf, updatable manual and an accompanying compendium of practice in 1985 and made a commitment to support use and updating of the format as needed.[12]

EXPLANATORY AND ADVOCACY GUIDELINES

A third category of guidelines might be characterized as explanatory or advocacy items intended primarily for an external audience, as discussed in chapter 10. *Who Is the "I" in Archives?* is a catchy SAA brochure that makes the point that archives are invaluable to just about everyone. Two NAGARA brochures, *State Government Records and the Public Interest* and *We Are Losing Our Past*, explain to state government officials and others why state records and archival programs are important and why their preservation warrants support. The state assessment reports discussed in chapter 3 were intended for government leaders and members of the public and therefore explain archival issues in terms that nonarchivists can readily comprehend. The New York State Archives and Records Administration's booklets, *Our Number One Client Is State Government* and *Archives and* You: *Practical Uses for Historical Records* are examples of publications aimed at a broad audience with the message of the value and importance of historical records. New York's *Let the Record Show: Practical Uses for Historical Records* and the Ontario Council of Archives' *The Archival Trail* are two examples of video productions that convey the same message.

Archivists Plan for Their Profession

Planning is a characteristic of professional maturity. The state assessment and reporting projects dramatized archival challenges and the need for a clear, shared vision as the basis for concerted action. The reports also encouraged planning in the individual states. Planning for the profession became a central concern in the 1980s. Profession-wide planning had been attempted earlier, with disappointing results that seemed to confirm archival parochialism and lack of consensus. In 1970, SAA established a Committee on the Seventies, which advanced recommendations for strengthening the Society, many of which were implemented but which gave little attention to archival work as a whole. A national conference on archival priorities in 1977 developed a thoughtful report but offered no recommendations for implementation.[13]

In the late 1970s and early 1980s, the NHPRC's records grant program helped turn attention to professional planning. The Commission issued a short statement on Categories of Need and Preferred Approaches for its national grants program, and it encouraged state historical records advisory boards to establish statewide priorities for grant application evaluation purposes.[14] The Commission-supported state assessment and reporting projects in the 1980s resulted in at least modest state-by-state archival assessment and planning. As interest in planning grew, SAA focused its 1982 meeting on archival planning and the same year established a task force on Goals and Priorities. The task force, with support from an NHPRC grant, drafted a report on goals and priorities that, after extensive review and discussion within the profession, was issued in 1986 as *Planning for the Archival Profession.*[15] This report ranks as one of the most important and influential publications in the history of archival work.

What Is an Archivist? Three Definitions

Despite all the progress in developing a true archival profession, there is no universal definition of "archivist." A working definition was provided in the Introduction to this book. Below are three other proposed definitions, each expressing varying perspectives on the essential nature of the archivist's work.

Archivist. A person responsible for or engaged in one or more of the following activities in an archival repository: appraisal and disposition, accessioning, preservation, arrangement, description, reference service, exhibition, and publication (William L. Rofes, ed., "A Basic Glossary for Archivists, Manuscripts Curators, and Records Managers," *American Archivist* 37 [July 1974]: 418).

Archivist: A Definition. The archivist is the trustee of the present and the past for future generations. The archivist is a saver and a destroyer, a holder and a sharer, a student of the past and an assessor of the future, a member of society and a documenter of it. The archivist's purpose is to preserve the evidence of the activities of individuals and institutions in order that others may know and understand them. The archivist's mission is not to seek truth but to preserve truthfully those materials in which others may seek it. The archivist balances the needs of the records, the records creators, the record keepers, and the public served, assisting the many while keeping faith with the needs of the few. The archivist is a guide and a mentor but not an interpreter, a skeptic and a doubter, perhaps, but a steadfast keeper of the record held in trust ("Archivist: A Definition," Society of American Archivists *Newsletter* [January 1984]:4).

What Is an Archivist? An archivist is a professional who is responsible for the management of important records. Five basic activities define an archivist's function. Archivists:

Appraise. They determine which records are permanently valuable and should be retained. Often they work closely with key administrators and records managers in making these decisions;

Acquire. After deciding which material should be kept, they add it to the organization's archives;

Arrange and describe. Following established archival principles, archivists refine the order of the files and then prepare finding aids which enable users to locate material;

Preserve. Preservation encompasses a wide range of activities, including the simple storage of materials in safe areas with controlled climates, the transfer of files to acid-free folders and boxes, special handling of individual pages, and consultation with professional conservators on preservation treatments;

Provide access and reference services. Whether the archives are open to the public, to a limited category of researchers or scholars, or only to the staff of the organization, the archivist makes the holdings of the archives available to the individuals who need to use them.

Professional archivists combine the talents and abilities of information specialists, librarians, editors, records managers, conservators, researchers, and historians (Archivists' Round Table of Metropolitan New York and Mid-Atlantic Regional Archives Conference, "Selecting an Archivist" [pamphlet, n.p., 1985]).

Planning for the Archival Profession begins by asserting that "present conditions, which are inadequate to ensure the identification and preservation of archival records, will not improve unless there is greater support for archival activity from outside the archival community." Increased support depends on public understanding, and that understanding, in turn, requires clarification of the archival mission. Archivists need to rely on the broad strategies of planning, cooperation and mutual assistance, research and development, and advocacy in order to advance their profession. Archivists' professional obligations are not restricted to their own programs; they must work with others to improve their profession. Planning "is critical to give archivists the tools to approach their work in a more systematic and efficient fashion, to better utilize limited resources, and to deal with problems and opportunities created by the challenging way in which society creates and stores information."[16]

The report represents a consensus on major archival goals and objectives, gives individual programs a context within which to plan, and provides resource allocators and others on the outside an indication of the nature and purposes of archival work. It articulates a central archival mission: to ensure the identification, preservation, and use of records of enduring value. The report also articulates three goals for the archival profession: (1) identification and retention of records of enduring value; (2) administration of archival programs to ensure the preservation of records of enduring value; and (3) availability and use of records of enduring value.

IDENTIFYING AND RETAINING RECORDS

"The selection of records of enduring value is the archivist's first responsibility. All other archival activities hinge on the ability to select wisely," notes the report under goal 1.[17] In order to do this crucial work satisfactorily, archivists need to educate themselves about the records of modern society; analyze the creation, administration, and use of records by their creators; study users; and analyze how archival records fit in with the larger documentary record that includes all potentially useful informational resources. In addition, the impact of information technology must be assessed.

A second objective is to develop and apply appraisal and documentation strategies to "foster the integration and coordination of collecting programs across individual repositories . . . transcend the concerns of any one repository and to plan coordinated and cooperative retention programs . . . [and] compile a more balanced and representative record of society."[18] This should be done through development of improved appraisal techniques, case studies to develop appraisal guidelines for particular subject areas, and sharing of appraisal reports and information. Beyond that, archivists need to work at developing cooperative documentation strategies and coordinated, planned collection of records.

Third, archivists must influence records creators to accept responsibility for saving their historically important records. They must convince records creators that they have a responsibility to themselves and to posterity to provide for the identification and preservation of these materials. This step entails educating records creators about the obligations and benefits of preserving historically valuable records, assisting institutions in determining the best approaches to preservation of their own archival records, participating in policy development in the area of modern information technology, and promoting legislation, regulations, and guidelines to encourage historical records preservation and management.

Archivists also need to obtain public support for the retention and sound management of historical records. The most common public attitude toward archives is one of unconcern, notes the report, echoing a familiar refrain from the state assessment reports. This apathy undermines archival work, results in thoughtless destruction of valuable records, and deprives archival programs of needed resources. It must be counteracted by educating the public about the benefits of historical records programs.

ADMINISTERING ARCHIVAL RECORDS

The second goal broadly defines an agenda for addressing administrative responsibilities. The profession needs to establish, evaluate, and strengthen archival training and education through the development of standards and comprehensive educational programs. It must prepare program managers as well as archival practitioners. It must develop guidelines and standards for both archivists and historical records programs. Research and development efforts are needed in areas such as new technology and program monitoring and reporting. The profession needs initiatives in program planning, fund raising, and advocacy work. Archivists need to promote interinstitutional sharing of expertise and resources and technical assistance and advice on program development. Finally, there must be efforts to improve the management of archival records, including wider adaptation and use of automated systems and wider use of archival conservation technology and procedures.

MAKING RECORDS AVAILABLE

The third goal is based on the premise that "the use of archival records is the ultimate purpose of identification and administration.

Outreach—promoting use of these materials—is a fundamental goal of the archival community. This commitment rests on a belief that access to information contributes to the strength and well-being of a democratic society and that knowledge of the past contributes to a better future."[19] Because historical records are underutilized, archivists need to promote their broader and more imaginative use.

The first objective is to develop educational and promotional programs to encourage the use of archival records. Archivists themselves may need to be educated about the importance of reaching out to researchers. New approaches must be developed to improve researcher services. Archivists should cooperate with educational institutions to encourage students to use historical records. Databases with descriptive information on historical records need to be improved and broadened, and more and better finding aids developed to enhance access to historical records. Laws, regulations, standards, and guidelines should promote maximum access consistent with right to privacy, security, and other appropriate considerations. Archivists also need to identify and publicize innovative uses of historical records in order to stimulate even broader and more imaginative uses.

The report notes that planning should be a central, ongoing archival effort. The Society of American Archivists now maintains a standing committee on goals and priorities to continue assessing needs, to build consensus, to report on major actions taken, and to promote and coordinate plans of action. Other professional associations, federal funding agencies, and individual repositories have either adopted or recognize the report and its three goals as the overall framework for their archival endeavor. Though very ambitious, the report constitutes a central frame of reference for the archival profession. This planning document did not transform the profession, but it has helped define what archival work is and what its objectives ought to be. It has served as a point of departure and justification for many of the most exciting and promising new archival initiatives in the years since its publication. It has also helped solidify planning as a legitimate and central part of archival work.

Toward Educational Standards

The requirements that a profession establishes for entry into the field and the educational standards it sets combine to play a major role in defining the profession itself. Archivists have debated the role of archival education since the profession was organized, and the archival literature is replete with dozens of articles on the topic.

Much of the discussion has centered on whether history departments or library schools are the best settings for archival training, a debate that has produced more heat than light. Probably the most common formal training is a one-course introduction to archives, mostly offered by adjunct professors who are practicing archivists outside the universities where they teach. These courses typically touch on appraisal, arrangement, description, preservation, and reference services and have only enough time to provide a grounding in these fundamentals. Most students who take a summary course then go on to learn on the job and to piece out their training through reading, attendance at professional meetings, and other professional experience.

There are only about a half dozen full-time archival professors in the United States at this time. More full-time faculty positions are needed; as in other professions, faculty "hold a unique position as intermediaries between a scholarly community, which has the resources and intellectual orientation to tackle complex problems comprehensively, and professional practitioners, who have specialized approaches to problem solving, knowledge, and skills."[20] Education poses a dilemma: the profession wishes to maintain an independent approach to training, yet that training must be based in history, library, or other departments because the profession is too small to support its own separate departments. Adjunct professors may be adept and leaders of their field, but by definition they are outsiders and cannot build the strong academic base that is needed for sustained professional success.

In 1977, SAA developed general guidelines for graduate archival training that slowly became outdated. In 1988, after extensive study, new and stronger guidelines were issued, *Guidelines for Graduate Archival Education Programs*. Like *Planning for the Archival Profession*, the new guidelines attempt to set the profession onto a higher plane. "The work of an archivist represents that of a profession, not a craft or applied vocation," the introduction to the *Guidelines* asserts. "Theory is not only just as important as practice but guides and determines that practice." The times demand a comprehensive approach to archival education, and that means multicourse offerings taught by full-time faculty. "Archivists belong to a relatively young profession, but one that is seeking a stronger profile in society and that demands more stringent standards and guidelines and a broader base of theory."[21]

The *Guidelines* prescribes the curriculum elements that are needed. These elements are intellectually rigorous and important, for they prescribe what the archivists of tomorrow should study and, indirectly, presage how they will handle archival work. There are five curriculum elements: nature of information, records, and historical documentation; archives in modern society; basic archival functions; issues and relationships that affect archival functions; and managerial functions.

Students need to study information on the origins of humanity's efforts at writing, development of records-keeping systems, and the social and cultural utility of archives, if they are to build a true documentary record for the future. Archival education should cover the development of written, oral, and other forms of communication and should show how information has been preserved, transmitted, and employed by past and current societies. Students need to understand the changing nature of records, the development and use of classification systems, the nature of documentary evidence, and the skills required for critical analysis of documentary sources.

Archival students should study the wellsprings and dynamics of the profession they are about to enter and also understand the challenges the profession faces. Students need instruction in the origin and development of modern archival principles, methods, and institutions. They also need to understand the types and variety of archival repositories and holdings, the relation of archives to other professions, and "the present condition of the archival profession . . . its size and resources, position in society, variety of professional associations, and contemporary trends and priorities. . . . Students should [also] learn to appreciate the nature of current issues and unresolved problems confronting the profession."

"To achieve its objective of maintaining a usable documentary heritage, the archival profession has developed a number of basic archival functions, each with an evolving set of standards and accepted practices," says the *Guidelines*. Courses need to cover five basic areas:

Appraisal and acquisitions. Students need to be introduced to the theoretical basis of appraisal, the criteria and processes by which selection decisions are made, the applicability of records management techniques, and the concepts of documentation strategies and adequacy of documentation.

Arrangement and description. The objective here is to teach students about the nature of physical arrangement and the intellectual basis for description. Instruction should also highlight the concepts of provenance and original order and introduce automated descriptive formats and standards.

Preservation management. Archivists need to understand the physical nature of the various media they may work with, the role of proper environment, storage, use, and security, the application of techniques such as cleaning, mending, and microfilm or other reproduction, and the fundamentals of preservation management.

Reference and access. Students need to learn how to identify the various constituencies their programs will serve, how to render reference service, and also how to expand the use of their holdings over time.

Advocacy and outreach. It is important to introduce students to basic promotional and outreach techniques such as exhibits, publications, audiovisual productions, and other public programming efforts that can be used to "educate, to create alliances with specific constituencies, and to gain resource support" for the program.

The *Guidelines* covers legal considerations that affect access, use, and government records programs, and the ethical concerns that they may face as custodians of sensitive information. Students should be provided with information on how to build inter-institutional cooperation, particularly in the areas of appraisal and collecting, and to learn the advantages and benefits of sharing resources and cooperating with allied professions. Students should be prepared to face issues introduced by new information technologies and should be aware of emerging standardization in some areas of archival work, e.g., descriptive practices.

The final area of archival education concerns management. "Most archivists have administrative responsibilities to varying degrees," even in one-person operations, the *Guidelines* observes. All students should be introduced to fundamental management principles and the basics of how institutions function. They should study program planning, human resources management, resource development, and buildings and facilities maintenance. The *Guidelines* also discusses course formats, the makeup of practica and independent study, facilities needed, and the role of an archival education program director.

The new educational guidelines establish a measure of academic respectability, and they attempt to put archival education on a par with its allied disciplines, history and library and information science. They establish expectations for new programs that may be established in the future. Even though there are few (perhaps no) universities that offer all the training that the *Guidelines* requires, they at least provide students and archivists with a vision of what training is needed for people entering this complex and rapidly changing field.

Certifying Archivists

One distinguishing trait of a profession is a formal designation or credential to identify people who are competent to carry out the work. Like the issue of educational standards, archival certification has been debated since the profession's earliest years. The SAA proposed a certification program in the mid-1980s. The Society's committee that advanced the final proposal sounded a note of caution:

> The program is meant not as a form of regulation but only as a service to the profession. It will provide individual archivists and their employers with a new means of gauging basic competence and its improvement through experience, continuing education, and professional activity. It will provide the profession with a new means of stimulating developmental activity for the common good. It is not intended to control entry into any professional position or to force archivists to meet the requirements if they wish to retain the respect of their peers. . . . [The committee] does not anticipate that certification will become the routine credential of professional archivists in the near future.[22]

For two years, there was a spirited debate among archivists over certification. Some saw it as elitist, unnecessary, expensive, difficult to administer, and probably ineffectual in making for real change. Others—eventually, the majority—viewed it as a logical step forward for the profession that would strengthen its capacity to secure resources, deal with issues, and improve its standing in society as a whole. In the formal presentation of the plan, the SAA noted:

> A distinguishing mark of a profession is its willingness to set standards. A profession views its practice as a public charge and maintains the performance standards of its practitioners through formal procedures controlled by the professional peer group. Standards show that the profession as a whole takes seriously its responsibility to the public. Accountability, responsibility, and competence are the fundamental premises behind the program of archival certification. The program proposes both a service offered by the profession to its members, who wish to demonstrate a basic level of competence, and a service to a society which depends on professional archivists to keep in trust its documentary heritage.[23]

The certification plan, adopted in 1987, provided for two years of certification by petition (or "grandfathering") and, thereafter, certification by examination. For certification by petition, one of the following was required: five years' professional experience plus a master's degree, plus or including graduate study in archives administration; six years' professional experience plus a master's degree; or seven years' professional experience plus a bachelor's degree. The petition form noted that

> A professional archivist actively exercises responsibility for one or more of the following: the acquisition, preservation, management, reference, and control of archival materials. A professional archivist should have a comprehensive understanding of basic archival principles and the ability to apply or implement these principles while performing the above functions in an official capacity.[24]

"Professional experience" is based on the classification system and job description of the employing institution.

Certification by examination has lower prerequisites but requires a full-day examination. The examination tests candidates in seven major "domains of archival practice": selection of documents; arrangement and description; reference service and access; preservation and protection; outreach and promotion; program assessment; and professional, ethical, and legal issues.[25] The SAA's description of those "domains" represents one of the most comprehensive statements ever drawn up on the nature of archival work; it is reproduced in Appendix A.

The knowledge required is both broad and deep. In selection of documents, for instance, candidates are expected to be able to identify sources of documents by researching subjects, individuals, and organization; to make retention recommendations by appraising records for legal, fiscal, administrative, evidential, and informational value; and to implement disposition recommendations through such legal instruments of transfer as schedules, deeds of gift, and deposit agreements. They are also expected to know how the holdings and acquisitions policy of an institution affects appraisal; techniques for surveying and locating documents of historical value; how to find information pertaining to the role and history of document-creating sources; factors that should be considered when defining collecting areas and developing an institutional collecting policy; the past and potential uses of records; and sampling and scheduling techniques. The certification is for a limited duration; maintenance will depend on continued professional attainment.

Certification is administered under the oversight of the Academy of Certified Archivists, an independent, nonprofit organization founded at the 1989 meeting of the Society of American Archivists. The ACA is separate from SAA but maintains strong ties to it. The ACA is expected to promote professional archival standards, increase the visibility of Certified Archivists, and establish a certification maintenance program. The Academy believes that certification will have broad implications over the coming years. According to an ACA statement, certification will:

> Signify achievement of a high level of archival knowledge and skills.
> Provide employers with an additional method of evaluating prospective and current staff.
> Identify knowledge areas that must be included in any comprehensive archival education program.
> Establish a primary professional standard by which to judge the knowledge of archivists.

By a certification maintenance program, ensure that certified archivists remain current in their knowledge of new technology, techniques, and policies affecting archives.[26]

It is too early to judge the impact of certification, but it can certainly be expected to strengthen archivists' professional identity in the years ahead. Certification joins education, planning, and a stronger archival infrastructure as factors leading toward a stronger archival profession.

NOTES

1. Wilfred I. Smith, "Broad Horizons: Opportunities for Archivists," *American Archivist* 37 (January 1974):11.
2. A. M. Carr-Saunders, "Professionalization in Historical Perspective," in Howard M. Vollmer and Donald L. Mills, eds., *Professionalization* (Englewood Cliffs, N. J.: Prentice Hall, 1966), 4. For a discussion of archivists as professionals, *see* Richard J. Cox, "Professionalism and Archivists in the United States," *American Archivist* 49 (Summer 1986):229–247.
3. Philip Elliott, *The Sociology of the Professions* (New York: Herder and Herder, 1972), 94, 130.
4. Social Research, Inc., *The Image of Archivists: Resource Allocators' Perceptions* (Chicago: Society of American Archivists, 1984), iv–v. This report is discussed in detail in chapter 10.
5. Elliott, *The Sociology of the Professions*, 130.
6. *See* Larry J. Hackman, "A Perspective on American Archives," *Public Historian* 8 (Summer 1986):10–28.
7. Patrick H. Quinn, "Regional Archival Organizations and the Society of American Archivists," *American Archivist* 46 (Fall 1983):433–440.
8. James Gregory Bradsher, ed., *Managing Archives and Archival Institutions* (Chicago: University of Chicago Press, 1989).
9. Ann Pederson, ed., *Keeping Archives* (Sydney, Australia: Australian Society of Archives, 1987).
10. Sue E. Holbert, *Archives and Manuscripts: Reference and Access* (Chicago: Society of American Archivists, 1977), 1.
11. "A Code of Ethics for Archivists," *American Archivist* 43 (Summer 1980):414–418.
12. Nancy Sahli, *MARC for Archives and Manuscripts: The AMC Format* (Chicago: Society of American Archivists, 1985, with periodic updates); Max J. Evans and Lisa B. Weber, *MARC for Archives and Manuscripts: A Compendium of Practice* (Madison: State Historical Society of Wisconsin, 1985).
13. Society of American Archivists, Task Force on Goals and Priorities, *Planning for the Archival Profession* (Chicago: Society of American Archivists, 1986), 2–3.
14. Frank G. Burke in "The Forum," *American Archivist* 41 (January 1978):125–126.
15. Society of American Archivists, Task Force on Goals and Priorities, *Planning for the Archival Profession* (Chicago: Society of American Archivists, 1986).
16. Ibid., 4.
17. Ibid., 8.
18. Ibid., 10.
19. Ibid., 22.
20. Paul Conway, "Archival Education and the Need for Full-Time Faculty," *American Archivist* 51 (Summer 1988):257–258.

21. Society of American Archivists, *Guidelines for Graduate Archival Education Programs* (Chicago: Society of American Archivists, 1988).
22. "Certification," Society of American Archivists *Newsletter* (July 1985).
23. "Archival Certification Plan," Society of American Archivists *Newsletter* (August 1986).
24. Society of American Archivists, *Certified Archivist Petition* (Chicago: Society of American Archivists, 1988), 1.
25. "SAA Role Delineation," Society of American Archivists *Newsletter* (January 1989):6–8. *See* Appendix A.
26. "What Is the Academy of Certified Archivists?" *History News* 46 (March–April 1991):35.

5 Administering Historical Records Programs

Historical records programs face challenges that call for a high degree of organizational and administrative skill. They carry out important functions with significant implications for a wide range of human activity and obligations to future generations. Expectations for service to their parent institutions and researchers are likely to continually increase without a corresponding increment in staff and other resources. In fact, archivists face increasing competition for support, particularly in the public sector. In hard times, they need to be vigilant and assertive just to avoid reductions. The character of the work force is changing as the nation's demographic makeup changes, educational and skill levels change, and people seek more opportunities for part-time work, flexibility in assignments, and other approaches to work that differ from past patterns. Changes in information technology are transforming the nature of the record itself, and the archival function may be blending into an undifferentiated information management field.

The historical records program administrator acts within an even broader context of national and worldwide complexities and unpredictability. "This is an era marked with rapid and spastic change," notes one recent study of leadership. "There are too many ironies, polarities, dichotomies, dualities, ambivalences, paradoxes, confusions, contradictions, contraries, and messes for any organization to understand and deal with."[1] Historical records program administrators, buffeted by changes in their profession, in the missions and tactics of their parent institutions, and in the research communities they serve, must attempt to change, adapt, and marshal available resources to move toward desired goals.

These challenges occasion and require well-developed administrative skills, including leadership, program management, planning, working with people, and monitoring and reporting. The definitions of these administrative areas are not precise, but *administration* means something more than interacting with records and researchers and managing a program day to day. Administration of a historical records program involves taking the lead, coordinating planning, helping shape and define the nature of the program, taking responsibility for achieving defined objectives, and, in some cases, directing the work of other people. Administrative skills are needed for small programs, where the scale and magnitude of the challenges may be modest but where resources are also likely to be lacking, as well as for larger programs.

Most archivists carry out some administrative work every day even if they work alone and also directly provide services. The librarian in charge of historical records at our model Salem Public Library must spend some time planning and setting priorities and expectations for his own work even if he works alone—a "lone arranger," a term archivists sometimes use to refer to colleagues in "one-person shops." The Westlake City Clerk's hours spent on budgeting, planning, establishing work objectives, and supervising staff (even if they are part-time clerical and support staff) working on archival records are time devoted to administration. Many archivists have not given enough attention to administration because they regard it as beyond their work as professionals, they lack the skills and training to do it, or they believe that administration is at its heart nothing more than applied common sense. In recent years, however, emphasis on profession-wide planning, cutbacks and financial retrenchments in many institutions, a demand for cost-efficient performance, and other factors have provided incentive for the development of administrative approaches and skills.

Leadership

Successful programs aren't just *managed*; they're also *led*. Sound management and leadership skills are often found in the same person, but they are not the same thing. Managers tend to focus on control and maintenance, while leaders influence, guide, initiate change, bring innovation, appeal to both their employees and their bosses, and move their institutions ahead. As one book puts it, "managers are people who do things right and leaders are people who do the right thing." The leader creates "a mental image of a possible and desirable future state of the organization . . . a view of a realistic, credible, attractive future."[2]

Leaders are future-oriented. "The dream or vision is the force that invents the future. Leaders spend considerable effort gazing across the horizon of time, imagining what it will be like when they have arrived at their final destination. . . . There is a desire to make

A Vision for the Archival Future

How important is it for the leader to paint a picture of the kind of program that his or her institution should strive to create? The answer is: very important, for it gives everyone something to work for. Below is part of a statement by the director of the fictional Auburn Research Library to his staff early in his drive to develop the historical records element of Auburn's program.

I'd like you to share with me a vision of an exciting new direction for our library. The trustees have authorized the development of a historical records collecting program, concentrating on art history and the performing arts, areas of human accomplishment compatible with Auburn's other collecting and documentation efforts. The new program should enhance Auburn's reputation for excellence and service and its long-established tradition of encouraging and supporting primary research. I ask you to join me in welcoming this challenge. It is a reflection on the well-known talents and energies of this staff that the Trustees have entrusted this endeavor to you. In a very real sense, this will be *your* program to launch and to shape and it will reflect your pride and commitment.

Our collecting efforts will probably concentrate initially on the records and papers of accomplished artists and leaders in the fields of arts and performing arts—people who gave of themselves, who influenced colleagues, who excelled in carrying an artistic message to a broad audience, and who showed exceptional creativity. These people are gone, but their spirits and minds are still accessible, to a degree, through their archival legacies. Like their paintings, music, and other manifestations of their work, their historical records should give us insight into the people, their times, and their achievements. Of course, we expect to collect selectively and carefully, in line with a collection policy, to appraise and select only what is of lasting value, and to arrange, describe, and make the records available in accord with the very best archival practices. The prospect of passing on a legacy of the past to future generations is thrilling to contemplate!

In our new endeavor, as in our existing ones, we will aim for a high standard of excellence for Auburn. As the collections grow, we will launch outreach and publicity efforts so that people interested in this field know what we hold and feel invited to come here for research use of the materials. Research traffic would include scholarly researchers, people who enjoy the arts and want to learn more about them, students, and others who will approach our materials with the excitement and expectation of people who anticipate making discoveries. Not everyone will find the information he or she is seeking, of course, but there will be garnering of information that broadens and deepens insights and discoveries that help unlock historical mysteries. Eventually, resources permitting, we will also try to include exhibits, public presentations, and possibly even publications which showcase our materials. We also expect to collaborate with other libraries, universities, and others to identify approaches to improved documentation of arts and performing arts on a continuing basis. This new program's future—caring for records of the past—is full of promise!

something happen, to change the way things are, to create something that no one else has ever created before."[3] The leader has a compelling vision and an agenda, a sense of destination, and a desire to take the institution on a journey to it. Leaders must be able to "relate a compelling image of a desired state of affairs—the kind of image that induces enthusiasm and commitment. . . . The management of meaning, mastery of communication, is inseparable from effective leadership."[4] Anyone desiring to lead the development of an archival program must be able to make a concrete and attractive vision of what the program should look like and accomplish. There needs to be a multipart vision of its facilities and resources, collections, services, and overall impact on a continuing basis.

Leadership of a historical records program must be inspirational, uplifting, and motivational. The leader must develop, present, and secure allegiance to a vision for the program that encompasses mission, collecting policies, overall program size, and service to researchers and the public. The leader must articulate a clear notion of funding and support, what will be collected and why, how it will be cared for, and what people or groups it will serve. He or she has an obligation to "preach" the importance of archival work to the staff, to hold out a vision of excellence and attainment, and to reinforce aspirations and feelings of pride in the program and its accomplishments. This task should be comparatively easy because it is in harmony with the pride that archivists usually feel naturally in their work.

Leadership also requires spirited appeals to resource allocators in the parent organization who control the program purse strings and therefore its destiny. The leader of a historical records program is likely to need to compete for attention and resources with other worthy causes and programs—possibly even with the justifiable need for more staff and books by other divisions in a library. The most effective leaders "understand that the fundamental responsibility of archival administration is to build resources. Their role is *not* to appraise, acquire, arrange, and describe historical records but to obtain the needed resources to develop programs that will systematically and adequately perform their function."[5] Archival leadership implies program growth, transformation, and new and better approaches.

Of course, the leader must also know how to deal with setbacks and disappointments and how to cushion their impact on employee morale and on the program. Leaders should establish realistic (but high) expectations to ensure that attainment can actually match objectives and to minimize the chance of serious, disappointing shortfalls. Leadership requires having ready persuasive arguments to meet potential threats such as budget or staffing reductions. The leader must be able to articulate to administrators and resource allocators up the chain of command how important the historical records program is and the probable dire consequences of a reduction.

If this and other defensive strategies fail, the leader's role may become one of minimizing or containing the negative impact on the program through carefully planned and managed reductions in nonessential areas. Leaders who must preside over program reductions or other threats need to carefully prepare employees ahead of time by explaining the background of the event or development leading to the reduction. There must be an explanation of how the impending problem is being handled so that the best interests of both the program and the people involved are protected. No matter how serious the consequences of the problem, the leader must also have strategies to keep employees from becoming dispirited and to recover from the problem and continue building the program. The process of meeting problems and dealing with retrenchments or other threats may result in increased commitment, new insights for improving program performance, and new strategies for program development in the future.

Program Management

Management and *leadership* are closely related; in most historical records programs, which are small or modest in size, they will need to be combined in the same person. "A person in a management job contributes to the achievement of organizational goals through planning, coordination, supervision, and decision making regarding the investment and use of corporate human resources. A manager is someone who 'gets things done through other people.' The results of the manager's actions can be linked to performance of an organizational unit."[6] Management skills vary from one individual to the next and management demands from one program to the next. In some programs, the manager has risen through the ranks, and his or her outstanding technical background and proficiency as an archivist must be matched by development of good management skills. It is not uncommon for accomplished archivists, used to working directly with historical records and serving researchers, to feel uncomfortable when promoted to a management position that involves planning, budgeting, supervising staff, and other functions that have no direct relation to records.

Management skills must be learned and refined. Whatever the program setting, managers need to carry out five interrelated functions:

Managers plan. Managers lead a process to establish goals, objectives, and priorities, and communicate the plan to people who must carry it out and to those whose support is essential for it to be carried out. Managers also determine how best to carry out the plan. They follow it, and get their staff and colleagues in the historical records program to follow it, as the central blueprint and road map for the program's work.

Managers organize. A manager "analyzes the activities, decisions, and relations needed . . . classifies the work . . . divides it into manageable activities and further divides the activities into manageable jobs . . . groups these units and jobs into an organizational structure . . . [and] selects people for the management of these units and for the jobs to be done."[7] The historical records program manager assesses people, records, and service needs and then matches available resources to the work at hand and makes continual adjustments on the way to desired objectives. Organizational skills are also needed for short-term projects. For instance, the transfer and accessioning of a large new collection may require finalizing legal transfer documentation, preliminary sorting and cleaning, boxing the materials, keeping track of them, arranging for transportation, and sorting and formal accessioning at the repository.

Managers exercise control. Control requires establishing quantitative and qualitative guidelines, supervision, monitoring performance, providing feedback and critiques, and rewarding or disciplining based on performance. Control of this sort is needed to get the work of the historical records program done, but it cannot go so far as to stifle creativity and initiative.

Managers encourage self-motivation. Managers have well-developed "people skills." They build loyalty and commitment, stimulate an interest in the work, help develop subordinates, and keep people working together as a team toward common objectives. Archivists who enjoy their work and are self-starters who take pride in what they accomplish have considerable potential self-motivation; the manager must find a way to appeal to it.

Managers coordinate. Managers facilitate communication, encourage team play, and make certain that the work proceeds according to plan, that program elements work with each other and reinforce each other as appropriate, and that there is balanced program development. Coordination is particularly important for historical records programs where a program initiative in a given area has ramifications in other areas. For instance, development of an exhibits program needs to be coordinated with preservation staff if the documents to be exhibited need preservation work beforehand. A major promotional publication may bring expanded research traffic, which the researcher services unit needs to anticipate and prepare for.

A common analogy in management literature is a conductor who appeals to talents and motivations, gets individuals to function as a harmonious team, and produces a satisfying performance. In archival work, management is usually not that simple. Many archivists might agree with a slightly different view:

> [The manager] is like a symphony orchestra conductor, endeavouring to maintain a melodious performance in which the contributions of the various instruments are coordinated and sequenced, patterned and paced, while the orchestra members are having various personal difficulties, stage hands are moving music stands, alternative excessive heat and cold are creating audience and instrument problems, and the sponsor of the concert is insisting on irrational changes in the program.[8]

Often, the manager must think and work in terms of "relative emphases and priorities among conflicting objectives and criteria; relative tendencies and probabilities (rather than certainties); rough correlations and patterns among elements (rather than clear-cut cause-and-effect relationships)."[9] Archival program managers must be flexible, able to deal with the unexpected, and prepared to take advantage of unforseen opportunities. In fact, the manager often plays the roles of reactor to surprises, settler of disputes, and snap decision maker, choosing among options, none of which may be totally desirable. In the course of a day, the manager of a historical records program might have to respond to the library director's decision to reduce the program's budget, soothe a valued archivist who feels her work has not been recognized, decide on whether to alter arrangement and description plans to accommodate a donor's demands that her grandfather's papers be made available immediately for research, decide which microfilm camera best fits the program's requirements for quality, lasting microfilm, and respond to a staff member's request to attend a professional seminar. These real-life situations pose hard choices and certainly refute the popular impression that all archivists do is deal with old records. A firm grounding in archival training and experience, steady good judgment, coolness under pressure, and an eye to fundamentals and priorities, are needed to ensure smooth sailing in rough managerial seas.

One tool that supports smooth program management is a procedures manual that indicates how the program deals with administrative matters as well as how it approaches its archival work. A loose-leaf, updatable format with two distinct sections, one for administration and the other for archival practices, or two separate manuals, will serve the purpose. The manual, developed by program

Outline of "Manual of Administrative Procedures for the Department of Special Collections/Division of Archives and Manuscripts, Madison University Library"

I. Program Planning
   A. Trustees' resolution establishing department of special collections
   B. Mission statement for the archives and manuscripts division
   C. Description of the planning process
   D. Current long-range plan
   E. Current annual work plan

II. Personnel Administration
   A. Educational and experience requirements for Archivist, Senior Archivist, Associate Archivist, and Principal Archivist
   B. Job descriptions for Archivist, Senior Archivist, Associate Archivist, and Principal Archivist
   C. Qualifications and job descriptions for technical positions
   D. Qualifications and job descriptions for support staff positions
   E. Performance planning and evaluation system
   F. Professional development policy
   G. Disciplinary procedures
   H. Tenure and promotion
   I. Ethical and conflict-of-interest statement

III. Program Administration other than Personnel
   A. Purchase procedures
   B. Travel
   C. Printing and publications
   D. Program reporting procedures and requirements
   E. Security
   F. Disaster preparedness and recovery

IV. Program Procedures
   A. Criteria and process for appraising records
   B. Accessioning
   C. Procedures for arrangement
   D. Procedures for description and development of finding aids
   E. Automated data bases
   F. Preservation
   G. Archival microfilming
   H. Electronic (machine readable) records
   I. Researcher services and searchroom rules
   J. Outreach and public programs
   K. Liaison with other university departments

Note: In some areas, this manual reprints or summarizes the broader administrative procedures manual for the Madison University Library. It also reflects university policies as a whole.

managers in consultation with staff and reviewed and approved by the highest level program supervisors, facilitates consistent, predictable program administration. Above is an outline of an administrative manual from our model program at Madison University.

The Heart of the Program: Human Resources

Experts on administration sometimes refer to "human resources"—the people who make up the program and do its work. Administration requires well-developed people skills—the ability to understand, work with, and provide support and motivating circumstances.

Administrators must work at building up employees' self-esteem, confidence in their own ability, high expectations, and a feeling that they have a measure of influence and control over their own work. These skills are essential even in small historical records programs where the boss and employees work side by side.

The program director needs to concentrate on the program's emotional and spiritual assets and the aspirations of its employees. The director must develop and convey a sense of vision, which in turn gives direction, imparts a sense of purpose, and makes everyone feel special and part of a team effort that is leading to important advances and products. Archival managers need to work to maintain a high level of pride and *esprit de corps* in their organizations. Archival work is an important and inspired calling, and the people doing it, often under pressure and with limited resources, need to understand that they are contributing to an effort with broad ramifications for human advancement. How people feel about themselves and their work is important. "An old story tells of three stonecutters who were asked what they were doing. The first replied, 'I am making a living.' The second kept on hammering while he said, 'I am doing the best job of stonecutting in the entire country.' The third one looked up with a visionary gleam in his eyes and said, 'I am building a cathedral'."[10]

Some archivists, used to functioning as dedicated professionals with minimal supervision, may chafe at what they perceive as too close or extensive oversight of their work. In some instances, there is a "clash of cultures." The management culture stresses performance and efficiency, career specialization that limits professionals to particular tasks, and promotion of professionals only within a relatively narrow hierarchy of technical positions. The professional culture, by contrast, stresses mastery of knowledge and its related skills, adherence to principles and standards, and loyalty to the profession.[11] A historical records program manager might insist that processing of a collection meet a particular deadline; the archivist might counter that the presence of several series, numerous physical formats, and important research information warrants stretching the deadline in favor of a more thorough, high-quality job of arrangement and description. A manager might insist on simple explanations of archival work for the lay readers of a proposed program brochure; the archivist might respond that archival work is not simple and that its complexities need to be portrayed.

Balance and compromise between the two positions are essential. Archivists must apply their abilities within an organizational setting, according to a plan, and under supervision. However, a substantial measure of self-motivation and self-direction is highly desirable in archival work, which requires flexibility in application of training, skills, and good judgment. Modern managerial theory holds that coercing or driving employees is counterproductive, particularly in knowledge industries, such as archival work, where a high degree of commitment and involvement is needed to carry out the work. "The dominant principle of organization has shifted from management in order to control an enterprise to leadership in order to bring out the best in people and to respond quickly to change. . . . It is a democratic yet demanding leadership that respects people and encourages self-management, autonomous teams, and entrepreneurial units."[12]

Studies of motivation have demonstrated that people respond poorly to threats, coercion, and overly strict direction. Positive motivational factors include a variety of tasks; a feeling of contributing to completing a whole, identifiable piece of work that measurably contributes to the overall production of the organization; recognition from the boss and peers; the inherent interest of the work itself; a high degree of autonomy and responsibility; potential for advancement and personal growth; and feedback in terms of information about the quality of the work and its impact. Archival program staff need to feel that they have control over their own destiny and that their work is valued and important. For some people, these intangible, feedback factors actually count more than salary level and opportunities for promotion.[13]

The popular management consultant Tom Peters emphasizes the need to involve employees in all planning activities, to remove stifling bureaucratic restrictions, to encourage suggestions and listen to employees, and to establish high expectations that employees are expected to produce excellent work. The key to employee satisfaction and continuing high volume and high quality productivity is for the manager to empower employees—to give them latitude, to encourage them to innovate, and to get them to identify with their work and the organization's progress. Beyond that, says Peters, recognize achievement and celebrate progress and victories to strengthen a sense of team play.

The most effective managers make their employees feel a sense of self-esteem, pride, and accomplishment. They play the role of coach: encouraging, guiding, articulating objectives, and encouraging a sense of team plan and of operating as one. Recognizing contributions and linking rewards with performance are essential. The brief comment or note to the archivist who prepared a particularly outstanding finding aid or who put special effort into assisting a researcher, is a small but helpful gesture. "Cheerleading," "encouraging the heart," and "celebrating team victories" are means of encouraging continuing concerted efforts toward agreed-upon goals. This encouragement applies to all employees, including clerical and

Madison University—Department of Special Collections/Division of Archives and Manuscripts

Annual Performance Workplan for Emily Baker, Senior Archivist, for July 1993–June 1994

Introduction. At the direction of her supervisor, Associate Archivist Maureen Kerwan, Ms. Baker is expected to divide her time among arrangement and description work, facilitating use, and serving researchers. Ms. Baker is expected to operate with a high degree of initiative and independence within the objectives and guidelines established by her supervisor, to pace herself and move ahead with a minimum of detailed supervision and review, and to ensure that work is carried out to the department's high standards for accuracy, timeliness, and helpful service. The work is tied to the Department of Special Collections' Annual Workplan for 1993–1994, and is to be carried out in accord with the department's *Manual of Administrative Practices,* especially Sections 4-C (arrangement), D (description and finding aids), I (researcher services), and K (liaison with university departments).

Tasks/Performance Indicators

1. Arrange and prepare a finding aid to the box and folder level for approximately half of the New Holland Tractor Company Records held by the Department of Special Collections.

    In accordance with the department's procedures, weed duplicative and non-record material, identify and restore original order where it has been lost, refolder and rebox all material into standard folders and boxes, prepare accurate labels, and produce an accurate, detailed guide following MARC/AMC format. Enter into the RLIN database information on the collection. Complete processing and draft of guide for review by Jan. 1, 1994. Complete work on guide within two months after review of draft is completed by supervisor.

2. Arrange and prepare finding aids to the records of university presidents from 1850 to 1950.

    In accordance with the department's procedures, arrange and describe the materials of the seven men and women who served as Madison's President during this century. Give priority to President Henry Mattice, the university's first president. Produce a standard finding aid for each president's materials and a summary brochure for publication: *A Proud Educational Legacy: The Records of Madison's Presidents in the University Archives, 1850–1950.* The brochure must be succinct and appropriate for a lay audience. It must include information on each president, the highlights of his or her administration and his or her major reforms or initiatives, and an overview of the records with particularly interesting materials highlighted. Ms. Baker should also select photographs and other materials to illustrate the brochure and collaborate with the library's Public and Educational Programs Office on its production and distribution.

3. Serve as liaison to the History and Public Administration Departments.

    Visit department heads and faculty members to apprise them of the Special Collections Department's holdings that might support research in their fields and in the topical areas of their courses. Make arrangements if possible to visit their classes to discuss holdings, emphasizing those that are likely to be of most interest to the students. Upon request, provide follow-up advice to students on particular holdings that may be of interest to them.

4. Respond to written inquiries for information about materials in the Archives and Manuscripts Division.

Answer inquiries promptly, accurately, and thoroughly, with the objective of being as helpful as possible in providing information about the division's holdings and services.

5. Provide services at Reference Desk as assigned on rotational basis.

Conduct entrance and exit interviews, direct researchers to finding aids and explain their use, suggest particular records that may be of interest, retrieve records as requested, carefully oversee their use to ensure their security and prevent harmful handling, check materials to ensure that they are all turned in, return material to stacks, and answer inquiries from researchers.

6. Carry out other duties as assigned by supervisor.

Carry out assignments in a timely and accurate fashion in line with department objectives and procedures.

---

support staff as well as dedicated professionals. Everyone should feel pride at being part of the team.[14]

Beyond these general approaches to motivation and building confidence and incentive, historical records program managers need to give attention to personal workplans, performance measurement, feedback and evaluation, and training and professional development. Individual staff workplans should be developed, discussed, and finalized on a regular basis, e.g., annually, and should be tied to the program's workplan activities as closely as possible. The plan should include quantitative performance indicators, such as quantities of records expected to be arranged and described or turnaround time for responding to researcher requests, and also qualitative indicators relating to quality, proficiency and effectiveness of services. The box above illustrates the elements of a desirable personal workplan for a midlevel archivist.

Qualitative indicators differentiate between acceptable work and truly outstanding work. They include such things as the clarity and validity of appraisal recommendations, thoroughness of finding aids, helpfulness and extra attention to assisting researchers, and innovation in public programming. They should, to the degree possible, be agreed upon between employee and supervisor, spelled out in the workplan, covered in day-to-day discussions, and addressed in formal performance evaluations at least twice a year. Though it needs appropriate detail, the workplan should not be a straitjacket and should allow plenty of room for individual flexibility. The strongest incentives for initiative come from situations in which "job charters are broad; assignments are ambiguous, nonroutine, and change-directed; job territories are intersecting, so that others are both affected by action and required for it; and local autonomy is strong enough that actors can go ahead with large chunks of action without waiting for higher-level approval."[15]

Supervision should also entail continual feedback—communication from the supervisor on how well the employee is doing in moving toward agreed-upon objectives and in meeting qualitative standards. Feedback can be informal, as in brief comments of praise, criticism, and suggestions, and studies have shown that people appreciate and react positively to sincere, accurate, and timely feedback. Some of the best supervisors practice "walk-around management"—informal face-to-face discussions at work sites that involve questions, encouragement, and suggestions. This approach keeps the manager in touch with the work and provides opportunities for addressing minor problems on the spot.

There should also be more formal and structured performance reviews on a timely basis, perhaps once a quarter or once a year. This evaluation compares what was accomplished against what was laid out in the workplan, analyzes the reasons for any shortfalls, explores how the employee might improve in the future, and also addresses how the supervisor might improve and how the work might be reorganized or new priorities established.

Programs should also build in provisions for advancement and promotion. One approach that has worked in many other settings where professional employees are involved is the so-called dual ladder, which includes a managerial ladder leading to increased managerial responsibility and a parallel professional ladder for positions of comparable rank, salary, and responsibility. The objective is to encourage and compensate professional achievement in a way comparable to that of managerial achievement. This approach holds out the promise that professionals such as archivists can advance without having to take on managerial responsibilities that may not interest them and for which they may not be suited by temperament or training.[16]

Another aspect of working with people is providing opportunities for professional development. The archival world is constantly in flux, with large-scale changes being wrought through adaptation and use of information technology. It is increasingly difficult to be master of all archival trades. People working in historical records programs need opportunities to expand and sharpen their skills. Formal university courses, attendance at seminars and workshops, and attendance at meetings of professional associations can all provide professional development. In fact, because of the relative scarcity of formal courses and seminars in this field, active participation

Sample Statements of Qualifications for Archivists

There are no standard national job descriptions or minimum qualifications for archivists. However, the following descriptions and qualifications statements, based on New York State Civil Service guidelines, provide an indication of job descriptions and qualifications for archivists at several levels.

Archivist

Responsibilities. Under the direction of a Senior or Associate Archivist, Archivists accession, arrange, and describe archival material, prepare finding aids, evaluate preservation needs, assist in records appraisal, provide reference services, conduct historical research into the offices and activities that originated records, and assist in the selection of materials for exhibits and/or other public and educational program functions.

Minimum qualifications. Education: A bachelor's degree in history, government, economics, public administration, political science, American studies, or library and information science, including or supplemented by 15 credit hours in history, 9 of which must have been in American history. (A master's degree in any of the above fields may be substituted for these credit hours in history.) Experience: one year of experience in one or more of the following areas: (1) archival appraisal, arrangement, description, or preservation; (2) providing reference services in an organization whose primary focus is archival services; and (3) providing educational programs or technical assistance in the administration of archival records.

Senior Archivist

Responsibilities. Under the direction of an Associate Archivist, Senior Archivists analyze records and information systems to identify valuable records, prepare records series descriptions and administrative histories, plan and supervise or directly carry out processing, develop finding aids, write and edit public information materials, present workshops and other training on archival methods, provide reference services, and assist in developing automated descriptive systems. The Senior Archivist may also supervise staff.

Minimum qualifications. Education: Same as for Archivist. Experience: Three years' experience in the areas noted under Archivist.

Associate Archivist

Responsibilities. Under the general direction of a Principal Archivist, Associate Archivists serve as the administrative supervisor of a major program area or technical service function. The Associate Archivist develops annual workplans and budgets; assigns and evaluates staff work; develops policies, procedures, and guidelines; conducts research and analysis to improve archival methods; directly carries out particularly complex and difficult assignments; and supervises staff.

Minimum qualifications. Education: A master's degree in history, government, economics, public administration, political science, American studies, or library and information science. Experience: Four years of experience in the areas noted under Archivist, two years of which must have included supervising archives staff or managing an archival program or function.

Principal Archivist

Responsibilities. Under the general direction of a Division Director, Principal Archivists plan, organize, and supervise programs for the preservation and research use of archival records. The Principal Archivist interprets statutes and regulations, updates policies and procedures, refines and approves budgets, coordinates activities among major program areas and technical service functions, and supervises staff.

Minimum qualifications. Education: Same as for Associate Archivist. Experience: Five years of experience in the areas noted under Archivist, three years of which must have included supervising archives staff or managing an archival program.

---

in professional associations is a good way to enhance skills, exchange views on how to meet particular problems, build up an informal network of contacts who can be helpful in providing consultation and advice, and, at the same time, contribute to the growth and progress of the archival profession itself. Archivists who are the most active in associations, as officers, members of task forces and committees, and presenters of papers at meetings, often tend to be the most highly motivated and most energetic members of their programs' staffs. Professional participation is also a way of reinforcing pride in archival work and identification of the individual with that work.

Anticipating the Future: Planning

Historical records program administrators must try to anticipate and prepare for the future. Planning is the management technique of systematically establishing program goals, organizing staff, and allocating resources to meet those goals by established deadlines. Planning is important because it enables managers to establish direction and overall control, ensures that everyone involved has a common understanding of program purpose and goals, permits effective marshalling of staff and other resources, ensures that the program proceeds according to established guidelines rather than in reaction to everyday pressures and problems, and furnishes a framework for staff assignments and for ensuring accountability. A program plan also provides a clear way to explain the archival program to governing boards, researchers, and the public. Regardless of size, age, or circumstance, an archival program needs a plan to help focus resources and actions. Appendix B provides an example of a long-range plan and an example of an annual plan.

It is useful to distinguish between strategic planning, which concentrates on broad issues of direction, priorities, resource allocation, and destination over a long term, and short-range or operational planning, which concentrates on a more immediate time period, such as a year. The term *strategic* is often used in planning discussions, but seldom defined or explained. The term has a military connotation; in that context, it refers to the science or art of military command that is used to meet the enemy under conditions advantageous to one's own forces. In a historical records planning context, it has a sense of means or methods to get from one point to another or to achieve something that the program manager wants to achieve. It indicates *how* things are to be done rather than *what* is to be done. The term is associated with roughly similar terms such as tactic, method, design, and expedient. Strategies are associated with the dynamic nature of growing programs. They are also related to innovation, nonconventional approaches, and new tacks that depart from old ways of doing things.

There is no surefire approach to planning, but some important criteria for success are:

Be sure everyone involved understands the need for, benefits of, and timetable for completing, the planning process.

Try to involve everyone who has any direct connection with the program, including people in charge of its destiny and all employees.

Make sure the planning process is completed in a timely fashion.

Disseminate the final written product and reiterate its importance as a central operational tool.

Revisit the plan from time to time during the period that it covers to ascertain progress, shortfalls, and needed revisions.

At the end of the planning period, assess accomplishments and shortfalls before beginning the next planning cycle. Continue the planning and evaluation approach to determine how well the program is progressing and as a basis for making changes as needed.

A useful prelude to planning is a program self-analysis of the type prescribed in the SAA's *Archives Assessment and Planning Workbook*.[17] This manual provides a series of questions to help analyze the status of the program in ten essential functional areas. These areas are similar to the basic elements described in chapter 2 of this book. The areas are legal authority and purpose; governing authority and administration; financial resources; staff; physical facilities; building archival and manuscript holdings; preserving archival and manuscript holdings; arrangement and description; access policies and reference services; and outreach and public programs. Besides the evaluative questions, the manual also provides a planning worksheet for each element for listing program strengths, areas that need improvement, and recommended actions to address those areas. The self-analysis aims to answer four general questions about the program elements:

What is the program doing now in this area?

What are the most important aspects that need strengthening or improvement?

What resources are available for this work?

What additional resources and new approaches seem to be needed?

This thorough self-analysis provides an appropriate starting point for the planning process.

After the self-analysis, the next logical step may be to prepare, revise, or update the program's mission statement. A mission statement describes the fundamental nature, scope, functions, and *raison d'etre* of the program. It should include information on:

Why the program was initiated. This part of the statement should indicate the purposes and general objectives of the program as perceived by its founders. While the nature and direction of the program may change over time, this part of the mission statement documents the vision for the program at its origin.

The program's relationship to the parent agency's work. The mission statement should indicate how the program is expected to contribute to the agency's mission and goals. This provides justification for the program, demonstrates that it is related to the parent institution's work rather than being an add-on solely to serve external purposes, and establishes general expectations for what the program is expected to contribute to the progress and well-being of the parent agency.

The program's administrative setting in the parent agency. If this is not established by charter, law, or other document, then the mission statement should indicate where the program fits in the parent agency's administrative structure.

The types of groups, activities, developments, or experiences that the program aims to document. This provides basic information on the program's fundamental documentation purposes. Usually, it should identify, and provide descriptive information on, broad topical areas.

The types of records and information that the program aims to collect, maintain, and make available. This aspect of the mission statement, closely related to the statement of documentation purpose, provides a general indication of what the program will collect and maintain.

The research groups or interests that the program supports and serves. While most historical records programs should serve researchers without discrimination, a mission statement should indicate preferences and priorities. This does not mean that other groups will be excluded or slighted. It does, however, provide a basis for program priorities in areas such as description, researcher services, and outreach and public programming.

From the mission statement, the planning process should move to define overall *goals* for the program; for each goal, a set of *objectives*; and for each objective, a set of *activities*. The three levels should fit together logically in a hierarchical, pyramidal arrangement.

Goals, tied closely to the mission statement, are broad statements of desired outcomes or destinations to be achieved during the planning period. The goals, taken together, should clearly point the program toward the broad aspirations laid down in the mission statement, but they should also be realistic in light of the program self-analysis and the likely availability of program resources. Unrealistically high goals will discredit the plan and lead to frustration; goals that are too modest will discourage maximum contributions and efforts. Examples of goals statements are:

> Continually appraise and schedule records in accord with the repository's documentation strategy and collection policy.
> Ensure maximum use of holdings through effective finding aids and outreach programs designed to reach researchers with information needs appropriate to the repository's holdings.

Within each goal, the plan should establish objectives—clear, measurable, and attainable targets intermediate to the goal. Objectives are more immediate, tangible, and concrete than goals. Achieving all the objectives under a given goal would put the program at or near the goal. Examples of objectives, tied to the two generic goals mentioned in the previous paragraph, are:

> Appraise, and prepare and secure approval of a records retention and disposition schedule for the records of the president's office.
> Develop and distribute finding aids with descriptions at the series level within six months after collections are accessioned.

Under each objective are activities—specific, distinguishable work units that must be carried out in order to meet the objective. Activities—the most numerous, concrete, and immediate elements of the plan—should be precise enough that they can be tied to unit or individual employees' work plans. Employees should feel that the activities are sufficiently close to their everyday work that they can directly relate that work to an activity. Examples of activities, tied to the objectives summarized above, are:

Survey, appraise, and write a report recommending and justifying a retention period, for the President's Office Correspondence series.

Prepare an acceptable finding aid in standard format at the series level for the Matthew Nealon Papers by June 30, 1994.

How can a strategic approach be applied? As noted above, strategies are broad statements of how to reach program objectives and goals. If one of the program's priorities is to accelerate the arrangement and description of its backlog, strategies might include developing a volunteer program and arranging with a local university for students from an archives class to arrange and describe records as part of an internship or practicum. If greater visibility is desired, an archivist might devise a strategy for attracting the attention of local television stations to public programming events. A general strategy for preservation might be to copy (e.g., microfilm) records rather than carry out hands-on work. As a strategy for improved identification of archival records in state agencies, a state archival program might adopt a general strategy of training and working closely with agency records management officers. A strategic approach for electronic records, discussed in chapter 11, might be for the archivist to join discussions of planning for electronic information systems to ensure that archival concerns are considered and addressed.

Accountability and flexibility are the keys to successful implementation of the plan. Accountability entails tying activities to individuals' workplans, continual feedback, and periodic meetings to discuss and evaluate progress on the plan. Flexibility implies continually evaluating the program and the environment in which it operates for evidence that change is needed. Problems and unforseen difficulties will arise to confront every program, but they are easier to solve with a thoughtfully prepared plan that has been developed and represents a settled consensus on where the program should be headed.

Planning is an ongoing process. "Your plan should be a living document. . . . [If it] is more than a year old, chances are that it will seem more like a history lesson than an operating plan."[18] Long-range strategic plans should be revisited and revised as needed at least once a year, and workplans based on them should also be reworked on an annual basis to keep them current and fresh.

Monitoring and Reporting

There is at least one additional aspect of sound program administration: monitoring work against the workplan and reporting that progress as appropriate. Archivists do not have well-developed monitoring and measurement tools and are searching for better ways of meaningfully reporting on progress and service. Weak reporting procedures put historical records programs at a disadvantage in appealing for and explaining and justifying the use of program resources.

Many archivists attempt to quantify their work and monitor and report on it in statistical form. The SAA and NAGARA have both developed statistical program reporting guidelines and forms.[19] In general, historical records programs should keep track of and report on the following areas:

Appraisal activity. Reports should include information on records appraised; on the development of records retention and disposition schedules, where appropriate; on the number of series and quantity of records covered; and on records identified for accessioning or collecting by the program.

Total holdings. Programs should standardize on linear or cubic feet as reporting units and should report on the volume of new accessions and total holdings. The SAA guidelines recommend breaking down this part of the report by formats: textual materials (primarily paper records), microfilm, photographs and other graphic materials, cartographic materials, audio materials, motion pictures, video materials, and machine-readable records.

Arrangement and description. Programs should report on the work accomplished during the reporting period. The SAA guidelines recommend reporting arrangement and description by level of access, that is, the percentage of holdings covered by finding aids at the collection or record group level, at the series level, and at more detailed levels.

Preservation. The NAGARA guidelines for preservation are especially helpful. They recommend reporting in three areas: (1) holdings maintenance, covering basic activities such as unfolding, foldering or refoldering, and boxing or reboxing; (2) conservation treatments, including numbers of pages cleaned, repaired, deacidified, encapsulated, or laminated; numbers of volumes bound, rebound, otherwise treated; number of protective enclosures constructed; and number of audiovisual and machine-readable units (by media type) reproduced; and (3) preservation microfilming, including number of cubic feet of records filmed, number of images produced, and number of microforms (rolls, microfiche, jackets, aperture cards, and other formats) produced.

Reference services. Reference services are discussed in more detail in chapter 9. Statistical reports should include numbers of daily visits (users who spend all or part of a day in the repository—a user is counted only once a day and is reported again on each subsequent day he or she visits); requests received by telephone; requests received by mail; types of researchers; types and purposes of research carried out; materials consulted by or for users (numbers of collections and series accessed, and numbers of folders, boxes, reels, disks, or other units delivered to researchers and then returned to the shelves); and numbers and types of copies made for researchers.

Public and educational programs. The reports should include numbers, titles, and brief description of publications, including newsletters, special reports, and other publications; description of document exhibits, including numbers, themes and records used, number of visitors, media coverage if any, and documents loaned to other institutions for exhibits; and other public and educational program activities, including numbers (and brief descriptions) of guided tours, workshops, lectures, seminars, press releases, newspaper and magazine articles, and radio and television spots.

Problems and obstacles. Not necessarily suitable for an external audience, a report that includes a section on problems and obstacles can be useful for an internal audience where the intention is to apprise staff and resource allocators of problems and, perhaps, to appeal for their aid and assistance.

Other areas. Reports should include information that program administrators feel is important to highlight and communicate. This section might include special events—the accessioning of a particularly notable collection, the research visitation of a famous historian. It might include notice of awards and commendations for the program. Employee activities and accomplishments, especially those that go beyond routine, everyday work, might be good candidates for inclusion.

Program monitoring and reporting efforts have several beneficial purposes. Staff see the reports as opportunities to let people know what they have accomplished and, in addition, should see them as documentation and recognition of their work. Reports can thus be a motivational device. Second, reports help managers gauge progress against projected timetables set out in workplans. Third, they are vehicles of accountability for archival programs with their parent agencies, helping to justify the existence of the program to the institution in terms of the services it provides. The final point ties reporting back to leadership. Program managers should act as champions and advocates for their programs, using reports and other evidence of progress in newsletters, speeches, other presentations, and other ways to call attention to the program and its accomplishments.

NOTES

1. Warren Bennis and Burt Nanus, *Leaders: The Strategies for Taking Charge* (New York: Harper and Row, 1985), 8.
2. Ibid., 21, 89.
3. James M. Kouzes and Barry Z. Posner, *The Leadership Challenge: How to Get Extraordinary Things Done in Organizations* (San Francisco: Jossey-Bass, 1987), 9.
4. Bennis and Nanus, *Leaders: The Strategies for Taking Charge,* 33.
5. Edie Hedlin, "*Chinatown* Revisited: The Status and Prospects of Government Records in America," *Public Historian* 8 (Summer 1986):57.
6. Richard E. Boyatzis, *The Competent Manager: A Model for Effective Performance* (New York: John Wiley and Sons, 1982), 16–17, quoting L.A. Appley.
7. Peter F. Drucker, *Management: Tasks, Responsibilities, Practices* (New York: Harper and Row, 1974), 400.
8. Leonard R. Sales, *Managerial Behavior* (New York: McGraw-Hill, 1964), 162, quoted in Henry Mintzberg, "The Manager's Job: Folklore and Fact," *Harvard Business Review* 53 (July/August 1975):57.
9. Robert L. Katz, "Skills of an Effective Administrator," *Harvard Business Review* 52 (September/October 1974):101.
10. Drucker, *Management: Tasks, Responsibilities, Practices,* 341.
11. Joseph A. Raelin, *The Clash of Cultures: Managers and Professionals* (Boston: Harvard Business School Press, 1986), 5–6.
12. John Naisbitt and Patricia Arburdene, *Megatrends 2000* (New York: William Morrow and Company, 1990), 218.
13. Frederick Herzberg, "One More Time: How Do You Motivate Employees?" *Harvard Business Review,* January/February 1968, reprinted in Beverly P. Lynch, *Management Strategies for Libraries* (New York: Neal-Schuman, 1985), 613–630; J. Richard Hackman et al., "A New Strategy for Job Enrichment," *California Management Review* 18, reprinted in Lynch, *Management Strategies for Libraries,* 551–575.
14. Tom Peters, *Thriving on Chaos: Handbook for a Management Revolution* (New York: Knopf, 1987), chapter 4.
15. Rosabeth Moss Kanter, *The Change Masters: Innovations for Productivity in the American Corporation* (New York: Simon and Schuster, 1983), 143.
16. Raelin, *The Clash of Cultures,* 185–186.
17. Paul H. McCarthy, ed., *Archives Assessment and Planning Workbook* (Chicago: Society of American Archivists, 1989).
18. Siri N. Espy, *Handbook of Strategic Planning for Nonprofit Organizations* (New York: Praeger, 1986), 124.
19. "Final Report of the Task Force on Standard [Program Reporting] Practice," Society of American Archivists *Newsletter* (November 1983):13–16; National Association of Government Archives and Records Administrators, *Program Reporting Guidelines for Government Records Programs* (Albany: NAGARA, 1987).

6 Identification and Selection of Historical Records

All archival work depends on archivists meeting their primary obligation: identifying and selecting that small percentage of records whose enduring research value makes them worthy of continuing preservation. Careful selection is essential because the huge volume of records produced, especially in our modern, information-rich society, makes it impossible to retain everything. Even were this possible from a cost and storage capacity standpoint, it would defeat its own central purpose, for the volume and complexity would make it difficult or impossible for researchers to locate and retrieve needed information. The expanding volume of records produced in a growing variety of formats with a broadening array of potential uses vastly increases the selection challenge.

The identification and selection process has broad implications. Through deciding what to save, archivists contribute to the many types of research discussed in chapter 1, some of which have broad implications for legal and social matters and quality of life. They help determine what information future generations will be able to study about their predecessors and therefore have an impact on the future of historical understanding. Selection is essential for archivists' mission of connecting the past with the present. Despite its historical and cultural implications, however, this central responsibility is not always met on a systematic basis. There is no surefire line of analysis or formula that can be applied to guarantee the right decision in every case; experience and sound professional judgment are keys to success. Like other aspects of archival work, selection combines theory and practice in a somewhat inconsistent pattern. Uneven training and resource limitations affect selection work and, therefore, the quality and volume of the nation's historical record. Archivists are developing new strategies to address the most important issues and concerns.

Issues and Concerns

Archivists confront several issues as they go about their appraisal and selection work. The first issue is *how to deal with an overabundant record*. The sheer volume of records created by individuals and institutions presents a staggering challenge. While the telephone, other means of communication, and improved means of transportation may have reduced the need for creation of records, other forces, such as the use of computers and photocopiers, have more than compensated by increasing the volume. According to one source, the United States alone each year creates about 1.3 trillion documents—enough to wallpaper the Grand Canyon 107 times—and 95 percent of it is in paper form.[1]

Faced with a paper avalanche, the archivist, in order to responsibly carry out the mission of identification and preservation, must actively encourage disposal of records that have outlasted their usefulness. Ironically, systematic destruction of the mass is the reciprocal of selection and preservation of the best. This consideration has encouraged an expansion of the archivist's role in cooperating with records managers on such issues as development of records retention and disposition schedules for institutions and organizations. Schedules that prescribe how long records must be retained should be based on analysis of records and consultation regarding their administrative, legal, fiscal, and historical values.

The small percentage designated for continuing preservation is eventually transferred to the care of the archivist or otherwise designated for special attention on a continuing basis. The original National Archives Act in the 1930s stressed preservation, but later amendments expanded the Act's authority to authorize destruction of records, store inactive records, and advise on other aspects of records management. The interlocking relationship between records management and appraisal, and scheduling and identification of archival records, may be especially evident in the institutional and organizational archival programs described in chapter 2. Many institutional programs that begin with an exclusive archival mission gradually branch out to include schedule development and other records management activities. This development may blur the archival program's mission or even transform it into a hybrid records management–archival program, but it recognizes the essential connection between retention and destruction.

There are less direct, but important, implications for historical records collecting programs. Records that are systematically managed and organized as they are created and used are much easier to evaluate and appraise later than those that are not. Moreover, a records scheduling system may lead to an agreement to transfer particular series of archival records from an entity of origin to a collecting program, after a specified period of years, under an agreement worked out between the originating entity and the program. For instance, the Madison Chamber of Commerce's records schedule might include this item: "Board of directors' minutes: transfer annually after twenty years to Madison University Department of Special Collections pursuant to the records transfer agreement between the chamber and the university."

A second issue is *how to achieve balance, representative documentation, and a reasonably objective historical record*. Historian Daniel Boorstin writes about "how partial is the remaining evidence of the whole human past and how accidental is the survival of its relics. Survival is chancy, whimsical, and unpredictable." Furthermore, the archival record is likely to be abundant for some topics and bare for others. "We know little about what and how much earlier Americans drank. Yet the history of the temperance movement and the prohibition of alcoholic beverages has left an abundant literature." Boorstin and others have expressed concern at the sometimes arbitrary "survival of the collected and the protected."[2] The archival record is naturally relatively strong on institutions that create and save records, such as state and federal government and colleges and universities, but weaker on women, minorities, the poor, working people, everyday events, and ordinary communities.

One archivist notes bluntly that most of what has survived pertains to the "elite and powerful, white and male" and slights women, minorities, and the disadvantaged.[3] A study of social history sources notes that:

> Huge areas of recent American social history are virtually untouched by archival work, including the development of suburbs; the workings of political machines; the experience of the black and European migrations; popular culture; evangelical religion; and the impact of various government programs, from education through transportation, on the community or neighborhood level. . . . We have acquired relatively little on the key elements of an advanced capitalist society, the corporations and the unions, and on the places where most Americans now live, the suburbs.[4]

Another expression of concern about bias and distortion observes that "if archival accession programs continue on their present course, it is only a slight exaggeration to say that historians 500 years from now will assume that Americans were either politicians or people who passed their days at the academy."[5] Archivists in Arizona concluded that their libraries, universities, and other repositories may have saved enough material on topics such as Anglo pioneer reminiscences, "Tombstone–Wyatt Earp," and "Crimes and

Notorious Personages of the Territorial Period," but not nearly enough documentation on agriculture, blacks, current social issues, tourism, water and irrigation, the history of women, and other topics of high social significance.[6]

The archivist must cope with this problem of relative abundance on some topics as opposed to relative scarcity on others. Historical records programs may deliberately decide not to acquire and preserve seemingly important materials on a given topic because that topic is already well documented. On the other hand, the discerning archivist may seek out and accept materials that may be less information-rich but still worth acquiring and retaining because their subject is important but poorly documented. The challenge is one of degree, balance, and the optimal use of limited archival resources tied to institutional or other priorities.

A third issue is *how to cope with the complexity of modern records*. Our modern, complex, information-laden society, with its continuous changes in responsibilities and relationships coupled with advances in information technology, makes selection anything but simple. Piecing together a reasonably complete national "archival record" is a bit like trying to assemble a 1,000 piece jigsaw puzzle with pieces that were not manufactured with any common design in mind and that don't necessarily fit together, and where many pieces are missing or unavailable. For instance, in the subject of space technology, government, industry, and academic institutions are tied together in complex and continually evolving relationships that make appraisal of records in any single institution practically meaningless. To take just one example, records pertaining to the first moon shot are scattered among the John F. Kennedy Presidential Library, the Martin Marietta Company (which built the craft), the files of individual scientists, and elsewhere, rather than in any single institution or location. Any archivist or historical records program seeking by itself to identify and collect all the important records pertaining to the moon shot would find the task nearly impossible. Archivists are trained to identify and collect, but applying these two processes is difficult for complex, modern records and information systems.[7] As discussed below, cooperation among historical records programs holds promise as a means of coping with the complexity of modern records.

There is another, growing challenge. Many systems are based on electronic records and in turn are connected to other systems and databases and feature information that is constantly in flux. This complexity poses even greater challenges for the modern-day archivist.

A fourth issue is *lack of coordination among historical records programs*. Except in a few cases, such as the networks in Wisconsin, Ohio and some other states, cooperative collecting is rare. Many programs follow an introspective, isolated approach rather than consulting and cooperating in collection of records. Even within a particular city, the public library, the historical society, the museum, and the local university may all seek and collect historical records to suit their own institutional purposes and with little or no regard to neighboring programs only a few blocks away. Selection decisions often reflect reactions to records becoming available or being offered to the historical records program, as opposed to collecting pursuant to a carefully worked out plan. As documented by the state historical records assessment reports, most repositories lack settled collecting policies and, in the words of one report, "most institutions passively accession rather than actively collect" historical records.[8] Lack of coordination and a passive rather than active collection strategy may intensify problems of unevenness and gaps in the record. As discussed below, cooperative collection development efforts can help obviate this problem.

A fifth issue is *how to anticipate and provide for future research needs*. Historical records have value primarily because of their potential usefulness for purposes other than those for which they were created. The archivist must consider source, purpose of creation and informational content, and must also anticipate future research uses. "By his training and his continuing intellectual growth, [the archivist] must become the research community's Renaissance man. He must know that the scope, quantity, and direction of research in an open-ended future depends upon the soundness of his perceptions about scholarly inquiry. But if he is passive, uninformed, with a limited view of what constitutes the archival record, the collections that he acquires will never hold up a mirror for mankind."[9] The archivist must not only be aware of current research interests and trends, but must also act as the agent on behalf of future generations of researchers.

A final issue is *how to balance institutional and research priorities* in appraising and selecting records. Here, there may be a divergence between institutional and organizational archives, and collecting programs. In the former, archivists are concerned with institutional memory and continuity and with saving documents that have potential legal or financial significance. The appraisal archivist at a computer or software development company, for instance, would give particular attention to research and development files that might be needed in the distant future if the company became involved in patent or copyright litigation. The archivist would also be concerned with future research use of the company's archival records, of course, but his or her primary concern might well be documentation for the company's own needs. An appraisal archivist reviewing official records at our mythical Madison University would give high consideration to records likely to be needed on a continuing basis for the university's own retrospective policy analysis, legal documentation, or other university purposes. On the other hand, archivists in collecting programs are likely to be more interested in the informational content of records and in their usefulness for research purposes, both in the present and in the future. To return again to our model programs, the manuscripts librarian assigned to appraisal at Auburn Research Library would concentrate on records that fit the library's stated collection policy and would certainly try to anticipate research by people other than library personnel.

Selection is an unsettled area of archival work where traditional approaches have been challenged but not replaced and where new approaches have been put forward but are still being tested in practice. It combines elements of art and science. Systematic selection needs to proceed with four considerations. First, there should be a broad design or scheme that provides a framework for what is to be documented through records identified as worthy of preservation. Second, there needs to be a sensible acquisitions policy. Third, there are practical considerations involving the program's capacity to care for records and serve its researchers. And, fourth, there is the process of appraisal of particular records to determine their value.

Cooperative Documentation Strategies: The Context for Selection

Until comparatively recently, archivists usually appraised records collection by collection or series by series as they became known or available (the concepts of *collections* and *series* are explained below). Some years ago, archivists began seriously questioning this approach and identified at least three deficiencies. The first is the absence of any mechanism for continuing consultation with either the creators of the records (who know the circumstances of the records' creation and, in some cases, can influence their institutions' and organizations' retention decisions) or with users (the beneficiaries of selection work and knowledgeable about research uses and trends). The second missing element is *context:* how can an archivist decide on the value of a given set of records without knowing about the documentation on the topic, place, or people covered by other records?

Archivists now recognize the need for having criteria for documenting culture lest they simply react and select from records that come to their attention, which may not be representative or indicative of reality. They are pulling away from the restrictive vision of

Theodore R. Schellenberg and the other pioneers of the profession who concentrated on analysis of records but did not consider broader contextual issues. "Why couldn't archivists determine the documentation needed to study contemporary religious life, thought, and change, and then advise denominations and congregations on how their records selection can contribute to this objective?" asked F. Gerald Ham.[10] Archivists drew other insights from the library world, which is pursuing coordinated collecting strategies to reduce duplication and stretch budgets. Further analysis drawing on these and similar perspectives found traditional approaches to appraisal wanting.

The third missing element in the traditional approach is *time*. Manuscript programs usually were not able to appraise records until near the end of their life cycle—a writer nearing the end of his career is interested in donating his papers, or a civic leader dies and her family approaches the repository. Government and other institutional archivists had endeavored to appraise and schedule records in their institutions early in their life cycles, but often this step was not possible. In fact, often records did not come to the archivist's attention until their custodians were ready to decide on their disposition or some other event, such as running out of storage space, forced a decision. Practical considerations of lack of time and resources also affected appraisal strategies. Archivists' time was so absorbed by appraising older records that they devoted little time to the broader issue of documenting present-day, continuing activities and developments. They had given little thought to the related issue of documenting the *future* by ensuring the *creation* of appropriate documentation. Archivists' insights into the value and research usefulness of information was not being applied to the question, "What records and other documentation should be created now in order to ensure adequately broad and deep recordation of our times for the future?"

Larry J. Hackman of the New York State Archives and Records Administration and Joan Warnow-Blewett of the American Institute of Physics have noted that archivists need to establish guidelines for repositories to collect within broader documentation contexts, pursue cooperative collecting, and consult records creators and users when appraisal decisions are made. Appraisal decisions are often made late (after related documentation is gone) and under pressure (offices need to move, or space has run out.) Along with Helen Samuels of the Massachusetts Institute of Technology, Richard Cox of the University of Pittsburgh, and others, they elaborated the notion of "documentation strategy" as a partial basis for selection. They defined documentation strategy as:

A plan formulated to assure the documentation of an ongoing issue, activity, or geographic area (e.g., the operation of the government of the state of New York, labor unions in the United States, the impact of technology on the environment). The strategy is ordinarily designed, promoted and in part implemented by an ongoing mechanism involving records creators, administrators (including archivists), and users. The documentation strategy is carried out through the mutual efforts of many institutions and individuals influencing both the creation of the records and the archival retention of a portion of them. The strategy is refined in responses to changing conditions and viewpoints.[11]

The proposed new approach transcends and informs appraisal rather than replacing it. It is an ongoing process rather than a series of one-time evaluations of records. It means broadening participation beyond archivists to creators, users, and other interested parties; influencing the creation and retention of records on an ongoing basis; encouraging cooperation; and sharing responsibility for appraisal and collection decisions beyond archivists themselves.

The documentation strategy development process can begin whenever a group of concerned individuals comes together to assess and improve documentation. The group should include records creators, representatives of user groups, concerned professionals, and others, as well as archivists. For instance, a manuscripts librarian in a county public library could initiate discussions on documenting the county. The group constitutes the catalyst and moving force in the development and maintenance of a documentation strategy; the archivist plays a leadership role. The first step is to define a documentation area, usually a topic or defined geographical area. The next step is information gathering and analysis of present records practices; past, present, and projected uses; degree of identification of archival records; programs collecting records in this area; and new policies and practices needed to improve the creation, identification, retention, and use of archival records.

The findings and recommendations are then drawn together and presented as an action report, including a statement of the subject, functional area, or geographical scope; information and opinions drawn on; findings on major matters; recommended actions and practices, including suggested actors and the role of the documentation group itself; and a rough timetable for implementation. The report should address such far-reaching questions as "What new policies and practices would be most likely to improve the future condition of archival documentation?" and "How can records creators, existing repositories, and other parties be influenced to act individually and collectively to refine present policies and practices in appropriate ways?" The report should be both a blueprint and a springboard for action.[12]

The next hurdle is the most difficult: begin implementation of the report. This step requires convincing records creators "to create, retain, and appropriately administer and dispose of archival documentation vital to the creator and to others"; encouraging repositories to refine their acquisitions policies and practices and to cooperate with other repositories in light of the strategy; and urging institutional archives to take the same steps.[13] The documentation group eases the way by acting as advocates and garnering public support for the strategy and by providing coordination, oversight, and encouragement. A system of monitoring, reporting, and reevaluation ensures that the system stays fresh and responsive to changing needs.

Developing a documentation plan requires much in the way of initiative and leadership, resources to carry out the study and develop the plan, and lobbying and influence to ensure its implementation. Success is achievable only if the archivist and the other participants are willing to invest time, energy, and work. There are only a few approximate models for documentation plans: a project in the City of Milwaukee, a multi-institution labor history documentation effort in New York State, the work carried out by the American Institute of Physics and possibly other discipline centers that exist to help document a given professional field, and a few others. The notion of developing a full-blown documentation strategy for something as complex as, say, the state of California or the American banking industry seems daunting and perhaps impossible. Archivists are still debating how best to adapt and apply the documentation strategy approach.

But the insights suggested by this approach are helpful even if the results are something less than a full-fledged documentation strategy. The approach involves cooperation and discussions with archivists at the center but including other parties, encouraging the sharing of responsibilities and possibly the marshalling of far more resources than archivists can marshal on their own. It points toward consideration of a documentation universe as a context in which to appraise individual series of records. It encourages plans to document the present and the future as well as to collect from the past. Finally, it holds out the promise of more comprehensive and systematic documetation in the future.

The approach also relies on communication and cooperation rather than isolationist, single-repository competitive approaches. "Manuscript solicitors rival the foreign service in the diplomatic arts," writes Frank G. Burke. "As professionals, they are quite ready to discuss old conquests with glee, recent acquisitions with circumspection, but planned campaigns or past failures not at all."[14] A better approach would rely on openness, planning, and cooperation.

Agreements and protocols short of full-fledged documentation strategies could include such things as: periodic meetings to assess documentation and collecting; an understanding that repositories will inform each other about collecting policies and plans; and development of joint finding aids on topics where documentation is scattered. Repositories should agree to consider transferring holdings that don't fit their collecting mission to other programs where they are more appropriate. They should exchange appraisal reports with a view to sharing information not only on what is retained but on the appraisal process for reaching retention and disposal decisions. Looking beyond collecting, they should encourage the development of ancillary documentation work, such as oral history programs, to round out and enrich the historical record.

Acquisition Policy: Criteria for Selection

The second basis for systematic selection is a program acquisition policy or plan. This requirement applies to historical records programs that collect outside historical records as well as to institutional archives that accession materials from their parent organizations. Acquisition policies help ensure that collecting will be consistent, that the repository's holdings will relate in a logical way to each other, that holdings will grow gradually and systematically, that unnecessary competition with other programs will be avoided, and that program sponsors and researchers can have reasonable expectations for future growth of the holdings. Acquisition policies have three bases or sources of derivation: the program's mission statement, the program self-analysis (both discussed in chapter 5), and the documentation policy discussed above. Even if not all three sources are present, an acquisition policy can and should be developed to guide program development efforts. It needs to be developed in sufficient detail to provide continuing guidance for archivists in their day-to-day work of deciding which materials to accept and which to reject. An acquistions policy should include the following elements:

> *Statement of purpose or rationale.* An acquisition policy should begin with a statement that is tied to and derived from the program's mission statement. It should provide "carefully defined objectives for a rational collecting program," usually limited by geography, topic, timeframe, or some other "common denominator."[15]
>
> *Topics and areas of emphasis.* Historical records can be sought and collected for almost any topic where there is enough documentation to support research. The idea is to collect related records that

A Sample Acquisition Policy: Institutional Archival Program

As noted in the text, both institutional archival programs and programs that collect historical records need acquisitions policies. The following statement, for the imaginary City of Westlake, is intended to serve as a sample for institutional archives.

**City of Westlake
Office of the City Clerk
Department of City Archives**

*Acquisitions Statement
for the City of Westlake Archives*

The City of Westlake Archives is part of the city's records management program, authorized and described in a Resolution of the Westlake city council, June 11, 1992. It is a department of the City Clerk's office and functions under the direction of the City Archivist.

The archival program's primary mission is to systematically document the operation and services of the city government and to ensure the identification, preservation, and availability of documents needed on a continuing basis for administrative, fiscal, legal, or other purposes. Its secondary mission is to serve historical research and scholarship.

In line with this mission, the archival program concentrates on identification, acquisition, and sound administration of Westlake city government records with obvious importance for continuity of government, documentation of key decisions, substantiating legally binding commitments, development and implementation of important policies, and delivery of services to the people of Westlake. The program also seeks city government records with information on the people, groups, communities, and institutions of the City, and on its continuing historical development and evolution. In particular, the city archives gives emphasis to documentation of the offices and functions of the mayor and the city manager, planning and development, the functions of public works and community services, and issues pertaining to education, culture, and quality of life in Westlake. While the City Archives is interested in nongovernment records and keeps in close touch with the Westlake Library System, the Old Westlake Historical Association, and other historical programs, it acquires only city government archival records.

The City Archives seeks and accepts letters, memos, minutes, directives, reports, files on projects and services, journals, ledgers, and machine readable files. Records are identified in the course of inventorying and development of records retention and disposition schedules for city offices, in accord with state schedules issued by the State Archives. The City Archivist carries out these functions in concert with the records management coordinator in the city clerk's office.

The City Archives operates on the assumption, derived from professional archival practices, that records must clearly have enduring informational or research value to warrant their continuing retention and maintenance by the City. Records are carefully appraised to determine their importance and informational content before a decision is reached on retention or disposal. The City Archives also operates under realistic assumptions regarding space and financial resources available to the program on a continuing basis. Therefore, only a small portion of all city records can be expected to be acquired by the Archives for permanent preservation.

The City Archives is open to the general public, with appropriate restrictions on records deemed to be confidential under state freedom-of-information and personal privacy statutes, and the Archives staff answers researcher inquiries and assists on-site researchers. However, in acquiring materials, the Archives regards as its primary researcher clientele officials of the City of Westlake government who may need to seek and use records in connection with city business or operations, and members of the public seeking information on government policies or services. The Archives also considers the teachers and students of Westlake to be among its primary constituency and makes special attempts to encourage educational uses of historical records.

A Sample Acquisition Policy: Collecting Program

The following historical records acquisition policy for the model Auburn Research Library described in the Introduction illustrates a statement for a collecting program. The major and obvious difference between Auburn's statement and the City of Westlake Archives' statement is that Auburn seeks and collects historical records in particular topical areas and serves a specialized research community, while the Westlake Archives accepts only materials from its own city government and serves city government and general researchers.

Auburn Research Library
Division of Historical Records
Acquisition Policy for Historical Records

Auburn Research Library exists primarily to collect materials and support advanced research about the cultural history of this state and region. Its historical records program concentrates on primary materials pertaining to artists, performers, and the performing arts.

The historical records program seeks materials that will help researchers understand the creative spirit, reveal how artists viewed and interpreted their own artistic creations, document the origin and development of ideas and trends and the influence of people in the field on each other, and show how creative and artistic people dealt with and related to museums, galleries, theatres, performing arts production companies, and the general public. Auburn's collecting is very selective, based in part on this tightly defined focus and in part on a determination to give excellent care and attention to all the materials it acquires.

Auburn collects materials directly from individuals, from their associations and professional groups, and from institutions that organized and presented their work. Among the materials accepted are collections of letters, diaries, scrapbooks, sketchbooks, notebooks, photographs, slides and videotapes, oral history tapes and transcripts. (Note: Auburn does not have an oral history program of its own and does not support oral history interviewing or transcribing.)

Like all of Auburn's holdings, the historical records are open to all serious researchers during the library's normal hours of business. The historical records program staff serves any and all serious researchers who write, call, or visit. However, the main researcher audience is expected to be historians, scholars, and other experts in the arts and their history, and the library's approach to collecting reflects this priority. Materials are also used frequently for exhibits as part of the library's continuing exhibit program, including exhibits in the library rotunda and exhibits that travel throughout the state and, in some cases, nationally or internationally. The materials may also be the focus of scholarly seminars or symposia built around particular topical areas or individuals documented in the collections.

illuminate the topic, that augment each other, and that can be considered together by researchers. The discussion of areas of emphasis is the heart of the acquisition policy statement and deserves as much detail as possible on the topical, chronological, and geographical priorities of the collection. "What manuscripts, fields, types, or subjects are collected to an exhaustive or comprehensive degree? Is the collection's purpose to collect all manuscripts relating to a particular person or subject, or is it to collect a representative sample of all fields and subjects for a particular time or region?"[16] In the case of an institutional archival program, this part of the statement might detail what aspects of the institution's work are identified as priorities for documentation.

Forms of material acquired. The policy should indicate what physical types of historical records the program seeks and maintains, e.g., letters, diaries, photographs, ledgers, and computer records.

Types of activities supported by the historical records. The statement should provide insight into the anticipated users of the materials. First and foremost should be research; for instance, legal documentation and administrative continuity for a business archives, research use by faculty and students for a university collecting program, use for legal and administrative purposes by a corporate archives. Other uses might include exhibits (an important potential use that should be made known to potential donors); publications; and other public and educational programs (slide presentations, lectures, workshops, tours, etc.). The statement does not have to delineate all potential uses; the objective is to indicate priorities and probable patterns of heaviest or most significant use.[17]

The statement should be reviewed periodically when long-range workplans are revised, and revised in light of changing research interests, uses, and needs.

The Program's Capacities: Anticipating Impact

Selection needs to be based in part on practical realities relating to the program's staff, other resources and storage and materials-handling capacity.[18] If a program has a backlog of unprocessed material and no plans for processing it, should it continue to solicit or accept more material? If the stack area is almost full, should a program actively seek more material before addressing that need? If preservation work is far behind schedule, and old pages literally crumble in the hands of even the most careful researcher, what will be the result of taking more material that needs extensive preservation? Any potential new accession needs to be scrutinized in realistic terms of cost of handling and retention. How much, and what type, of storage space will be required? How long will it take to arrange, describe, and carry out necessary preservation work on the records to ready them for use? Will additional staff and special expertise be required? How much will it cost for supplies and materials?

What are the implications for reference service in terms of probable increase in use resulting from new holdings? Related to this question is, what will need to be done by way of promotion and outreach? Aggressive promotional efforts require resources and time and can be expected to increase researcher traffic. If a given cache of records is taken, what may be the implications for work that will need to be deferred on the existing holdings and for records that may need to be passed up in the future?

There are, of course, compromises between policies of "take it all" and "reject it all." For instance, a library whose stacks are bulging but that anticipates constructing a new wing in a few years might simply slow down its rate of new accessioning, become more selective especially when confronted by large collections, or postpone some major new accessions and arrange instead for the records to remain in place but in secure storage. A hospital archives might arrange for designated archival records to remain with their offices of origin longer than anticipated while it accelerates an archival microfilming program. Once the filming is completed, the filmed records can be sent to the hospital's inactive records storage center, freeing up space in the archives' storage area for the records held by the offices. A program that is about to install an automated access system may feel it can take additional materials because archival staff time formerly needed to assist researchers in the use of paper finding aids can be shifted to care for the new material. A university library that anticipates receiving information in the form of computer tapes in the future rather than paper copy may anticipate storage space savings (which, however, may be more than overbalanced by the need for special storage vaults and procedures as well as equipment to read the tapes). These questions do not have simple answers in most cases; they need to be considered as the archivist balances various factors and compromises between taking too little and taking too much.

Appraising Records: Determining Values, Anticipating Uses

Appraisal is "the process of determining the value and thus the disposition of records based upon their current administrative, legal, and fiscal use; their evidential and informational or research value; their arrangement; and their relationship to other records."[19] It is often considered the most intellectually demanding part of archival work because it entails analysis, judgments of value, knowledge of research interests, and anticipation of future research trends. It is best accomplished in the context of documentation strategies, collection policies, assessment of program resources, and anticipation of impact on the program.

Appraisal can be carried out on small or large categories of records but probably it is most often applied at the series level. A series is defined as "file units or documents arranged in accordance with a filing system or maintained as a unit because they relate to a particular subject or function, result from the same activity, have a particular form, or because of some other relationship arising out of their creation, receipt, or use."[20] Series can be expected to have a high measure of coherence and unity because they were established and developed for a single, fairly well defined purpose. Beginning in the 1930s, archivists at the National Archives—particularly G. Philip Bauer, Philip Brooks, and Theodore R. Schellenberg—developed the principle that records appraisal is essentially an analytical process to identify values and that the appraisal process is best applied at the series level. If records have sufficient value in the judgment of the archivist, they should be retained on a continuing basis; if not, the records need not be saved. Schellenberg's articulation of this approach to appraisal is probably best known and most influential because it is presented in his books. With some modifications, this approach is still the basic one used in appraising records today.[21]

Records possess two kinds of values. The first is called "primary value"—the administrative, fiscal, legal, and operational value for which the record was originally created or received. They also have "secondary" values—importance for others beyond the current users. Secondary values—key for archivists—are of two types: "evidential" and "informational." Appraisal archivists invest their time, talent, and mental energies to determining the degree to which records fit these abstract concepts.

Evidential value pertains to the functioning and organization of the person, group, or institution that produced them. Schellenberg described the multiple levels of importance of government records with high evidential value:

> Records containing information on organization, functions, activities, and methods are indispensable to the government itself and to students of government. For the government, they are a storehouse of administrative wisdom and experience. They are needed to give consistency and continuity to its actions. They contain precedents for policies, procedures, and the like, and can be used as a guide to public administrators in solving problems of the present that are similar to others dealt with in the past. They contain the proof of each agency's faithful stewardship of the responsibilities delegated

to it and the accounting that every public official owes to the people whom he serves. For students of public administration who wish to analyze the experiences of an agency in dealing with organizational, procedural, and policy matters, they provide the only reliable source.[22]

Records with high evidential value include policy documents that have wide applicability and have determined organizational directions and priorities. They encompass organizational records—statutes, orders, directives relating to organization and reorganization, budgets, planning documents, administrative and legal opinions, organizational charts, and so forth. Also included are documents such as annual and special reports, hearings, and minutes that discuss organizational activities. In general, the higher up in an organization, the more important the records-creating person or office and therefore the more substantial and information-laden are the records. The archivist should be particularly concerned with records in offices where major "policy, procedural, and organizational decisions are made" rather than with more voluminous records from lower levels concerned with "detailed and often routine operations."[23] Institutional archivists are likely to be much concerned with evidential value, assuming their primary mission is to serve their program's parent agency.

The second broad category, informational value, is of more significance to most archivists—and to most researchers. Researchers usually seek information on a particular topic; the pertinence of the information is of greater concern than documentation on the creating entity. Informational value pertains to the significant information in the records on people, places, or topics. The focus is the content and probable research usefulness rather than the person, agency, or institution that created the records. Records need to be evaluated on the basis of the extent and uniqueness of their information, its importance, and its relationship to other sources of similar information. In judging informational value, archivists review the following:

Identity of the creator. What person, group, office, or other entity created the records? Knowing the identity of the creator helps authenticate the records and may provide insights into the extensiveness and reliability of the information.

Purpose of creation. Why were the records created in the first place? What were the intentions, intended audience, documentation need, and information transmittal need that the creator had in mind? How does the purpose of creation affect the nature and level of the information in the records? Is there evidence that the records were created to convince someone of a certain point of view or to appeal to a certain audience and, if so, how might this slant the informational content?

Accuracy and reliability. Is the information in the records likely to be reliable and complete? Did the creator actually see, hear, or have firsthand experience or information about the event, development, and so forth that is being described? When did the person create the record in relation to the time of participation or observation of the event or development? Is there evidence the creator had preconceptions and biases that might influence the accuracy of the records? Is there evidence of care and attention to details, or signs of carelessness and gaps?

Past and current use of records. If it is possible to determine, it is helpful to ask who has used the records, and for what purposes. Who refers to them either fairly continually or occasionally, and for what purposes? The answers may provide some clues to the importance, extent and usefulness of the information in the records.

Intensity of information. How much detailed information do the records provide in relationship to their bulk and volume? The higher this information intensity factor, the more valuable the records are likely to be for research. Records that are concise and compact but that have much information to offer are likely to be better candidates for permanent preservation than bulky records with sketchy information.

Relationship to other records. What is the relationship between these records and other records with information on the same topics, developments, people, and so on? Is the information duplicated or summarized in another series of records? These are essentially documentation strategy questions but, even in the absence of a documentation strategy, it is still worthwhile to consider them. If desired information is presented in another series of records, the archivist needs to decide whether to accept the ones being examined or seek out the alternative records.

Nature and quality of the information. What information is captured and presented in these records? To what extent do the records provide significant information on people, topics, and developments of interest to the historical records program? How important is the information? Is the information easy to identify, clearly presented, and capable of being interpreted by researchers? These are subjective, judgmental questions where the archivist brings to bear his or her training, experience, ability to gauge the importance of information, and knowledge of research interests and trends.

A related series of appraisal questions should focus on the anticipated uses of the records—essentially, who is likely to use these records, how frequently, and for what purposes? These questions fall into at least four headings:

Relationship to the program's researcher priorities. While it is possible to imagine a use for just about any record, the repository's primary researcher groups, as defined and presented in the mission statement, should be kept in mind in reaching appraisal decisions. This does not mean that records that do not fit these needs will be rejected; it does mean that those that fit the needs will be given priority over those that do not.

Usability. These practical questions pertain to whether the records can actually be used. Are the records legible? Are they indexed? Do they require an intervening device such as a computer or microfilm reader, to read and interpret?

Access restrictions. Are there legal or other access restrictions, tied to sensitivity or confidentiality of information or other considerations? If so, do the restrictions pertain to some or all of the records? How severe are they—do they forbid access or instead add requirements, for instance, a prohibition against disclosure of sensitive information such as individuals' names? In general, the more extensive and limiting the restrictions and the longer the time period for which they are imposed, the less potential research usefulness the records will have.

Anticipated descriptive and promotional activities. To what extent will the program's descriptive and promotional activities focus on and encourage use of the records? This difficult question depends on broader plans and priorities as indicated in chapters 9 and 10. Records that are merely accepted and processed and whose existence and research potential are never promoted are unlikely to be extensively used. Key questions are: how soon will these records likely be arranged, described, and at what level, so that they can be used? What sorts of finding aids will be developed? Will the records be described in a database or other central place where the descriptions will be accessible to people with an information need that could be satisfied by consulting the records? How much promotion will take place, for instance, announcements and descriptive articles in newsletters and journals of professional associations interested in the topic, presentations at meetings, tours, exhibits, and other promotional activities? It is impossible to answer all of these questions with precision in advance of every selection decision, and these answers should not be the primary determinants of whether records are designated for permanent preservation or not. But the questions are important considerations when trying to anticipate potential use of the records in the future.

Appraisal requires a thorough knowledge of the records and also awareness of active research in the field or fields where they may be used. Appraisal decisions should be shared; the archivist appraising the records should write a report and advance recommendations but then consult with colleagues in the program before making a final determination. This consultative process provides opportunity

To Retain or Not to Retain? An Appraisal Report That Concludes "Yes"

How is one to balance all the factors that need to be considered when deciding whether particular records are worthy of permanent preservation? There are no simple answers, only a systematic analytical process that takes into account as many of the factors noted above as possible. In this sample appraisal report, the archivist, and her supervisor, contended that the records in question were worth accessioning into the library's historical records holdings. The situation is a simpler one than most appraisal archivists encounter in their daily work but it illustrates the analytical process.

Auburn Research Library
Historical Records Appraisal Report

Name of collection or series: Malcolm Hayden Records

Inclusive dates: 1960–1990

Volume: Approximately 50 cubic feet

General physical condition: Generally excellent. Most of the records have been stored in the Hayden house in files and sturdy cartons and show little sign of wear through use, deterioration, or dirt, mold, or mildew.

Description and assessment of the records: Malcolm Hayden (1914–1991) was a well-known artist, an art teacher, a prolific writer on arts-related topics, and a philanthropist. He first proposed the Auburn Arts Museum, is generally regarded as responsible for its origin and development, and was the first chairman of its board of trustees. His career, which spanned nearly a half century, was marked by noted success and influence. His earlier papers were destroyed in a fire in 1959. The Auburn Arts Museum holds his official board of trustees' records but is not interested in collecting his additional material, which is held and owned by his daughter. The records apparently consist of the following:

Personal and miscellaneous correspondence, 1960–1990. This pertains to personal and business affairs and to Mr. Hayden's role as a benefactor of the state Republican Party and his attendance at various party conventions and meetings. It contains his views on various political, governmental, and cultural developments during these two decades.

Correspondence on paintings and exhibitions, 1960–1985. This series includes letters to and from a number of prominent artists on Mr. Hayden's painting and on their art work, and it also documents a number of shows and exhibitions of his work in several galleries and museums. Also included are diaries where Mr. Hayden maintained a daily account of his thoughts and progress as he produced several of his most important works.

Articles, books, media appearances, and lectures, 1960–1980. There are notes, rough drafts, and final versions of Mr. Hayden's many articles and his books on the history of art, and his lecture notes for the courses he taught at Olympia University and Harper State College.

Philanthropic activities and donations, 1965–1985. This series documents Mr. Hayden's participation as a member or chairman of several philanthropic fund-raising organizations and his own contributions to a number of art museums, galleries, and causes.

Correspondence on planning and development of Auburn Arts Museum,

1970–1975. This revealing correspondence demonstrates Hayden's behind-the-scenes role in raising awareness about the importance of the arts and stimulating interest in organizing the museum.

Records of chairman of the board of trustees, Auburn Arts Museum, 1975–1980. This material, from Mr. Hayden's tenure on the museum board, is revealing, but it consists of duplicate copies of material already accessioned by the Auburn Arts Museum Archives.

All of these records are well-maintained, well organized, and informative. They could be arranged and described with only a modest amount of staff work in relation to their volume. There is an index for some of the materials that refers to individuals and particular topics. Mr. Hayden was a prolific writer, and his correspondence often reflects his beliefs, summarizes affairs as he saw them, lays out courses of action, and tries to convince people to take certain action. He sometimes also conveys first-hand information, based on discussions with the people involved, of important developments in the arts and in cultural affairs in the Auburn area in general. Among the topics where there is extensive information are the following: the work of several prominent artists, art schools and art education, poverty and social action to combat it, Republican party politics, research and publication on art and art history topics, cultural developments in Auburn, government support of and policies toward culture,

and the founding of the Arts Museum. Several art history scholars have used the materials since Mr. Hayden's death, despite the difficulty of using them in the cramped space in the Hayden home, and they have been extensively cited in a number of dissertations and books. This extensive information on so many important topics is not even partially duplicated in any other records. Mr. Hayden's daughter is willing to turn over title of all the material to the library and to have the material open without restrictions. She intends to sell her father's house soon and does not want to move the records.

Recommendation: These materials are important historical documents, they are well-organized and in good shape, and they clearly fit the collection policy of Auburn Research Library. It is likely that they would be frequently used and would support important scholarship. It is recommended that they be accepted and accessioned, with the exception of the duplicate Auburn Museum records. Because the originals are safe and accessible in the Auburn Museum Archives, these duplicates may safely be destroyed. All the other material should be accessioned but it is probable that some of the research notes for the publications will be weeded and disposed of during processing.

Appraisal report prepared by: *Mary Frances, Senior Manuscripts Librarian*

Report reviewed and recommendation __XXX__ accepted _____ rejected _____ revised by: *Michael Johnson, Library Director*

To Retain or Not to Retain? An Appraisal Report That Concludes "No"

Not all records are historical and not every cache of material that an archivist encounters is worthy of preservation. In fact, only a small percentage of the totality of records warrants the appellation "archival" and the resources required for permanent maintenance. This appraisal report reaches the conclusion that the materials in question are marginal at best.

Madison University
Department of Special Collections
Appraisal Report

At the request of the University's Records Management Officer, I visited the office of Buildings and Grounds to appraise a series that the department calls its "Central Files," dating from 1940 to the present, and encompassing approximately ten filing cabinets. The Superintendent of Buildings and Grounds stated that the records have historical value because they document the functioning of his department over a half century, which has seen many physical changes in the university as well as continuing upkeep and maintenance. This series was omitted from the university-wide records survey and schedule development initiative carried out some years ago; the Superintendent indicated that his predecessor did not believe in records management and simply declined to fill out the inventory forms.

The Central Files appear to comprise all the major recordation generated by the department except purchase, personnel files, capitol construction, and renovations and reconstruction of buildings and facilities (which are maintained in separate files.) The files are broken by year, and, within year, by topic in an alphabetical filing system. However, purely administrative topics (e.g., budgets and planning) are included along with work files (for instance, on snow removal) and minor repairs to buildings. Most of the materials have information on routine work and there is nothing with outstanding significance. The files appear to have little fiscal significance, since purchase records are separately maintained, though they might be desirable for audit purposes. They apparently lack legal significance, since documentation pertaining to legal actions (e.g.,

lawsuits resulting from injuries in campus buildings) is held by the university counsel's office. It is difficult to identify any significant research that is likely to draw on these records or to anticipate any significant use by the university after a few years. They are bulky and the use of a single filing system for so many diverse topics would make them difficult to use by any researcher. This department, while important to the physical operation of the university, is not central to its academic life, and its records appear to document only routine matters of passing significance.

I discussed these records with Grounds and Maintenance personnel, who stated that they never referred to records more than a few years old. I also consulted with Professor Edwin Lowell, a well-known expert on the history of the university, who does not believe the records have historical significance. I recommend that I consult with the Records Management Officer and then meet with the Superintendent of Buildings and Grounds to review these findings. I am prepared to recommend a retention period of ten years for these materials—five years in the Superintendent's office, then transfer to the University Records Center for another five years—and then destruction. If this approach is acceptable, the description of these records and the retention period should be added to the University's records retention and disposition schedule.

Richard Golden, Senior Archivist

Reviewed and approved: Robert Evans, Director, Department of Special Collections for discussion of the appraisal recommendation as well for anticipating impact on the program. It is sometimes helpful to consult with outside experts in the field or even to impanel a group of experts to discuss particularly difficult appraisal decisions. The importance of this aspect of archival work makes the extra time and effort worthwhile.

The appraisal process usually results in one of three decisions: identify the records for permanent retention because of their value; reject the records because they have insufficient value; or retain a portion and reject the rest. This third option may involve weeding to eliminate duplicates and extraneous material, or sampling to obtain a representative portion of all the records. Sampling involves the application of systematic approaches to ensure that the sample retained typifies the records as a whole, an important consideration for researchers who, later on, will need to be certain that the sample is truly representative of the original body of records.

Finally, after the decision is made, the reasons for the appraisal decision should be written down and retained in the program's collection or accessioning files as a permanent record of why the materials were judged to have continuing value. A record should also be kept, if possible, of what related or accompanying records were appraised and determined not to have sufficient continuing value and were, therefore, not retained. Archivists should share information with each other on appraisal practices and, as appropriate, on particular appraisal decisions.

Accessioning: Legal and Physical Custody

Once the appraisal is completed and the selection decision is made, the archivist still has one more obligation: effecting transfer of the records to their new home, the historical records repository. *Accessioning* is the process of transferring legal and physical custody of selected records to a historical records repository.

While accessioning practices vary from one repository to the next, essentially three activities are involved. The first is a preliminary survey and listing of the records. The listing does not aim to be definitive or detailed, but it should include enough information to clearly identify the records. It may take the form of a list of series if that is possible, but if not a box list will suffice. The listing serves as a preliminary finding aid until a more detailed one can be created. When the work of arrangement and description begins in the repository, the preliminary listing provides a point of departure for the processing archivist.

The second aspect of accessioning is a physical analysis of the records. The archivist should describe the general condition of the records and note whether they appear to be in reasonable order and intact. The report should also note outstanding preservation problems such as water damage, mold, mildew, or insect or rodent damage.

The third aspect of accessioning is the legal transfer of custody. Records selected for preservation become the legal custodial responsibility of the historical records program, unless some other arrangement is desired and made. Legal documentation of ownership should be created and filed with the repository. In the case of an institutional archives, documentation might take the form of a transfer agreement showing that the records were transferred from the creating agency to the custody of the archives pursuant to an existing records retention and disposition schedule, or pursuant to a law or administrative directive. In the case of a historical records collecting program, documentation might be a deed of gift that identifies the owner and the recipient, describes the records being transferred, specifies whether there are any restrictions on use, addresses copyright issues if any, and formally transfers custody and ownership. Examples of a "deed of gift" transferring private records to a repository, and of a "record transmittal form" officially conveying records to an institutional (in this case, state) archives, are shown in figure 2. The receiving program should also prepare a receipt acknowledging that it received the records.

The file created for each accession should also include the appraisal report, notes on the program's decision to take the records, conditions of transfer if any, documentation of payment for the records if they are purchased, and statements of restrictions on access and use, if any. Repositories should also maintain accession logs or alternative register and tracking systems that record the origin, date of receipt, number and size of boxes, contents, and other descriptive information for each accession. The objective is to provide complete written documentation of the transfer.[24]

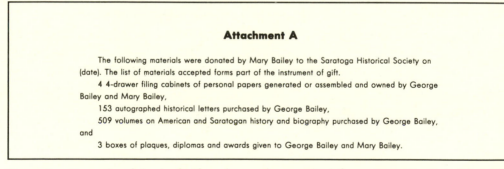

SARATOGA HISTORICAL SOCIETY

DEED OF GIFT

I, Mary Bailey, hereby donate the books, papers, and other historical materials described in Attachment A to the Saratoga Historical Society. I am the owner of these materials and now give and assign to the Historical Society legal title, property rights, and all rights of copyright which I have in them, including the rights to reproduce, publish and display the materials.

The materials shall be maintained, organized and made available for research under the usual procedures of the Historical Society. I understand that any time after delivery of the materials I shall be able to examine them during the regular working hours of the Historical Society. The papers will not be made available to researchers until a standard inventory of their contents has been prepared and a copy received by me.

The Historical Society may dispose of any materials which its representatives determine to have no historical value or permanent interest, providing that prior to any disposal and during my lifetime I shall be notified of such determination, and that at my request the materials proposed for disposal shall be returned to me.

Signed: *Mary Bailey*
Date:

This gift of books, papers and other historical materials is accepted on behalf of the Saratoga Historical Society, subject to the terms and conditions above.

Signed: Curator of Manuscripts
Date:

Attachment A

The following materials were donated by Mary Bailey to the Saratoga Historical Society on (date). The list of materials accepted forms part of the instrument of gift.

4 4-drawer filing cabinets of personal papers generated or assembled and owned by George Bailey and Mary Bailey,

153 autographed historical letters purchased by George Bailey,

509 volumes on American and Saratogan history and biography purchased by George Bailey, and

3 boxes of plaques, diplomas and awards given to George Bailey and Mary Bailey.

Figure 2.   Example of deed of gift and record transmittal form. From Frederic M. Miller, *Arranging and Describing Archives and Manuscripts* (Chicago: Society of American Archivists, 1991), 35, 36. Reprinted with permission of The Society of American Archivists

SARATOGA STATE ARCHIVES RECORD TRANSMITTAL FORM	D81789	89-767
	Leave blank – Archives use only	

AGENCY REQUESTING TRANSFER:

Agency Department of Natural Resources

**Major
Subdivision** Bureau of Parks and Recreation

**Minor
Subdivision**

Office/Unit Office of Park Planning

Person with whom to confer about contents, location, and shipping of records:
Name F. Olmstead

**2. RECORDS DISPOSITION SCHEDULE
NUMBER: 12-345**

3. CURRENT LOCATION OF RECORDS:
[ ] State Records Center
[X] Agency Space (specify):
Room 27 of DNR Building

Phone number 706-1234

4. DESCRIPTION OF RECORDS: (Give overall title of records, contents of individual containers and volumes, dates, or attach Office of General Services Records Center Transfer List if the records are now in the State Records Center.)

[ ] OGS Records Center Transfer List attached   [X] Additional sheet(s) attached
General Title–Planning Files

Box #	Records	Dates
1	Departmental/Divisional Files, A-F	1976-1980
2	Departmental/Divisional Files, G-L	1976-1980
3	Departmental/Divisional Files, M-P	1976-1980
4	Departmental/Divisional Files, P-Z	1976-1980
5	State Park Plans, A-C	1972-1978
6	State Park Plans, D-G	1972-1980

5. ESTIMATED VOLUME: 15   cubic feet   items (specify)

6. STATEMENT OF AGENCY REPRESENTATIVE: The records described above and on the attached pages are hereby transferred to the Saratoga State Archives in accordance with Section 142 of the State Records Law. It is agreed that these records will be administered in accordance with the provisions of this law and the rules and regulations of the Commissioner of Records and the State Archives. The State Archives may dispose of any containers, unused forms, blank stationary, duplicate records, or other nonrecord material in any manner authorized by law or regulation without further consent of this agency. I certify that I am authorized to act for this agency on matters pertaining to the disposition of agency records.

SIGNATURE _____ TITLE Administrator ____ DATE 8/15/89

7. REMARKS CONCERNING SHIPPING/DISPOSITION: Note pickup of Planning Files at State Records Center (Acc89-768) and coordinate storage

8. RESTRICTIONS: Unrestricted

9. RECORDS RECEIVED AT STATE ARCHIVES:

SIGNATURE _____ TITLE Archivist I _____ DATE 8/15/89

SR 1-80-3

NOTES

1. Alvin Toffler, *Power Shift: Knowledge, Wealth, and Violence at the Edge of the 21st Century* (New York: Bantam Books, 1990), 88.
2. Daniel Boorstin, *Hidden History* (New York: Harper and Row, 1987), 3–9.
3. Linda J. Henry, "Collecting Policies of Special-Subject Repositories," *American Archivist* 43 (Winter 1980):58.
4. Frederic M. Miller, "Archival History and Archival Practice," *American Archivist* 44 (Spring 1981):118.

5. F. Gerald Ham, "NHPRC's Records Program and the Development of State-wide Archival Planning," *American Archivist* 43 (Winter 1980):38.

6. Arizona State Historical Records Advisory Board, *Preserving Arizona's Historical Records: The Final Report of the Arizona Historical Records Needs and Assessment Project* (Phoenix: Department of Library, Archives, and Public Records, 1983), 58.

7. Helen W. Samuels, "Who Controls the Past," *American Archivist* 49 (Spring 1986):112–114.

8. Wisconsin State Historical Records Advisory Board, *Planning to Preserve Wisconsin's History: The Archival Perspective* (Madison: State Historical Society of Wisconsin, 1983), 14.

9. F. Gerald Ham, "The Archival Edge," *American Archivist* 38 (January 1975):13.

10. Ibid.

11. Samuels, "Who Controls the Past," 115. The most extensive discussion of the documentation strategy concept is Larry J. Hackman and Joan Warnow-Blewett, "The Documentation Strategy Process: A Model and a Case Study," *American Archivist* 50 (Winter 1987):12–47.

12. Hackman and Warnow-Blewett, "The Documentation Strategy Process," 24.

13. Ibid., 23.

14. Frank G. Burke, "Collection Building and Acquisition Policies," in Robert L. Clark, Jr., ed., *Archive–Library Relations* (New York: R.R. Bowker, 1976), 128.

15. Megan Floyd Desnoyers, "Personal Papers," in James Gregory Bradsher, ed., *Managing Archives and Archival Institutions* (Chicago: University of Chicago Press, 1989), 80.

16. Faye Phillips, "Developing Collecting Policies for Manuscript Collections," *American Archivist* 47 (Winter 1984):41.

17. Ibid., 40.

18. *See* Frank Boles and Julia Marks Young, "Exploring the Black Box: The Appraisal of University Administrative Records," *American Archivist* 48 (Spring 1985):139. Boles and Young provide excellent suggestions for new approaches to appraisal, including considering the practical implications of appraisal decisions and their impact on the program. Much of the discussion in this section is based on the insights and implications in this article.

19. William L. Rofes, ed., "A Basic Glossary for Archivists, Manuscript Curators, and Records Managers," *American Archivist* 37 (July 1974):417.

20. Ibid., 430.

21. The best overview of appraisal practices is Maynard Brichford, *Archives and Manuscripts: Appraisal* (Chicago: Society of American Archivists, 1977). An excellent summary of more recent approaches is in Maygene Daniels, "Records Appraisal and Disposition," in Bradsher, ed., *Managing Archives and Archival Institutions*, 53–66.

22. Theodore R. Schellenberg, *Modern Archives* (Chicago: University of Chicago Press, 1956), 140.

23. Ibid., 142.

24. Daniels, "Records Appraisal and Disposition," 64–65; Brichford, *Archives and Manuscripts: Appraisal and Accessioning*, 21–22; Gary M. Peterson and Trudy Huskamp Peterson, *Archives and Manuscripts: Law* (Chicago: Society of American Archivists, 1985), 24–38; Frederic M. Miller, *Arranging and Describing Archives and Manuscripts* (Chicago: Society of American Archivists, 1991), 33–41.

7 Arrangement and Description of Historical Records

The ultimate purpose of all archival activity is the *use* of the historical records by people with an information need that can be satisfied in full or in part through such use. In order for these materials to be used, they need to be physically and intellectually accessible. Accessibility is the purpose of what archivists refer to as arrangement and description. Arrangement follows a few fundamental principles derived from nineteenth-century European archival practice and changed very little during the past half century. Descriptive practices were, until recently, much less standardized. The arrival of computers, automated description, and the use of databases have propelled the profession toward more standardization in recent years.

There has been a *de facto* amalgamation in description of what are sometimes called the Historical Manuscripts Tradition and the Public Archives Tradition. The former, emerging from library practices and historical societies that relied on library techniques, focused on individual documents, describing them according to arbitrary classification schemes; arranging them according to subject, geographical area, chronology, or other categories; and in general treating them as akin to library materials. The Public Archives Tradition, by contrast, took a top-down approach to the magnitude of records that confront archivists typically working in institutional (particularly governmental) settings, whose main challenge is working with large quantities of records. This approach stresses dealing with and describing records collectively rather than document-by-document. It also holds that describing the origin, context, purposes, and informational content of the records is a better descriptive approach than trying to make them fit predetermined classification schemes.[1] In general, the second tradition has displaced the first, and most archivists today follow it, with some variations.

In both arrangement and description, archival approaches differ from library practices, to which they are often compared. The librarian's universe may be larger in terms of numbers of volumes, but the

The Difference between Library and Archival Practice

There are significant differences between library and archival descriptive practices, resulting from the differences between library and archival materials. From Kathleen D. Roe, Guidelines for Arrangement and Description of Archives and Manuscripts: A Manual for Historical Records Programs in New York State (*Albany: New York State Education Department, 1991*), 3.

When librarians catalog books, they basically transcribe information from the item in hand and provide a physical description of the item. For example, they take the title from the title page, list the number of pages, and provide the year and date of publication. They analyze the book to identify subjects that may be of interest to users and they classify them according to the major topic of the book. Librarians, however, do not research beyond the item being cataloged itself.

Archival description involves describing the physical characteristics of the materials, the intellectual contents, and the context in which the records were created. In order to do this, the archivist must look through the records and then interpret, extract, or extrapolate information about them. This may involve creating a descriptive title, determining who created the records, summarizing the contents of the materials or explaining when and why they were created. Archivists also identify subjects that may be of interest, but they also identify other access points unique to archival research needs such as form of the material and function. Archival materials are not classified the way books are because they generally do not have one single topic of focus. The process of archival description requires providing much more information than is common when cataloging library materials.

archivist's is more unsettled, unstandardized, and complex. Books, serials, and other library materials usually cover diverse topics and are created to be read and used by people other than their creators. Records, on the other hand, are byproducts of human activity, created to meet the needs of the creators and their organizations and institutions rather than later researchers. They often cover a single topic. Library materials usually exist in multiple copies, while historical records by definition are one-of-a-kind.

The primary challenge with library material is to catalog it, meaning to assign it a classification number and physical location within pre-existing classification schemes. The comparable challenges for archival records are to arrange and describe them—to ensure orderliness and to provide enough information about their nature and contents that archivists and researchers can discern whether the records are germane to a given research topic. Archivists do not classify their material, and there is no master archival subject classification scheme resembling the Dewey or LC systems familiar to librarians. Moreover, archivists usually describe their material collectively—for instance, at the record group or series level—rather than one single item at a time, the way books are described. Historical records are described this way because they were created, maintained, and used together by the person or institution where they originated. The nature of archival description is covered in more detail below and illustrated by the several examples in appendix C.

Arrangement

BEDROCK PRINCIPLES

Arrangement of historical records is defined as:

> The process and results of organizing archives, records, and manuscripts in accordance with accepted archival principles, particularly provenance, at as many as necessary of the following levels: repository, records group or comparable control unit, subgroup(s), series, file unit, and document. The process usually includes packing, labeling, and shelving of archives, records, and manuscripts, and is intended to achieve physical or administrative control and basic identification of the holdings.[2]

"Arrangement . . . is largely a process of grouping individual documents into meaningful units and of grouping such units in a meaningful relation to one another," wrote Theodore R. Schellenberg.[3] The objective is to make records physically accessible and usable. In a sense, description follows arrangement, for finding aids and other access tools must relate to and explain arrangement schemes.

Two fundamental principles have been adopted by archivists to guide arrangement work. They both are based on the assumption that the archivist should retain and follow the natural order of the records.

The first principle is *provenance* or, as it is sometimes referred to using the French counterpart, *respect des fonds*. It is derived from approaches developed by French and Prussian archivists during the nineteenth century and interpreted and applied to American conditions by Schellenberg and other early leaders of the field. As the term *provenance* implies, this principle relates to the origin of records. It holds that records of a given creator should not be intermingled with those of other creators, or, more simply, that records should be kept according to the person, organization, office, or administrative entity that created them. For instance, the imaginary Malcolm Hayden records accessioned by our model Auburn Research Library should be kept separate from the Jane Stapleton records, even though both might have information on the development of the local community arts council.

At first consideration, provenance appears little more than common sense, but is actually a powerful guiding principle. For one thing, it rules out any desire to pull collections apart and reorganize them according to subject or other headings. Unlike library materials, historical records are not gathered together by subject by the archivist. Instead, access must be gained via descriptions and indexing approaches that either reveal the subjects directly or permit users to get at them indirectly by describing the origins, purpose, process of creation, and the functions that resulted in the records' creation. Reliance on provenance assumes that records result from organized, purposeful activity, and that they are created organically and have a relationship to one another. It assumes that important information can be derived from examining the records in context of their creation and their relationships. It keeps related groups of records intact, enabling a review of them in their totality.

The second principle is that of *original order*, which holds that records should be kept in the order in which they were created or that was imposed on them by the person, organization, or institution that created or assembled them. Presumably the original order documents the sequential development of organic activity, reveals organizational approaches, shows administrative processes, and in general documents relationships. Maintaining the original order allows the user to get at and use the information in the order it was created and in a sense to see the story unfold as the records are perused in order. The original order principle assumes that the archivist is simply taking advantage of the originator's self-interested need to organize and maintain records in some logical order reflecting the progress of activity and facilitating retrieval. Moreover, keeping original order simply saves time that would be needed to develop an alternative, artificial scheme and rearrange all the records to conform to it. Individual documents "achieve status as *records* through linkage with the entity which created or maintained them as records." If the link is broken, the value and reliability of the records are diminished.[4]

It is easy to follow both provenance and original order when records are accessioned intact from a responsible record-keeping entity that created and maintained them systematically. In fact, as one of the leading concept builders in this field remarked many years ago,

> Archives are already arranged—supposedly. That is to say, an arrangement was given them by the agency of origin while it built them up day after day, year after year, as a systematic record of its activities and as part of its operations. This arrangement the archivist is expected to respect and maintain. Arrangement is built into archives; it is one of the inherent characteristics of "archives," differentiating them from nonarchival material. Theoretically in

the archives of an agency of government, or of any organization—and therefore in the archival depository that has custody of such archives—each document has its place, a natural place, so that its association and relation with all other documents produced or received by the creating agency remain clear. The archivist preserves and uses the arrangement given the records by the agency of origin on the theory that this arrangement had logic and meaning to the agency and that if the agency's employees could find and use the records when they were active . . . the archivist surely can do the same.[5]

The same reasoning applies to personal papers; it assumes that people, for their own control and retrieval purposes, will keep their materials in a more or less orderly fashion and maintain them in the order in which they were created.

Of course, if the original order is difficult to understand and frustrates access, or if it has been lost, for instance through successive transfers of the records or disassembling and reassembling in the past, then the archivist should depart from it. In that case, the arrangement order should be tailored to the nature of the records, the subjects they cover, the probably access needs of users, and the amount of time and staff resources available to do the arrangement work.

The archivist should aim for a serviceable, practical arrangement that can be described clearly in finding aids and that will make for easy access and retrieval. Chronological, topical, or geographical arrangement might be considered. For instance, an individual's correspondence might be arranged by year and, within year, alphabetically by name of correspondent. Disarranged photographs might be grouped around the topics of their primary coverage. In the case of electronic records, discussed in chapter 11, information may be altered so often that the concept of original order has limited or no meaning.

A MULTITIERED ACTIVITY

Despite these principles, there is no single, prescriptive approach to arrangement or description. Archivists, unlike their colleagues in the library world, do not all follow a single, uniform set of rules. A repository's approach will depend in part on its mission, priorities, researcher traffic, and resources. In particular, the plans for arrangement will depend on the size of the holdings, their current arrangement, changes over time in the organizational structure of the materials before they reached the repository, variations in the filing structure, and the variety of physical formats represented.[6]

Furthermore, arrangement requires more than just following two precepts; it involves addressing the hierarchical nature of records both in their original settings and in the historical records repository itself. Moreover, *description follows arrangement* in the sense that it must reflect the manner in which the records are organized and retained. In 1964, Oliver W. Holmes, an archivist at the National Archives, wrote a seminal article offering an approach to arrangement that fits both the natural hierarchy of records and the administrative divisions in repositories.[7] With some variations, this approach is still followed today in approaching the arrangement of records. Because description goes hand in hand with arrangement, it is also a guiding influence for description.

Arrangement, Holmes claimed, is actually five different operations at five different levels:

> The repository itself
> Record group and subgroup
> Series
> Filing units
> Individual records

Modern archivists are inclined to add a sixth level, usually below the subgroup, of "information system." This term, primarily associated with electronic records and databases discussed in chapter 11, means "the organized collecting, processing, transmission, and dissemination of information in accordance with defined procedures, whether automated or manual. . . ."[8] Since relatively few historical records programs have yet accessioned significant quantities of electronic records, the other five levels are the basis for most descriptive work.

The first level, at the very top of a repository's organizational structure, is appropriate to larger repositories and might not be needed for smaller ones. It refers to a few major divisions along the lines of the repository's administrative breakdown or major divisions in the stacks. A university library's special collections program (for instance, our sample Madison University) might logically divide its historical records holdings into university archives (the archival records of the university itself) and nonuniversity historical manuscripts (collected from outside sources). Other logical major division breaks might be chronological (for instance, colonial period or national period) and type of material (for instance, photographs, maps, and manuscripts).

The next level of arrangement is that of record group or collection. For institutional records, a record group corresponds to the organizationally related holdings from an administrative division or branch, for instance a department of state government in the case of a state archives. Thus, all the records from the State Department of Agriculture would be called the Department of Agriculture Record Group.

Five Levels of Control: Examples

Here are examples of the five levels of historical records arrangement and description, from the hypothetical repositories cited in the Introduction.

Repository	**Auburn Research Library**	**Madison University/ Special Collections**	**Salem Public Library**	**Westlake City Clerk's/ City Archives Dept.**
Division	Historical Records Div.	University Archives	Historical Records Program	Executive Branch Archival Records
Record Group/ Collection	Malcolm Hayden Papers, 1960–1990	President Henry Mattice Records, 1850–1861	McAuliffe Family Papers, 1950–1993	City Treasurer's Office
Series	Correspondence on Painting and Exhibits, 1960–1975	President's Reports to Trustees, 1850–1861	Correspondence of Joseph McAuliffe on Religious Issues, 1950–1970	General Ledgers, 1900 +
Filing Unit	Correspondence on Painting and Exhibits, 1972–1973	Reports, 1861	Letters on Salem Ecumenical Council, 1969	General Ledgers, 1944
Individual Document	Letter to Hearst Gallery, 8/25/73	Report on Faculty Tenure Decisions, 1861	Letter to Rev. Henry Thatcher, 1/24/69	General Ledger, June 1944

For other historical records, the term collection is used, but it has two meanings, neither quite corresponding to record group. The first is a body of historical records having a common source. For instance, all the historical records created by choreographer Jane Stapleton might be called the "Jane Stapleton Collection" by the Auburn Research Library that accepted and maintained them. The second definition is "an artificial accumulation of manuscripts or documents devoted to a single theme, person, event, or type of record."[9] A collection may have been assembled by a particular person and later been accepted and maintained by the repository, or it may be assembled by the repository itself from small, scattered miscellaneous accessions. The Salem Public Library, for instance, may collect small caches of photographs from various sources and choose to group them together as an artificial collection, called "Historical Salem Photographs, 1900–1950."

Subgroups correspond to divisions within these entities, for instance, major divisions within a state agency, or to grouping established by the creator of non-institutional records on the basis of function, subject, geography, chronology, or some other factor. Within the record group for the city of Westlake's mayor's office, for instance, there might be subgroups for the records of each of the three deputy mayors. This approach follows both provenance and original order and arranges records according to origin and function.

The third level, series, is probably the most important from an archival standpoint. As noted in chapter 6, the series level is a common level at which to appraise and select historical records, and, as discussed below, it is often the most useful level for describing historical records. A series is defined as:

> File units or documents arranged in accordance with a filing system or maintained as a unit because they relate to a particular subject or function, result from the same activity, have a particular form, or because of some other relationship arising out of their creation, receipt, or use.[10]

A true series "is composed of similar filing units arranged in a consistent pattern within which each of the filing units has its proper place. The series has a beginning and it has an end, and everything between has a certain relationship."[11] Series may be small or large in volume, but they are marked by coherence and commonality of purpose and topic and/or relate to or spring from some identifiable activity. Series may be created and maintained in alphabetical, chronological, numerical, or topical order. Appendix C presents several series-level descriptions.

Below the series is the filing unit level: discrete assemblages of records pertaining to some person, case, subject, or transaction. Filing units may consist of folders, binders, dockets, dossiers, or other methods of holding individual records together. Filing units may be in chronological, alphabetical, numerical, topical, or some other logical order.

The final level is that of individual records or documents, i.e., the individual letters in a file in a correspondence series. At this level, usually the only arrangement work is to determine that a pattern exists and has been maintained.

Description

EMERGING UNIFORMITY

Description used to be regarded simply as "the process of establishing intellectual control over holdings through the preparation of finding aids" and finding aids as "the descriptive media, published

Containers and Shelving for Historical Records

Detailed guidance on shelving and containers is beyond the scope of this book. The size, shape, and physical condition of historical records vary so greatly that it is impossible to prescribe containers that will always be appropriate. Single-page documents should usually be kept in order, gathered together, and placed in sturdy, acid-free folders, usually either letter or legal sized. These protect the material, keep items together, and can be labeled to improve access.

Archivists often use standard-sized acid-free grey fiberboard cartons to accommodate either file folders or bound volumes. The most common dimensions are 12" or 15" long × 5" wide × 10" high. These cartons can be purchased with attached covers, and can accommodate letter-sized (12" dimension) or legal-sized (15" dimension) material. The cartons should also have metal-reinforced edges and corners to improve sturdiness. Several companies now manufacture these cartons.

Another standard carton, often used in records centers as well as archival programs and frequently called a "records center carton," measures 15" long × 12" wide × 10" high. These cartons will accommodate approximately one cubic foot of material; legal-sized material fits the long way and letter-sized material fits the short way. These rugged, double-walled cartons are made with fitted lids and many programs store them two-high on shelves. Like the cartons described in the paragraph above, these are available from a number of companies.

Also available are flat storage boxes and other special boxes to house maps, prints, photographs, and other material. Some historical records repositories custom-make or custom-order boxes to accommodate odd-sized records. In all cases, the boxes should be made of acid-free material and should be strong enough to last and to protect the materials they house.

Repositories may need large metal cabinets with sizeable drawers to accommodate oversized materials such as maps and drawings. These cabinets can store either rolled materials (for instance, maps on rollers) or large items that warrant flat storage (for example, blueprints). The drawers roll out for easy retrieval and refiling of materials. Use of such cabinets helps protect, and prolong the life of, large items. Other materials, such as microfilm, prints, photographs, and computer tapes, will need special storage equipment that is custom built for, and suited to, their storage and preservation needs.

Records cartons should, in most instances, be stored on steel shelving. Use of wooden shelving is not advisable because wood is combustible and its presence may be chemically harmful to records. While shelf size varies, many programs have adopted shelving that is 42" long × 30" deep, with shelves about 13" apart vertically. Each of these shelves will accommodate six standard "records center cartons," described above—three in a front row on the shelf, and three in back. Some programs save on shelving by spacing out the shelves more than 13" apart vertically and stacking cartons on top of each other. This is a practical approach if the cartons are not stacked more than two high. Stacking higher than that will lead, with the passage of time, to the bottom ones sagging from the weight of the ones above them. Records cartons can be retrieved from heights up to about 14 feet with the use of mobile ladders without resorting to catwalks or multiple floors. Space between the rows of aisles needs to be sufficient to permit the easy passage of a person with a records cart or ladder, usually at least three feet.

Repositories that have limited storage space may wish to consider "mobile shelving"—shelving that moves on tracks and that provides maximum density of storage on a per-square-foot basis.

and unpublished, created . . . to establish physical or administrative and intellectual control over records. . . ." A newer definition reflects the emerging view of the importance and complexity of historical records description: "the process of capturing, collating, analyzing, and organizing any information that serves to identify, manage, locate, and interpret the holdings of archival institutions and explain the contexts and records systems from which those holdings were selected."[12]

It is possible to describe historical records at any level of detail all the way from summary descriptions of collections or record groups on down through descriptions of each individual document held by the repository. Most archivists aim for something in between—often, for reasonably detailed descriptions of each series. Description at the series level is a good compromise between something that may be on too global a scale (e.g., descriptions of each collection) and something that is too detailed and loses a sense of context and relationship among records (e.g., description of each individual item). In recent years, two major factors have affected archivists' approach to descriptive practices.

The first is that the advent and increasing use of computers and automated systems have nudged archivists toward more standardized approaches. Until recently, many archivists took pride in their uniqueness and resisted the notion of standardization as somehow detracting from their independent, professional status. Despite their kinship with librarians, whose field was being transformed by automation, archivists persevered as "the last 'rugged individualists' of the information community."[13] However, computers and automated systems dedicated to information exchange are intolerant of idiosyncratic approaches. The use of automated approaches accelerates work, permits easy subject access or other retrieval, encourages updating as needed, and facilitates access by researchers. It enables archivists to achieve and maintain intellectual control over all of their holdings and to continually keep track of locations. The requirement imposed (or, depending on one's point of view, the price exacted) by automation, as discussed below, has been a shift toward standardization.

The second impetus toward more attention for description is the realization that most historical records are underutilized, amounting to an archival concern of major proportions. One explanation is that not enough records have been arranged and described and therefore researchers have no way of getting at them. Archivists have also come to realize that researchers often do not know about or use external finding aids, such as published guides and directories. Instead, users often find out about holdings through other means, for instance, referrals by colleagues or by archivists and librarians in other institutions or by noting citations in footnotes. Finding aids simply have not been very effective—in the absence of some accompanying promotional activity—in interesting researchers and guiding them to appropriate holdings.[14] As a result of this realization, archivists are stepping up production of finding aids but also devoting more attention to promotion of their holdings (see chapter 9).

The archival community is close to having a *de facto* standardized descriptive format. Like many recent archival developments, this one came about in part by chance and in part through careful planning. An SAA Committee on Finding Aids reported in 1975 that many finding aids were compiled through similar processes and had similar intended uses. Gradually, archivists began to realize that some kind of national system for describing historical records was needed and in fact likely to develop, given the state of automation and the development of library databases. In fact, it was automation that brought the necessity for more standardization of descriptive practices.

In the late 1970s, the Society of American Archivists became concerned about the seeming contradiction between a descriptive software system known as SPINDEX that was being promoted by the National Archives and the National Historical Publications and Records Commission, and the National Catalog of Manuscript Collections (NUCMC), maintained by the Library of Congress for summary description of collections. The Society established a National Information Systems Task Force (NISTF) in 1977 which "fumbled, thrashed about for a mission definition, and almost went out of business." It soon moved away from being an arbiter between two national offices and instead toward encouragement of a system to assist individual repositories with their descriptive needs and to permit national interchange of descriptive data.[15]

NISTF discovered that, despite variations among repositories, there were common threads in the way most repositories described their records. NISTF was primarily responsible for the development of two important products: a set of common descriptive data elements for describing records, and a new descriptive standard, MARC/AMC—*M*achine-*R*eadable *C*ataloging for *A*rchives and *M*anuscripts *C*ontrol. MARC/AMC joined a family of MARC formats developed and used by the library community for information interchange. It was approved by the American Library Association's Committee on Representation in Machine-Readable Form of Bibliographic Information (MARBI), and SAA, through its Committee on Archival Information Exchange, undertook to maintain it and to train archivists in its adaptation and utilization. Substantial grant support from the National Historical Publications and Records

Commission and from the National Endowment for the Humanities has helped move the work ahead.

MARC/AMC: A FRAMEWORK FOR DESCRIPTION

What is MARC/AMC? It is mainly a "structured container for information" with different variable data fields or "tags"—77 in all—for recording and presenting information.[16] While it is associated with automated systems, it can be used for any descriptive purpose, including handwritten or typed finding aids. It can be applied at any level of description, from the collection and record group level down through descriptions of individual documents. In fact, MARC/AMC is a systematic way of capturing and presenting descriptive information that archivists have created in varying formats for many years. Commercial software has been developed that is MARC/AMC compatible, and the format is used by participants in the Research Library Information Systems Network (RLIN) and the Online Computer Library Center (OCLC). Other software can be custom designed or modified to accommodate the format.

Each MARC record has a leader and a directory, used mainly by the computer for processing, and numbered, variable-length fields into which the archivist enters data on the records at hand. The fields are divided into eight groups.[17]

Identifying data. Fields 0–99 are used for coded or numerical data such as control numbers, geographical or subject codes, time periods, or unique numbers to identify particular records.

Creator of the records. Fields 100–199 include the name of the creator of the records, for instance, an individual, a corporation, a university, or a government agency.

Title of the records. Fields 200–299 cover the title, inclusive dates, and bulk dates of the records.

Physical attributes of the records. Fields 300–399 accommodate the physical traits of the records, including volume (in linear or cubic measurement) and state of physical organization or arrangement.

Description of the records. There are no fields in the 400 series. Fields 500–599 contain a variety of descriptive notes. Probably most important is field 520, which describes the "scope and content" of the records, including forms of material present, informational content, people, groups, institutions, and topics documented in the records, and notable or unusual information. Other fields provide biographical information on the person who created the records or historical background on the creating institution. There are also fields for describing existing finding aids and indexes, for indicating arrangement and description actions taken on the records, and for describing restrictions on access and use.

Indexing information. Fields 600–699 contain indexing information, such as the names of people or institutions documented in the records, geographical terms, and other topics represented in the material. A repository may use its own unique indexing and reference terms but is better advised to use standard terms, such as those recommended by the Library of Congress (see below), in order to facilitate sharing of descriptive information and foster access.

"Added entries." Fields 700–799 contain "added entries," such as the names of cocreators of the material, hierarchical relationships between the parts of a collection and the whole, and other information needed to facilitate access.

Location of repository. Fields 800–899 provides the name and address of the repository holding the material.

MARC/AMC may well be refined and changed over the years as increased use reveals the need for modifications.

Appendix C provides examples of MARC/AMC format records descriptions. Example 1 illustrates series-level descriptions; example 2, descriptions at the record group or collection level. The examples illustrate how the information is created by the description archivist under appropriate MARC/AMC tags. The examples from Kathleen D. Roe's manual also illustrate how the descriptive information is presented in a finding aid for researcher use, with the MARC tags absent. In the examples:

> The information is presented in a systematic fashion: identifying data, creator of records, title of records, physical characteristics, description of content, key terms used for indexing, "added entries" where needed, and location of the repository. The consistency and predictability of the format are obvious.
>
> The information is concise, straightforward, and clear.
>
> The level of detail is appropriate in the sense that enough information is provided to give the potential user a reasonably good impression of the origin, volume, and informational content of the records and thereby provide the basis for a decision on whether they are likely to be pertinent to his or her research.

Mastery of all aspects of MARC/AMC requires study and experience. However, at its heart, MARC/AMC is essentially a sensible tool for organizing and presenting descriptive information in a systematic manner. It is the format of choice for archival description.

TOOLS FOR CONSISTENCY

Use of automated systems for recording and interchanging descriptive information has also occasioned attention to two other matters of precision and protocol that many archivists had ignored. The first, to borrow a library term, is cataloging rules. Archivists do not catalog materials in the library sense of the term, but they do need to be consistent in use of titles and descriptive terms in their descriptive work. MARC/AMC provides standard fields and subfields, but not guidance about how descriptive information is recorded in them. As with MARC/AMC, the use of computers and the need for consistency for data entry into library databases dictated a more standardized approach than archivists had followed in the past.

An SAA manual—*Archives, Personal Papers, and Manuscripts: A Cataloging Manual for Archival Repositories, Historical Societies, and Manuscript Libraries (APPM)*—provides the guidelines and rules in wording that archivists can understand and follow.[18] The manual mediates among the archivist's descriptive needs and approaches, the MARC/AMC format, and the library world's bibliographic and cataloging practices, as articulated in the *Anglo-American Cataloguing Rules,* second edition *(AACR2)*. The manual provides rules for describing historical records and includes advice on formulation of personal, corporate, and geographic place names and on how archivists can interpret and apply *AACR2. APPM* is based on the realities of archival description: it directs users to archival finding aids rather than to the records themselves for descriptive information, and it provides for collective description rather than a document-by-document approach. On the other hand, it addresses issues that archivists had neglected, such as the consistent derivation of titles, added entries, and index terms. *APPM* provides guidance for how to describe creators, titles, volume, and format, punctuation, and the order for the information commonly found in an inventory or a MARC/AMC record. The *APPM* covers the fine points of archival description, but these are essential if information is to be processed and accessed by computer, and desirable even for noncomputer-generated finding aids because they provide for uniformity and consistency.

Less well settled is the issue of name and subject headings and access points. As noted above, archivists do not classify their material according to subject; rather, they maintain it according to provenance and original order. This preserves the integrity of the records but it does not solve the problem of the researcher who wants to access material according to subject or topic. Archivists have traditionally used two different approaches. The first, sometimes called the provenance method, assumes that the appropriate way to lead researchers into historical records is through "linking subject queries with provenance information contained in administrative histories or biographies, thereby producing leads to files which are searched by using their internal structures."[19]

For instance, a researcher at a state archives might be interested in the quality of milk in a particular county during a certain time period. The researcher would be directed to the archives' holdings from the state Department of Agriculture (a record group). There, the administrative history might note that milk inspection and quality control were the responsibility of the Office of Dairy Inspection (the records from this office constitute a subgroup). The finding aid for this office's records might include a series of dairy inspectors' field reports, in alphabetical order by county. The series description notes that the main responsibility of dairy inspectors was to check dairy herds, barns, and milk storage equipment for cleanliness and adherence to standards established by the department. The researcher surmises, correctly, that this series is likely to have information germane to the topic. The finding aids have led the searcher to the desired material, but the route has been through the natural hierarchy of the records and by explaining how records relate to the functions that produced them. Taking this provenance approach, the archivist's main descriptive challenge is to present information on the functions and activities of the creating entity.

The second approach, sometimes called the content indexing method, assumes that most users seek information on particular subjects, and that, therefore, the archivist's main challenge is to provide subject information in indexes or catalogs. Taking the research example discussed above, a detailed index listing all the series in the state archives under the heading "agriculture," the subheading "milk quality" and the further heading "county milk inspections," would have led the researcher directly to the desired material. The provenance method is more common and more compatible with other archival approaches in the sense that it follows the natural hierarchy of the records and relates the function that produced the records to their content. The content indexing method is less common and the indexing schemes it must construct often are an artificial fit for records.

Whether the provenance or the content indexing approach is used, it is highly desirable for archivists to use descriptive terminology consistently in finding aids. However, there is no lexicon of subject headings for archival description. The closest substitute is *Library of Congress Subject Headings (LCSH)*, originally intended as a list of headings for use by LC in cataloging books. Archivists have found problems using the headings, which are appropriate for books but not necessarily for archival material; for instance, many of the listings under "History," "Politics," and "Government" headings are too general for archival use.

A second Library of Congress publication, *Library of Congress Name Authority (LCNA)*, provides standardized forms of many personal, corporate, and place names. *LCNA* may not entirely meet archivists' needs, but its use is essential for entry into library bibliography networks. These national standard subject name and authority files have been supplemented for particular types of materials. For instance, the Getty Art History Information Program issues the *Art and Architecture Thesaurus (AAT)*, the National Library of Medicine publishes *Medical Subject Headings (MeSH)*, and the Research Libraries Group has issued *Form Terms for Archives and Manuscripts Control*.[20]

At the present time, the LC publications are the closest thing to a national standard for archival description and archivists find them serviceable for many purposes. To allow for local alternatives and variations, MARC/AMC offers a series of fields for local headings. Programs may use them but at a cost of undercutting one of the principal advantages of computerized description, the ability to search via standard subject and name indexing.[21]

TRAITS OF A DESCRIPTIVE PROGRAM

A systematic descriptive program, whatever the repository's size and holdings, should possess several characteristics. Description should be regarded as a core program element, should be scrutinized in any program self-analysis, and should be prominently addressed in planning processes and documents. The nature of the descriptive program will vary with the nature of the collections, the size of the staff and other available resources, and current and desired research use. It should be researcher responsive in the sense of being based on analysis of what information researchers seek, how they seek it, whether there are repeated requests for the same information, and whether researchers require summary or more detailed information to guide them to the records they need.

Descriptive work should be balanced in the sense that some attention is given both to current holdings and to new materials as they arrive. One of the most common obstacles to research use of holdings, and one of the greatest frustrations for archivists, is the presence of a growing backlog of materials that are accessioned and sent to the stacks or storage area but are not described so that researchers know about and can use them. Undescribed records exist in an archival "twilight zone"—they have survived but cannot be accessed and used. Description program planning should avoid this situation by ensuring that some resources are given to gradually reducing the descriptive backlog while at the same time tending to new accessions.

There is one other approach that prevents backlogs from developing or remaining as a problem: describe all holdings in summary fashion before describing any (or very many) of them in more detailed fashion. This approach is based on the assumption that a historical records program has an obligation to its holdings and its users to make known the existence of all of its holdings as soon as possible after receiving and arranging them so that they can be accessed and used. For instance, a state archival program probably should produce a summary guide to its holdings, such as a list of series titles and inclusive dates, before proceeding to more detailed description, such as description of each series. Appendix C presents examples of finding aids.

Finding Aids: Intellectual Routes to the Records

Historical records programs produce *finding aids*—items that provide researchers with information about the nature and content of historical records in their repository. There are what might be called external finding aids, such as published guides and directories which should be related closely to promotional publications and activities of the types described in chapter 9. These should be balanced by what might be called internal finding aids, designed for use by researchers themselves in the repository or for use by the archivists who assist them. These finding aids are typically unpublished and provide more detail than published ones. Their main purpose is to guide researchers to particular records that they will find useful, as opposed to inducing them to visit the repository in the first place.

Finding aids may be created at several levels of detail; examples are found in Appendix C. A summary guide, as noted earlier, provides sparse descriptions of all the record in a repository. There may be more detailed descriptions at the series or collection level or record group. One common finding aid, called an inventory, usually covers a collection or record group and has a description for each series, and sometimes for containers and folders within series. Many repositories rely on card catalogs, which may have one card for each collection, each series, each container or folder, or each item. Card catalogs, while serviceable for describing historical records, are inflexible and much less useful than other types of finding aids such as inventories. One final type of finding aid is the automated catalog or database, which includes descriptive information in a computer. Automated description provides quick, easy access and the ability to make the information available electronically via telecommunications networks.

Regardless of the approach and media, finding aids, broadly and generically defined as means of providing researchers with information about the content and nature of archival records, should present certain information on a consistent basis.[22] Finding aids can be constructed at any of the various levels of arrangement described earlier. A finding aid such as an inventory that focuses on the series level should typically include this information:

Finding Aids: Diversity for a Common Purpose

Finding aids are descriptive tools that describe records, attract researchers, and direct researchers to the historical records they desire. Thus they promote *the use of historical records (and as such are closely related to the public education and marketing efforts described in chapter 10); and they* facilitate *use and are thus closely related to reference services described in chapter 9. There is no standard listing of the types of finding aids. The list below describes the various types in general terms. For more information, see Frederic Miller,* Arranging and Describing Archives and Manuscripts *(Chicago: Society of American Archivists, 1991), especially pp. 91–108, and the examples in Appendix C.*

Finding Aids Intended Primarily for Use outside of the Repository

These finding aids are produced and distributed by repositories for use by researchers at remote locations. Usually they are either general summaries (e.g., summary guides), short overviews, or guides to particular types of records.

Introduction and Promotional Overviews. Some programs issue short general brochures or pamphlets, which provide an overview of the program, summarize its holdings, and perhaps point out its choicest materials. These short publications are usually produced in significant quantities, include layout and design features to make them attractive, and may be broadly distributed to potential researchers or made available at other research centers (e.g., local libraries), conferences, and other locations and events where potential researchers may see them and pick them up. They are really more promotional devices than they are finding aids *per se,* but they also serve as brief introductions to the holdings.

Summary Guides. Summary guide refers to published and externally distributed publications which provide at least limited information on all of a repository's holdings (or all of the holdings that had been processed and were available for research). Summary guides are often extracted and derived from more detailed finding aids, such as inventories, but they may also be based on preliminary information gathered at the time of accessioning, or on a cursory examination of the records. For instance, a research facility such as Madison University's Special Collections Division might choose to publish a summary guide that briefly describes each of its collections and lists all the series titles, inclusive dates, and approximate quantities. This summary would let researchers know at least generally about its special holdings and serve as a stop-gap until more detailed finding aids could be prepared.

Finding Aids to Particular Topics or Records. Historical records programs develop and issue special finding aids either to call attention to a particular collection or record group, to call attention to the program's holdings on a particular topic, or both. For instance, the Auburn Research Library might issue a special finding aid on its Malcolm Hayden records; the Westlake City Archives might develop one on its holdings (probably from several record groups) pertaining to environmental issues and policy. These special finding aids should be developed as part of the repository's overall planning process with an intention of engendering research use of particular records or giving them a higher profile because of a particular event. For example, a long government and community debate over local environmental issues might prompt the Westlake City Archivist to issue a special finding aid to her holdings in this area in order to call attention the historical roots of the issue and encourage retrospective research into the issue.

Automated Regional or National Databases. As discussed below, regional and national databases are a species of finding aid in the sense that they have descriptive information about a repository's holdings and are accessible to potential researchers. As automated description and access increase over the years, such databases may begin to upstage and overshadow traditional, paper based finding aids.

Finding Aids Intended Primarily for Use inside the Repository

These finding aids may be externally distributed, but they are more likely to be confined to use in the repository's search room. They are usually more detailed than their "external" counterparts, and are designed to help archivists and researchers link research interests and needs directly to appropriate records.

Creator-Furnished Finding Aids. In some cases, the originator of the records may have created an access tool, such as a register or an index to correspondence or a listing of ledgers, for his or her own access purposes. If they are accurate and complete, they may well be serviceable as finding aids once the records are accessioned and made available for use in the historical records repository. Viewed another way, they can serve as temporary finding aids until the archivist can develop others in line with the repository's policies.

Accession Documents and Preliminary Listings. As noted in chapter 6, in the process of accessioning—effecting the formal transfer—of records, archivists often make a preliminary listing of the materials, primarily for security and control purposes. Often these listings descend to the box and folder level of detail. These preliminary descriptions can serve as makeshift finding aids. Again, it may be sensible to use them as temporary guides until more formal and detailed ones can be developed.

Inventories. Inventories are descriptions of all the records in a collection or record group, usually at the series level, together with information on the person, organization, or institution that produced them. Often lengthy and detailed, they provide a historical context for the records by describing their originator and offer consider descriptive detail on the records themselves. Inventories, the heart of most well-developed descriptive programs, include the information on originator, identity, dates, volume, organization and arrangement, and informational content discussed for finding aids, below.

Card Catalogs. Many libraries use standard card catalogs to provide reference either to more detailed finding aids or directly to the records themselves. Because of their small format and limitations on the information they can hold, card catalogs are not considered to be an efficient form of finding aid. On the other hand, they are compatible in format with the finding aid that is used for most library holdings.

Automated Internal Databases. Automated descriptive systems may provide information at any level of detail. For instance, a repository may have all of its inventory information available and accessible via computer, saving researchers the trouble of having to handle paper records. Of course, the "internal" database may also be the repository's entries in a state or national database.

Originator of the records. Usually called main entry by descriptive archivists and catalogers, this indicates what person or group was mainly responsible for creating, collecting, or maintaining the material being described.

Title. The title of the collection or series as it was called by the originator or as the archivist has named it. It is helpful to indicate the form of material or type of records and the subject or topic covered (e.g., Correspondence on Political Matters, Student History Case Files, Reports on Pollution of Rivers, Photographs of Houses in Berne).

Dates. The beginning and ending dates of the records.

Volume. The volume of records, usually expressed in linear feet or cubic feet. This provides a general notion of the density of the information—the volume in relation to the time span covered. It helps researchers to gauge and anticipate how much material needs to be perused.

Organizational history or biographical information. The finding aid should have some information on the activities, events, and developments that took place as the records were being created or assembled. The intention is to provide enough information to provide a historical context for the records.

Organization and arrangement. The topical, chronological, alphabetical, numerical, or other arrangement of the records. This information helps researchers predict where information they need might be located.

Informational content. Sometimes called the scope and content note, this is the most challenging part of the finding aid, for two reasons. First, the archivist must make it up, that is, derive and describe it from review of the materials themselves. This involves being selective and interpretive and deciding what to highlight and what to only mention or to leave out entirely. Second, it is of central interest to researchers, who often will use it as the basis for examining or bypassing the records described. This part of the finding aid should describe the information that is found in the records. It should describe the people, places, events, and topics documented in the records at a significant level. If appropriate, it should offer additional information on the function or activity that resulted in creation of the records, as a means of assisting researchers to more fully understand the origin, nature, and extent of the information they are likely to contain. Finally, there should be a note on important information that is unexpectedly found in the records. Where appropriate, other information may be included, such as: how the records were generated, used, and maintained, interpretations of how the records reflect particularly important events, particularly important records, and surprising gaps in the records. Maintaining flexibility is important; the archivist should include whatever information seems appropriate and helpful, taking into account the nature of the records and their probable research use.[23]

Series descriptions. Inventories usually include a description of each series in a more or less consistent format. The description should be concise and yet detailed and informative enough to enable researchers to make a confident assessment whether the records are likely to yield information pertinent to their topic. The description should include the series title, inclusive dates, and information on the scope and content of the series—the activity that resulted in the creation of the records and the information they contain. It is also helpful to briefly describe the arrangement of the series, physical condition (particularly if there are conditions that make the records difficult to use), and especially important information.

Container listings. These list records boxes or other units and sometimes detail within boxes, e.g., folders or volumes.

Additional finding aids. It is helpful to note the existence of indexes or other finding aids, beyond the inventory itself.

Additional information. This final category is used by the archivist to present any further insights into the records or other information that might be helpful to researchers.

A New World of Access: Databases and Networks

State and national databases provide access to historical records by researchers. The pioneer national database was begun by the Library of Congress in 1959, the *National Union Catalog of Manuscript Collections. NUCMC* reproduces catalog card–length descriptions of historical records collections that are submitted to the NUCMC office. It is updated periodically and features a cumulative index. Its impact has been limited by its having separate volumes and the delays in getting those volumes published. It is, however, the only central source of information about manuscript collections in the United States, and is often consulted by researchers as a starting point in locating relevant collections. NUCMC lists over fifty thousand manuscript collections held by more than a thousand repositories.[24]

The National Historical Publications and Records Commission published a directory of archival and manuscripts repositories in 1978 and updated and reissued it in 1988.[25] The directory includes repository name, address, information on access and copying facilities, an indication of materials solicited, and a summary of holdings.

The directory's index provides a means of identifying repositories that hold records on particular topics. The NHPRC publication is helpful but its entries are too short to be of much assistance to researchers.

Use of the MARC/AMC format opens many possibilities. It provides the consistent format that is needed for the most effective use of computers to describe records, for the creation of databases, and for the interchange of information. It permitted archivists, for the first time, to actively join growing library databases. Pooling archival information with library bibliographical information has two advantages. It makes information on a given topic, whether in book, historical record, or some other form, available to researchers in a single place. It also takes advantage of an established and well developed information delivery system.

With MARC/AMC under development, the Research Libraries Group (RLG) began modifying its national bibliographic network, the Research Libraries Information Network (RLIN) so that it could accept information on historical records. The central RLIN database is an electronic union catalog that describes many of the materials held by RLG members and by nonmember subscribers to RLIN services. RLIN specified the use of MARC/AMC for entering data into its system, another incentive that spurred development and adoption of the format. By the early 1990s, nearly 100 repositories have entered a total of more than a quarter million AMC records into the RLIN database. In a notable expansion of data in RLIN, several state archives are now entering data describing their holdings, which has called increased attention to its usefulness for a wide variety of historical research. Other bibliographic utilities, including the Online Computer Library Center (OCLC), also accept MARC/AMC records.[26]

The number of repositories contributing to national databases continues to increase. Plans are also in place or under development for creation of statewide historical records databases, often as subparts of existing library databases. In New York State, Cornell University surveyed most historical records repositories in the state, produced county-level guides that are indexed in detail, and entered all the descriptive data into RLIN. Progress has been slow in most cases, due primarily to lack of funding. Archivists recognize notable advantages to having their data in state and national utilities; that is where researchers look for references to source material. In fact, some experts predict the eventual advent of an archival bandwagon effect, as programs realize that researchers may rely only automated databases and neglect or refuse to check further.[27]

There is a loss of some independence and archivists must now pay attention to descriptive standards, support changes in MARC/

AMC as needed, and participate in meetings of library database and bibliographic utility representatives. They must be concerned with cataloging rules, subject headings, name authorities, and other matters formerly beyond the arena of concern of most archivists. But this need for broader attention to matters in the library field is a small price to pay for the immensely increased access potential that goes with state and national databases.

More precise and exacting descriptive standards are also under development. Increasingly, archivists are finding that using computers, contributing to national databases, and adhering to library descriptive practices all impose a need for more attention to uniformity and consistency. This has led to a renewed discussion of the need for more precise descriptive standards, development of index and access terms appropriate to historical records, and new and more revealing approaches to description of records. As noted in chapter 9, it has also led to discussion of how to use the advent of computer access to encourage and assist broader use of historical records.

NOTES

1. Richard C. Berner, "Arrangement and Description: Some Historical Observations," *American Archivist* 41 (April 1978):169–181.
2. William L. Rofes, ed., "A Basic Glossary for Archivists, Manuscript Curators, and Records Managers," *American Archivist* 37 (July 1974):418.
3. Theodore R. Schellenberg, *The Management of Archives* (New York: Columbia University Press, 1965), 81.
4. Sharon Gibbs Thibodeau, "Archival Arrangement and Description," in James G. Bradsher, ed., *Managing Archives and Archival Institutions* (Chicago: University of Chicago Press, 1989), 68.
5. Oliver Wendell Holmes, "Archival Arrangement: Five Different Operations at Five Different Levels," *American Archivist* 27 (January 1964):21.
6. Frederic M. Miller, *Arranging and Describing Archives and Manuscripts* (Chicago: Society of American Archivists, 1991), 46.
7. Holmes, "Archival Arrangement," 21–41.
8. National Archives and Records Administration, *Managing Electronic Records* (Washington: National Archives and Records Administration, 1990), G-9.
9. Rofes, ed., "Basic Glossary," 419, for both definitions.
10. Ibid., 430.
11. Holmes, "Archival Arrangement," 30.
12. Society of American Archivists, Working Group on Standards for Archival Description, *Archival Descriptive Standards: Establishing a Process for Their Development and Implementation* (Chicago: Society of American Archivists, 1990), 15–16.
13. Janet Gertz and Leon J. Stout, "The MARC Archival and Manuscripts Control (AMC) Format: A New Direction in Cataloging," *Cataloging and Classification Quarterly* 9 (1989):5.
14. Roy C. Turnbaugh, "Archival Mission and User Studies," *Midwestern Archivist* 11 (1986):27–33; William J. Maher, "The Use of User Studies," *Midwestern Archivist* (1986):15–26.

15. Richard H. Lytle, "An Analysis of the Work of the National Information Systems Task Force," *American Archivist* 47 (Fall 1984):357–365.

16. Nancy Sahli, *MARC for Archives and Manuscripts: The AMC Format* (Chicago: Society of American Archivists, 1985). This looseleaf, updatable manual is the most comprehensive description of MARC/AMC. Supplements are issued periodically to update it.

17. This description of the groups of MARC/AMC fields is derived and adapted from Thomas E. Weir, Jr., "New Automation Techniques for Archivists," in James Gregory Bradsher, ed., *Managing Archives and Archival Institutions* (Chicago: University of Chicago Press, 1989), 138. Sahli, *MARC for Archives and Manuscripts,* also describes the MARC tags.

18. Steven Hensen, *Archives, Personal Papers, and Manuscripts: A Cataloging Manual for Archival Repositories, Historical Societies, and Manuscript Librarians,* 2nd ed. (Chicago: Society of American Archivists, 1989).

19. Richard H. Lytle, "Intellectual Access to Archives: I—Provenance and Content Indexing Methods of Subject Retrieval," *American Archivist* 43 (Winter 1980):64–75. This important article defines and explains the terms provenance method and content indexing method.

20. Miller, *Arranging and Describing Archives and Manuscripts,* 120.

21. Steven L. Hensen, "The Use of Standards in the Application of the AMC Format," *American Archivist* 49 (Winter 1986):39–40.

22. Miller, *Arranging and Describing Archives and Manuscripts,* provides extensive advice on both arrangement and description. A good summary of modern descriptive techniques is provided by Thibodeau, "Archival Arrangement and Description," in Bradsher, *Managing Archives and Archival Institutions,* 67–77. An excellent manual of descriptive practices is Kathleen D. Roe, *Guidelines for Arrangement and Description of Archives and Manuscripts: A Manual for Historical Records Programs in New York State* (Albany: New York State Education Department, 1991).

23. Miller, *Arranging and Describing Archives and Manuscripts,* 94.

24. Ibid., 108.

25. National Historical Publications and Records Commission, *Directory of Archives and Manuscript Repositories in the United States,* 2nd ed. (New York: Oryx Press, 1988).

26. Society of American Archivists, Working Group on Standards for Archival Description, *Archival Descriptive Standards,* 16–21; Research Libraries Group, Inc., *Government Records in the RLIN Database: An Introduction and Guide* (Mountain View, Calif.: Research Libraries Group, 1990).

27. Anne J. Gilliand, "Introduction," in Gilliand, ed., "Automating Intellectual Access to Archives," *Library Trends* 36 (Winter 1988), special issue.

8 Preservation of Historical Records

Archivists face a continuing dilemma in providing for the physical survival and maintenance of the materials in their care. The information has been judged to have continuing value and the records worthy of continuing retention, and yet their medium is fragile and their environment may hasten their deterioration. Historical records are meant to be used, and yet handling and use by people also pose a risk. That is the central challenge of preservation, a term that refers to measures taken to promote the protection, conservation, repair, restoration, and protective reproduction of historical records.

Archivists have always been aware of the problem of deteriorating paper, but recent studies have documented and dramatized its extent and seriousness. A National Association of Government Archives and Records Administrators' survey of state archival preservation needs turned up a series of problems, including the diversity in the formats of modern documentation, the inferior quality of paper used by government offices, wear and tear through repeated use and handling, unsatisfactory storage conditions, and significant deterioration of many of the records before they are transferred to state archives' custody. The state archives are countering the problem with microfilming and preservation treatments, but resource limitations permit work on only a small percentage of the records. In fact, the NAGARA study concluded that preservation work is not keeping up with the rate of new accessions.[1]

A study at the National Archives and Records Administration revealed that approximately one sixth of its holdings of nearly a half billion pieces are at risk of imminent deterioration and loss. The most immediate threat faces modern materials on highly acidic paper—and the continuing use of that paper is increasing the problem.[2] The gradual deterioration of historical records is much the same as the tragic and large-scale deterioration and loss of books and other materials in the nation's libraries. As many as a quarter of the books now in major libraries have been shown to be at risk, i.e., so embrittled that they will soon become unusable.[3] The issue of "brittle books" has become a central library concern and has been dramatized in the popular film, "Slow Fires," which compares the preservation threat to that of conflagration. Every historical records repository in the nation is afflicted by the problem.

Dramatizing the Archival Preservation Issue

Archivists recognize the need for help—from librarians, professional conservators, and others—to fight the "slow fires" in their stacks. Even more, they need broadened program support and improved, secure facilities. Therefore, like the library community, they have begun to interpret and present the archival preservation issue in engaging terms that their resource allocators, and members of the general public, can understand and appreciate. NAGARA and the Council of State Governments issued an eye-catching brochure based on the state preservation study, *Warning! We Are Losing Our Past!* "Our archives will literally crumble to dust by the mid-twenty-first century," it says. "The need is both critical and immediate, and, if it is not met, documentary resources that Americans depend on to establish their rights, understand their past, cope with their present, and plan for their future, will vanish forever."[4]

The Library of Congress and the National Archives and Records Administration prepared a slide-tape show, *Materials at Risk: The Preservation Challenge,* for advocacy use by the state archival programs and other historical records programs. The show, designed to raise audiences' awareness of preservation issues and provoke discussion, first describes the broad social value of historical records. "The threat to these documents is varied and complex," warns the narrator. "Their continued existence is in jeopardy." The show concludes:

> So, what's to be done? Overcrowded [*sic*] documents, brittle papers, deteriorating films—all are calling for our help. And for them to receive it, an organized, planned, and cooperative effort is needed. This effort must be supplemented by a willing commitment from professional associations, civic and cultural organizations, state and local governments, and concerned citizens. Archives and libraries need helping legislation. They need money and they need more trained staff. If archives and libraries are given these tools, they *will* get the job done. But we *all* must do more than simply explore the issues. We must dramatize the issues. We must inform and move those people and institutions that have the capacity to help. We must provide leadership if this challenge is to be met. It's up to all of us![5]

Advocacy efforts have another dimension: a growing campaign for the use of acid-free paper for documents of the future. Here, archivists are joining forces with librarians, who advocate acid-free paper for printing books. As discussed below, widespread use of high-acid paper is a leading cause of archivists' preservation headaches, and the objective of the acid-free paper campaign is to prevent the "slow fires" from having more fuel in the future. A symbolic victory was achieved when the U.S. Congress, by joint resolution, established a national policy on permanent paper. "It is the policy of the United States that Federal records, books, and publications of enduring value be produced on acid-free permanent papers," says the resolution, and Congress "urgently recommends" that federal agencies begin using such paper for enduring records and publications and that publishers and state and local governments follow suit.[6] Several states have taken similar action, and archivists, librarians, and others concerned with preservation of research materials are urging other states, business, and other producers of records to follow suit.

Use of long-lasting, nonacid paper may eventually reduce the rate of increase of the preservation problem but will not solve it. Preservation is a pressing, urgent need. Preservation entails careful planning and integration with the rest of the historical records program. It has an obvious relationship, for instance, to arrangement and reference use of historical records. It can include improved storage conditions, measured physical conservation efforts, selective reproduction onto more stable media, and disaster preparedness.

Sources of Problems: Chemistry, Environment, Humans

The major source of preservation problems is the chemically unstable nature of paper, the medium used for most records, historical and otherwise. Paper, which appears to most people to be a friendly, reliable and durable recording medium, is in fact created from materials and manufactured through processes that ensure its own destruction. Prior to the middle of the last century, most paper was made from rags and developed through procedures that ensured a reasonable longevity. Paper making was relatively expensive and time consuming. Beginning about that time, paper manufacturing changed to approaches that produced it more economically and in greater quantities for a growing market. The easy availability of cheap paper is one factor accounting for the proliferation of records during the past century and today's continued high-volume outpouring of records, but abundance brought problems with it.

The wood pulp that replaced rags as the main source of paper, the alum rosin sizing used to prepare it for ink, and the bleach used to whiten it all contribute to the formation of acids within the structure and fiber of the paper itself. High acidity leads to hydrolysis of the molecules that make up the paper, and this, in turn, leads the paper to discolor, become brittle, and deteriorate. Paper literally has within it the seeds of its own destruction. Much of the paper produced during the past century—and therefore a high percentage of the holdings of historical records repositories—has a short life expectancy. Even if the paper itself has low acidity, it may be threatened by storage in high-acid folders and boxes, because acid can migrate and affect the materials within these containers.

A second set of circumstances contributing to preservation problems relates to the environmental and atmospheric conditions that surround the records. Air pollutants, including ozone, carbon monoxide, sulphur dioxide, lead, and particles suspended in the atmosphere or emitted where the records are stored, all threaten their well-being. Absorption of certain acidic gases contributes to acidification of the paper. Sulphur dioxide, for instance, causes deterioration and accelerates the cracking of leather bindings. Paper can be soiled through deposit of dirt from the air, particularly in densely settled urban areas with high levels of atmospheric pollution. High levels of air pollution in urban areas from automobiles, factories, and other sources constitute a serious threat to records.[7] Since most records are created in or near urban areas, and most historical records repositories are also located there, the threat is serious.

Threats borne by air are augmented by fluctuations and extremes in temperature and humidity. High temperature speeds deterioration. It is estimated that the rate of chemical processes doubles for each 18 degrees Fahrenheit increase in temperature, and that the life of paper is reduced by half for every ten degrees increase. Historical records that have been relegated to attics or other hot places may, therefore, become brown and brittle long before an archivist can rescue them. The emulsion on photographs may become soft and damaged, and records in other media may also be harmed. Relative humidity is another potential threat. Paper relatively easily absorbs and retains moisture from the air. High humidity accelerates harmful chemical reactions and may cause inks to run, photo emulsions to become tacky, and coated pages to adhere to each other. High humidity coupled with high temperatures will accelerate deterioration and encourage mold and mildew growth.

On the other hand, dry air coupled with high temperatures will dry out paper, bindings, and adhesives. Rapid or extreme fluctuations in either temperature or humidity put historical records on a destructive roller coaster of expansion and contraction which shortens their lives. Exposure to light accelerates oxidation and breakdown of paper. Ultraviolet light—a major part of the sun's rays and fluorescent light—is particularly destructive. Paper bleaches, fades, yellows, or turns brown through lengthy exposure to strong light. The chemical actions initiated by exposure to light can actually continue after the light goes out and the materials return to darkness.[8]

Mold spores in the air can find a hospitable home on paper that is warm and moist. Mold can grow quickly, bore into the fiber of the paper, weaken and discolor it, and eventually completely ruin it. Roaches, termites, beetles, other bugs, mice, and rats, may soil paper, consume it, or bite off and carry away pieces of it. They can wreak havoc with historical records in short periods of time, leaving behind shredded paper and dirt. In summary, most historical records, weakened by their own internal degenerative disease of high acidity, are beset by external enemies that threaten to hasten their total destruction and loss.

To the menaces of chemistry and environment must be added a third set of threats: people. People may simply discard valuable and valueless records alike, effectively eliminating the historical record and depriving archivists of the chance to exercise care over the historical materials. This is the ultimate preservation threat. Inadequate binding or packaging techniques, careless handling, and even repeated touching of materials (body oils, even from apparently clean fingers, can harm sensitive paper) all constitute threats. Even under the protection of a historical records program, records are still susceptible to rough handling, marking, staining, defacement, and theft.

Preservation Administration

Archivists are responsible for meeting all these perils of preservation, but must do so within the practical limits of available resources. No archivist can reconstruct tattered records, reverse the results of years of acidic breakdown of paper, or guarantee that impermanent materials will last forever. Preservation needs to be approached in a practical manner, using a planned approach, just like other archival work.

The first step should be to gather and analyze information about the physical state of the records themselves and about their surroundings. The records condition survey might focus on a representative sample of the records, if the quantity is too great to include them all. Information should be collected on the quantities and physical types of records; on the types and conditions of their boxes, other enclosures, and bindings; on problems associated with age and use such as embrittlement and faded inks; and on significant damage, such as tears and water and mold damage.

The survey should aim to answer two basic questions. First, how many different physical problems exist with the historical records, and what are they? Second, approximately what percent of the material exhibit the two or three most significant problems?[9] Figure 3 provides an example of a detailed records condition survey, geared to the series level. The survey should lead to recommendations and priorities for preservation treatments.

The repository storage condition survey aims to assess the repository's temperature, humidity, handling procedures, security provisions, and disaster preparedness. This part of the survey should gather information in the following areas:

Effectiveness of heating, cooling, and other environmental control systems in maintaining steady environmental conditions suitable for the preservation of records. This entails checking the type, age, and apparent reliability of heating, ventilating, humidification, dehumidification, and air conditioning systems, and determining who is responsible for maintaining them.

Lighting, including proximity of windows to historical records and location, number, and types of lights and duration of exposure each day to light through windows and from internal lights.

Environmental monitoring devices, e.g., temperature, relative humidity.

Location of records in relation to water pipes, heating units, and other utilities that could imperil them.

Housekeeping procedures, including cleaning schedules, type of cleaning, and accumulation of dust and dirt on shelves, cartons, and records.

Shelving and records storage cabinets, including type, age, condition, and incidence of rust or other signs of deterioration.

Arrangement of space, including layout and distance appropriate for safe transport of materials and for adequate circulation of air.

Protection against fire, including fireproof storage, safe wiring, prohibition of smoking, and appropriate fire detection, alarm, and suppression systems.

General storage area security, including protection against unauthorized entry, appropriate locks and alarms, and surveillance or other oversight.

Cartons and folders in use, including whether acid-free, appropriate size, and condition.[10]

The records condition survey and storage survey should lead to a preservation plan that is integrated with the historical records program's overall annual, long-range, or other plan. The plan should be comprehensive, encompassing conservation treatment, needed reproduction, changes needed in the facility to improve the records' surroundings, handling practices, and reference and other policies designed to protect the records and extend their lives. It should include preventive measures to keep preservation problems from

NEW YORK STATE ARCHIVES

Office of Cultural Education
State Education Department

Acc # _____
Series # _____
Location _____

DESCRIPTION OF RECORDS

1. SERIES TITLE:_____

2. DATES:_____   3. AGENCY:_____

4. SUBDIVISION:_____

5. PHYSICAL FORM: [ ]paper [ ]card [ ]bound [ ]map [ ]photograph [ ]film [ ]microfilm _____mm.
   [ ]plan/drawing [ ]machine readable [ ]audiotape [ ]videotape [ ]other_____

6. FREQUENCY OF USE: [ ]high [ ]medium [ ]low

7. TOTAL VOLUME:_____ c.f._____ vols._____ items

8. VOLUME REQUIRING CONSERVATION TREATMENT: _____ c.f. _____ vols. _____ items

9. COPIES OF RECORDS AVAILABLE: [ ]yes [ ]no IF YES, FORMAT:_____

10. PHYSICAL CONDITION (check conditions present, explain, if necessary, and estimate volume)

[ ]surface dirt_____   _____ c.f./items
[ ]folds, breaks, tears_____   _____
[ ]losses, holes_____   _____
[ ]fading, discoloration_____   _____
[ ]staining:
    [ ]water   [ ]adhesive   [ ]foxing   [ ]mold
    [ ]other_____   _____
[ ]brittle_____   _____
[ ]fire or heat damage_____   _____
[ ]insect damage_____   _____
[ ]old treatments:
    [ ]varnish_____   _____
    [ ]mends (type)_____   _____
    [ ]backing (type)_____   _____
    [ ]lamination (date, if known)_____   _____
[ ]other_____   _____
_____   _____
_____   _____

1. RECORDS CONTAIN: [ ]paper clips [ ]staples [ ]attachments (pasted) [ ]other_____

2. ARE REPAIRS NECESSARY PRIOR TO REPRODUCTION? [ ]yes [ ]no

3. ARE REPAIRS NECESSARY PRIOR TO HANDLING? [ ]yes [ ]no RECOMMENDATIONS
   CONCERNING USE:_____

PREPARED BY:_____ DATE:_____ REVIEWED BY:_____ DATE:_____

Figure 3. Records condition survey form.

This survey form includes space for describing the records, noting their physical condition, and recommending preservation treatments. The information recorded here can provide the basis for setting priorities for preservation work and guide that work. (*Courtesy of New York State Archives and Records Administration*)

RECORD SERIES CONSERVATION SURVEY
SERIES CONDITION REPORT
CONTINUATION SHEET

Acc #	_____
Series #	_____
Location:	
Lab #	

1. SERIES TITLE:_____

2. DATES:_____ 3. AGENCY:_____

4. SUBDIVISION:_____

5. RECOMMENDATIONS FOR TREATMENT (check appropriate boxes and estimate volume)

Laboratory: c.f./items

    [ ]fumigate   _____

    [ ]clean   _____

    [ ]flatten   _____

    [ ]deacidify   _____

    [ ]repair   _____

    [ ]encapsulate   _____

    [ ]other_____ _____

    _____

    _____

Storage:

    [ ]acid-free folders   _____

    [ ]rebox   _____

    [ ]special storage (specify)_____ _____

    _____

    _____

Copy:

    [ ]microfilm   _____

    [ ]photostat   _____

    [ ]xerox   _____

    [ ]other (specify)_____ _____

    _____

    _____

Special (for records requiring special handling, check type and estimate volume)

    [ ]bound   _____

    [ ]maps   _____

    [ ]photographs   _____

    [ ]parchment/vellum   _____

    [ ]other_____ _____

Figure 3—*continued*

accelerating, as well as conservation, repair, and restoration needed to deal with materials that are afflicted with preservation problems. Preservation has program-wide ramifications:

> Because preservation concerns affect so many archival activities, most institutions will benefit from a program approach that influences the execution of almost all other archival functions. The goal of preservation is to assure that records in archival custody survive as long as possible or, in some cases, as long as is legally necessary. This can be most easily achieved when the goals and basic principles of preservation are understood by all staff involved with the records, including everyone from the head of the archives, to the search-room attendants, to the person responsible for the heating, ventilating, and air-conditioning system—and everyone else along the way.[11]

Preservation needs should be noted, and taken into account as an evaluative factor, when records are appraised. Minor preservation work, for instance basic cleaning, may be carried out at the same time as arrangement and description. The reference archivist needs to be concerned with the physical well-being of records while they are being used by researchers. Program administrators need to balance preservation needs against other demands on the budget.

The plan—backed by the authority and commitment of the program's leadership—must make it apparent that everyone has a measure of responsibility for preservation. However, to ensure a focused and coordinated approach, historical records programs should designate a single staff person as the Preservation Officer to centralize coordinating responsibility and also to dramatize the importance of the preservation issue, and to train their staff in basic preservation issues and techniques. A considerable part of the work involves consciousness raising about preservation needs and persuading colleagues to follow handling and security practices that are compatible with preservation needs. If possible, the preservation officer should be someone with advanced training in preservation issues and techniques. The preservation officer should be assigned some or all of the following responsibilities:

> Develop and coordinate the implementation of both long-term and annual preservation plans as part of the historical records program's overall planning process.
>
> Institute preventive measures, such as restrictions on handling in the research room, to promote the longevity of the historical records.
>
> Monitor environmental conditions and advocate changes where needed.
>
> Coordinate, oversee, or directly carry out conservation and preservation measures, especially those requiring particular experience and/or expertise.

Elements of a Preservation Plan

Preservation planning should encompass both long-term and short-term (usually one year) goals and objectives. It should be part of the broader historical records program planning discussed in chapter 5. The planning effort should factor in the analysis of records' preservation needs, the survey of the storage area and environment, probable growth in the preservation challenge as more records are accessioned, and a realistic assessment of the repository's human, physical, and fiscal resources. A long-term (e.g., five-year) preservation plan for a research facility such as Auburn Research Library might include the following goals and objectives. An actual plan probably would include considerably more detail.

Auburn Research Library
Division of Historical Records
Preservation Plan for 1993–1997

This preservation plan is an adjunct to the Comprehensive Plan for Auburn Research Library's Department of Historical Records, 1993–1997 and elaborates on the preservation activities summarized in that plan. This preservation plan is based on the survey of the physical state of historical records conducted in 1992 and the survey of the Department's storage area conducted in 1993. Implementation of the plan will be primarily the responsibility of the Department's Preservation Coordination Officer.

Goal I. Provide preservation training for all department personnel.

I-A. Develop a manual of preservation issues and procedures, including information on the care and handling of records, security, provisions for exhibits, and conservation methods.

I-B. Hold periodic discussion sessions with staff to explore preservation issues.

Goal II. Improve storage conditions and security in the historical records storage area to promote preservation and ensure the safekeeping of the records.

II-A. Develop, secure support for, and implement a proposal to provide air conditioning and an air filtration system for the stack area.

II-B. Improve security through installation of fireproof doors and intrusion alarms at all entry points into the stacks.

Goal III. In cooperation with Researcher Services personnel, upgrade security and reform records handling practices in the search room.

III-A. Develop, and then implement on a continual basis, a manual of Researcher Services procedures that provides for security, restrictions on handling of materials, and other safeguards.

Goal IV. Implement a "holdings maintenance" strategy for dealing with all new accessions.

IV-A. Unfold documents, place in acid-free folders and boxes, and place in secure shelving area within two months after accessioning.

Goal V. Selectively microfilm records, taking into account informational content, preservation needs, and researcher traffic and use.

V-A. Establish a priority listing of records for microfilming, taking the above-mentioned factors into account.

V-B. Microfilm records following the priority listing so far as practicable, ensuring that all filming is carried out to accepted professional standards.

Goal VI. Carry out conservation work on selected records.

VI-A. Carry out cleaning, tape-removal, and minor cleaning for selected records.

VI-B. Arrange for the West Coast Document Conservation Center to carry out deacidification and mending of selected maps and other records.

Goal VII. Prepare a disaster preparedness and response plan.

VII-A. Carry out a review of literature on disaster planning, consult with experts in this region who have prepared similar plans for their repositories, and secure copies of those plans to use as models if possible.

VII-B. Prepare the plan in consultation with other Department personnel.

VII-C. Implement the disaster avoidance aspects of the plan in so far as resources permit.

Train historical records program staff in preservation and conservation procedures.

Plan and carry out or oversee surveys of the conditions of historical records and the conditions of storage areas.

Ensure that accurate records are maintained on examinations and treatments of historical records.

Order and monitor quality of archival storage containers and conservation supplies.

Cooperate with public and educational programs specialists to ensure safe handling and exhibit of documents.

Coordinate the repository's security program, especially those aspects pertaining to security of stack areas.

Prepare and implement a disaster preparedness and response plan.[12]

In establishing preservation priorities, archivists must balance the volume of the records, their condition, resources available, and the value of the records and the likelihood that they will be actively used by researchers. Making decisions on what to do first, and how extensive work should be, requires experience and the ability to weigh and balance several factors. Full and complete preservation of all historical records in perpetuity cannot be accomplished, no matter how many preservation techniques are available or how many resources are applied. The basic goal is to make informed judgments and judicious interventions to save priority materials as long as possible.

It is usually advisable to proceed on the assumption that *moderate preservation work on the entire collection is in most cases preferable to intensive work on only part of it*. Historical records collections are characterized by their size and the variety of their physical materials, and modern information technology will introduce additional media into the mix. Preservation strategies must deal with mass and develop solutions on a large scale. Modest intervention on a broad scale is usually a more responsible approach than confining attention to only a few items. Archivists should avoid the temptation to carry out intensive work on only the choicest items with outstanding intrinsic value (for instance, expensive deacidification and encapsulation of a few early maps) if this means that there is not enough time and money to give any preservation attention to other materials.

Some years ago, the National Archives, faced with the challenge of preserving millions of documents, advanced the concept of "holdings maintenance." This means prolonging the life of documents through unfolding them, placing them in acid-free folders and boxes, and properly shelving them as soon as they arrive at the repository. This is a practical preventive maintenance approach for materials being received, and an approach that can be applied retrospectively as time allows to the backlog of holdings.[13] With all, or most, materials in a holdings maintenance state, the repository can turn to more exacting preservation work on selected items.

It is also advisable to recall that, in the final analysis, the archivists' mission is to preserve and offer the information in the record even if the record itself cannot be preserved or is so fragile that even gentle handling by researchers will endanger it. Desirable as it may be to preserve all historical records in their original form, preservation problems are too extensive, and they are growing too rapidly, to make this possible in every case. This means that reproduction copying should be considered as a viable preservation strategy.

Improved Surroundings: A Major Preservation Tool

The NAGARA study and other recent reports have concluded that the greatest single preservation intervention that archivists can practically make is to upgrade the surroundings in which historical records are stored. Temperature is one key variable. Cooler temperatures are conducive to long paper life, but, as a practical matter, since people and paper usually have to coexist together in the same facilities, atmospheric conditions that are good for people are also considered acceptable for historical records. A temperature in the range of 68 degrees Fahrenheit is a reasonable target. As noted earlier, the higher the temperature, the faster the rate of deterioration of the materials. Relative humidity around 47 percent is a reasonable target. The situation is more complex than with temperature, for higher moisture content increases the deteriorative chemical reactions, but reduced humidity reduces the flexibility of paper, thus increasing the chances of tearing through use.[14] Unnecessary fluctuations in either temperature or humidity should be avoided.

Historical records programs are often situated in substandard surroundings that cannot be upgraded as much, or as soon, as archivists might wish. As two preservation experts note, "the control of temperature and humidity is an expensive and complex undertaking and one that must be approached with judgment and common sense. The goal should be as even an environment as is economically feasible, with fluctuations that are as gradual as possible."[15]

Air cleanliness is important because impurities in the air are harmful to historical records. Air conditioning is highly desirable but if it is not obtainable an air circulation system should be provided to prevent stagnant air and to eliminate micro-environments where temperature and humidity are above or below desired limits. Storage areas should have filtration systems that remove particles and gaseous pollutants from the air.

Generally, historical records should be stored in darkened or low-light surroundings; exposure to bright lighting should be kept to a minimum. Storage areas should not have windows or, if they do, the windows should be equipped with shades, to reduce ultraviolet light. Fluorescent lights, sources of high levels of ultraviolet light, should have special filters.

Special provisions should be made for records that will be out on exhibit or otherwise exposed to light for extended periods of time. Materials should be copied before being exhibited to ensure survival of the information even if the original should be harmed. Time limits should be set for the exhibit. Light sources should be outside of, rather than inside, cases, to prevent heat buildup and reduce direct light.

Storage areas should be equipped with fire detection and alarm systems and, if possible, with a fire suppression system. These areas should be outfitted with steel shelving; use of wood and other materials is not advisable because they can contribute acid that can migrate to the records, and can add to combustible mass in case of fire. Historical records should be housed in acid-free files and cartons or, for oversized materials, in metal drawers or other containers that both protect them and insulate them from acid migration.

Preservation and Protection: Staff and Researchers

Humans may be the greatest continuing threat to the preservation of historical records. The well-intentioned researcher who inadvertently turns a weakened page too quickly, spills a bit of food, makes an ink mark on a document, or leaves fingerprints on photographs does not realize that he or she may be hastening the end of the document. Preservation consciousness should include consideration of threats to the well-being of the documents from all sources.

Staff training should include provision for imparting preservation mindedness—the recognition that preservation is everyone's job. Staff who deal with records should have general understanding of the physical nature of their materials, the causes of deterioration, and the practices and procedures that can help sustain the materials. Research room procedures should provide maximum protection for the records, but in a way compatible with encouraging maximum access and use. It is seldom justifiable, for instance, to close records indefinitely because of preservation needs unless a plan is also in place to eventually deal with those needs. On the other hand, it is prudent to postpone making records with extreme preservation problems available for research until those problems can be addressed.

Preservation concerns should be an integral part of researcher services in order to protect the materials through use. Security, preservation, and responsive researcher services should be developed in tandem. Historical records programs need clear policies for how much material a researcher may have on the table at a given time. As noted in chapter 9, research room rules should be available in writing and researchers should have to read and sign a statement to abide by them. The rules should include a statement that describes the fragile nature of the records and prescribes restrictions on researchers, a message that should be reinforced in the entrance interview. For instance, researchers must not use pens, must handle materials carefully, and must maintain individual documents in the order imposed by the repository. Eating, drinking, and smoking should be strictly prohibited. Coats, briefcases, etc., should be deposited in an area outside the search area to reduce possibilities of theft by concealment. Research room personnel should carefully monitor users, maintaining visual oversight at all times. Some historical records programs have installed surveillance cameras; their presence alone may be a significant deterrent to theft. Research room archivists should carefully check all returned material for order and completeness.

Preserving the Information: Copying Historical Records

Copying historical records is an effective means of protecting them against wear and tear while, at the same time, providing for broad dissemination of the information they contain. The decision to make copies should be based on their physical condition, the cost and effectiveness of other preservation approaches, and probable use. Level of use is a difficult factor to predict but, with some records, the archivist may conclude that research use would be increased significantly if the information were available in alternative format, for instance microfilm, that researchers could peruse quickly and that could be made available for loan or purchase. Historical records believed to be high security risks should be copied as a routine matter if possible. In fact, copying can in part compensate for less than desirable security, especially if the repository has a settled policy of making the copies rather than the originals available.

There are two primary approaches to copying. The first, sometimes called preservation photocopying, involves making photocopies of historical records onto a more stable paper that is acid-free and therefore long-lasting. It is popular for fragile materials and for related materials such as newspaper clippings in such an advanced state of deterioration that handling causes the materials to crumble. Copying involves handling one page at a time on a machine, so it is labor-intensive and slow. It is most effective where the volume involved is limited and the program desires to make the records available in a form that resembles the original.

A second copying approach is microfilming. This makes it possible to substitute the film copy for research, eliminating damage to originals from handling. Making copies of the film available means that the information can be accessed at several locations simultaneously. Relatively inexpensive copies can be produced and made available for loan or sale. Original records can be transferred to secure, off-site storage, freeing up tight storage space in the main facility. The economy, compactness, and other features of microfilm make it attractive. In deciding which records merit microfilming, archivists need to consider the significance of the information for a variety of research purposes, extensiveness of the information, research value compared to volume, actual (or likely potential) demand by researchers, possibility of loss or damage of original due to unsafe storage conditions or user theft or handling, and whether the records are sufficiently legible to be readable on film.[16]

Archival microfilming requires use of fine-grained, high-contrast silver halide microfilm with an emulsion capable of high resolution. The materials must be carefully prepared and organized. Special cameras are required to achieve high resolution and clarity and the camera lights must be calibrated to accommodate the color, texture, and contrast of the records. Film processing must ensure that harmful chemical residues that could later cause film deterioration are not left on the film. After processing, the film must be

Archival Microfilming: Technical Challenges

Microfilming of historical records requires adequate preparation of the materials, care in handling and microfilming them, and adherence to exacting technical standards. Below, some of the technical challenges are outlined. Reference is made to some of the technical publications issued by the two organizations that are primarily responsible for establishing standards in this area: the American National Standards Institute (ANSI), 1430 Broadway, New York, NY 10018 and the Association for Information and Image Management (AIIM) (formerly the National Micrographics Association, or NMA), 1100 Wayne Avenue, Silver Springs, MD 20910.

Microfilm stock. The original (camera-produced) film should be fine-grained, high-contrast silver film. It should be certified to meet the standards of the American National Standards Institute. See especially *Imaging Media (Film)—Silver-Gelatin Type—Specifications for Stability* (ANSI IT9.1-1989, or the latest revision); and *Imaging Media—Photographic Films and Papers—Characteristics* (ANSI IT9.3-1989, or the latest revision).

Completeness. Filming should be carried out carefully so that all the records are captured on the film. This may require a slow, careful approach, particularly if the documents are of varying sizes, but it is worthwhile to ensure that the final product is complete.

Identification. The film should be adequately identified and authenticated to indicate what information it contains and to attest to its authenticity. This is done through preparation of "targets" that are filmed along with the records. Identification is spelled out in *Recommended Practice for Identification of Microforms* (ANSI/AIIM MS 19-1987 or the latest revision.)

Readability and reproducibility. The film should be clear, sharp and legible and it should be possible to produce crisp, readable prints from it. This is a particular challenge for microfilm of old, faded records. An AIIM publication, *Practices for Operational Procedures/Inspection and Quality Control of First-Generation, Silver Microfilm of Documents* (ANSI/AIIM MS23-1991, or the latest revision), covers quality concerns,

processing, density, resolution, and inspection procedures.

Density. This term refers to the tonal contrast between the information and the background. Density, a major factor in the sharpness and readability of microfilm, is measured by a device called a densitometer.

Resolution. This term refers to the sharpness of the film. It is measured by using a microscope to read a special resolution test chart that should be filmed near the beginning of each roll of film.

Chemical residue. Processed film should be thoroughly washed to remove excess processing chemicals which, if left on the film could cause image deterioration later on. Standard MS23-1991, referenced above, describes the procedures for carrying out the tests.

Inspection. All microfilm of historical records should be thoroughly and completely inspected to ensure completeness and readability of the film. Standard MS23-1991, cited above, details quality controls and inspection procedures.

Duplication. It is essential to make at least one duplicate copy of all microfilm, because the original (camera-produced) film has a relatively soft emulsion coating that can be scratched through repeated use. Copies of the film (for instance, a copy for making other copies and/or paper printouts on request, or a copy for use in the search room) need not necessarily be silver, but they should meet appropriate quality standards.

Storage. Original film should be stored in specially made microfilm containers in secure, clean surroundings. Temperature and humidity should be controlled; temperature should be in the 60-70 degree range, and relative humidity around 40 percent. The film should be inspected periodically to ensure that there is no deterioration. Storage conditions are detailed in *Photography (Film)—Processed Safety Film—Storage* (ANSI PH 1.43-1985 or the latest revision). Inspection procedures are described in *Recommended Practice for Inspection of Stored Silver-Gelatin Microforms for Evidence of Deterioration* (ANSI/AIIM MS 45-1990 or the latest revision).

carefully inspected for readability and sharpness. The original camera-produced film should be used only to make duplicates for reference use, and should be stored under conditions that encourage longevity. The exacting quality and storage standards of the American National Standards Institute and the Association for Information and Image Management should be followed to ensure good quality, long-lasting film.

All of this work is time consuming and can be expensive but, if carried out properly, can lead to microfilm that is almost certain to outlast the original paper medium.[17] Microfilming is more economical in most cases than detailed, painstaking repair and restoration work on documents. It preserves and presents the information, not the medium, which should suffice for most research purposes.

Of course, microfilm also presents some disadvantages: it must be done to exacting standards to ensure it will last, it can be costly, and users may not appreciate it because inadequate viewing equipment coupled with prolonged viewing may cause visual fatigue and discomfort. Viewing equipment should be easy to use, well-maintained, and able to project an image that is visually sharp and easy to read. The repository should also have available reader-printers that make it possible to produce paper prints from the film. On balance, microfilm is a useful preservation and dissemination tool.

Recent technological developments have presented alternatives to microfilm, but none has yet proven a reliable and appropriate substitute for information that must be preserved and available indefinitely. The most impressive and promising is generally called optical storage, a term that encompasses technologies, equipment, and media that use laser-produced light to record and retrieve information. In most applications, lasers record information through altering an optical medium's light reflecting characteristics in a manner that a laser can subsequently "read."[18] Like microfilm, optical systems have the capacity for dramatic compacting of information, ease of copying and dissemination, and rapid retrieval of information. The most promising of the optical technology, Write-Once-Read-Many times (WORM) optical disks, permit recording of information, for instance from historical records, onto the disk, and its retrieval and access later by users. Advanced indexing methods and automated access and retrieval systems enhance the attractiveness of optical disk technology. Optical disk systems are increasingly common for information management applications where longevity of the information is not a significant consideration.

There is a major drawback, however, where continuing retention and use of the information is a requirement. Vendors claim a useful life of about five years for recording information on previously unused portions of disks and a useful life of ten to thirty years for the playback of previously recorded information.[19] The information will not survive indefinitely into the future unless it can be recopied. This is too great a gamble for archivists to take; until there are greater assurances of longevity, optical disks are not a good alternative for storage of permanent information unless information is duplicated in paper, microfilm, or other durable media.

Conservation Treatments

The Library of Congress developed the concept of phased preservation as a sensible approach to the issue of preservation. The term refers to pursuing collections maintenance (that is, refoldering, reboxing, and reshelving materials, and providing protective encasement for individual items) while devising surveys and establishing priorities for more intensive future treatments. The approach encourages repositories to take broad actions that will benefit all holdings in a protective environment while preparing for physical treatments of particular items as appropriate.

It is compatible with another strategic approach developed by archivists, referred to as mass treatment. Under this approach, documents of approximately the same age, the same paper and ink type, and having approximately the same conditions and problems are all given the same preservation treatment on a massive scale. This is contrasted with single-item treatment, which entails painstaking conservation and restoration work on particular items identified as having special value. A sensible compromise approach is to apply mass treatments only after careful analysis and to isolate special items requiring individual treatment for special care and attention.[20]

Archivists also try to follow an informal rule of reversibility: whenever possible, use only techniques that are reversible and add only materials that can be removed later if desired. This rule is in harmony with archivists' determination to keep records in their pristine state and to do nothing to harm their integrity. As a practical issue, it is sometimes difficult to apply, even for simple approaches like cleaning documents. In fact, even a cleaning process is not reversible unless the archivist is prepared to return the document to an unclean state!

It is desirable to fumigate records before bringing them into a historical records facility, particularly if they have been stored in surroundings that have evidence of insect infestation. However, the type of fumigant selected and the procedures used must conform to government safety requirements and the work carried out with a regard for human health. Soiled documents can be carefully cleaned of surface dirt with soft brushes or erasers, a simple process that will improve their appearance, make them more congenial to researchers, and prolong their lives. Washing will remove stains and deterioration but it may cause inks and colors to run and should be carried out only after analysis of the material reveals that it is safe to wash.

Since a high level of acid causes paper disintegration, removal of the acid (deacidification) is a desirable way of extending records' lives. Deacidification neutralizes the acids in paper and deposits an alkaline buffer that prevents the paper from returning to an acidic state. There are at least three types of deacidification process: aqueous (water), nonaqueous (nonwater solvent), and vapor. Any deacidification requires appropriate equipment, trained staff, careful testing of materials prior to beginning the processes, and monitoring of the process.[21]

Tears can be mended by a trained conservator, using long-fiber Japanese paper and a starch adhesive, but it is slow and exacting. There are two process for encasing documents to reinforce and preserve them. The first is heat-sealing lamination, used since the 1930s. Lamination involves placing a document between sheets of tissue and cellulose acetate and fusing the "sandwich" with heat and pressure into a single entity. Paper must be deacidified prior to lamination or else its deterioration may actually be accelerated. Lamination provides for a well-protected document, but it has several disadvantages, including the fact that the heat and pressure may harm the paper and the process is irreversible. The use of lamination as a preservation technique has declined in recent years. It has been upstaged by a simpler alternative, polyester encapsulation, a process which encloses a document between two sheets of polyester which are then sealed with tape. The polyester provides support, the document is unaffected, and the process can be reversed by removing the tape and freeing the document.

There is an unsettled debate in the archival community over the degree to which archival preservation should be carried out only by people with advanced training in conservation techniques. Proponents of restricting preservation work to trained experts point out the importance of the work, the need to understand paper chemistry and the physical and chemical aspects of various repair and restoration techniques, and the possible disastrous consequences of mistaken applications. However, trained conservators are in short supply. Smaller historical records programs find it difficult or impossible to budget positions to hire them or to send all materials that need preservation out for work. In some cases, a cooperative approach between two or more repositories may be the answer to securing the needed expertise. Several repositories devote part of their preservation budget to the hiring of a single preservation expert who serves them all.

A different philosophy holds that, while some exacting work must be referred to skilled archivists, much can be done by archivists with some training. George M. Cunha, a long-time leader in the field, has written that in-house staff and even volunteers—"careful and dedicated workers who are provided with necessary tools and suitable working conditions and are well supervised"—can carry out as much as 80 percent of the treatment work that needs to be done. He includes in that eighty percent such things as removal of pressure-sensitive tape, cleaning, deacidification, mending and reinforcing, cased books repairs, making portfolios and protective cases for books and documents, cleaning and repacking photographic materials, removal of acid cardboard and wood backs from framed items, and leaf casting repairs for damaged materials. Leave to the professional conservator, he advises, such work as hand bookbinding and binding restoration, treatment of illuminated book pages, parchment and vellum scrolls, hand colored antique maps, color prints and drawings, and works of art.[22] Archivists need to follow this debate within the conservation community. But they should realize that some modest, careful preservation work is preferable to neglecting preservation needs due to lack of professional conservation expertise on staff.

Planning for the Worst: Disaster Preparedness

There is one other aspect of preservation: taking steps to forestall disasters such as fires and massive water damage and, if one occurs, possessing the capacity to respond. These related concerns are often referred to as disaster prevention and disaster planning. "The disaster contingency planner must transcend the comfortable world of the office and situate him or herself in the frenzied, panic-stricken environment that prevails when disaster strikes. This person must think the unthinkable, foresee the unforseen, and expect the unexpected."[23] Archivists have come to recognize that disasters can be headed off, or their destructive impact minimized, through sound planning. Often, disaster preparedness is best effected through the cooperative efforts of two or more institutions.

Disaster preparedness planning should involve all key staff. The first step toward sound disaster preparedness is a survey of preservation conditions and needs, as described earlier in this chapter. In many ways, sound archival storage and security provisions, good preservation practices, and disaster prevention and avoidance activities are one in the same thing. Historical records should be safeguarded from fire by good housekeeping practices that prevent the buildup of dirt, papers, and other inflammable materials, and through the installation of fire detection, alarm, and suppression systems. A secure, well-maintained building, and security provisions such as closed stacks and surveillance in the search room, will help deter vandals and thieves. Prudent measures such as refraining from storing records in basements or beneath water or drain pipes, will help minimize the risk of water damage.

Every historical records program should have a disaster plan, with a disaster-prevention section (as summarized above) and a disaster recovery section. The disaster recovery section should make provision for the following:[24]

Designation of a disaster response coordinator and a disaster recovery team, and an indication of their responsibilities and the responsibilities of other staff members in the event of various types of catastrophes.

Appropriate floor plans, blueprints, and specifications showing the locations of gas, water, and electrical cutoffs, fire fighting equipment, and emergency equipment and supplies.

Periodic training for all staff.

Liaison with local fire and police officials.

Provisions for evacuation, relocation, and temporary storage of damaged holdings.

Priorities for salvage of various categories of historical records.

Written, step-by-step procedures for all salvage operations.

Location of each major category of historical records within the building.

List of individuals and companies to turn to for help and support, including possibly local electric, gas, water, and phone companies; plumbers, electricians, locksmiths, and glass companies; janitorial and guard services; and exterminators.

Location of commercial and other large freezers for freezing wet materials.

Procedures for freezing wet materials to stabilize them and for later freeze-drying them, if possible, as part of their restoration.

Location of large buildings in the vicinity that can be used for treatment and recovery sites.

List of supplies that would be needed to recover from a disaster and addresses of local suppliers.

Disasters are rare, but, when they strike the unprepared, their consequences can be much worse than if the archival program is prepared to respond quickly and systematically. Therefore, disaster preparedness is a worthwhile and necessary aspect of archival work.

NOTES

1. National Association of Government Archives and Records Administrators, *Preservation Needs in State Archives* (Albany: National Association of Government Archives and Records Administrators, 1986), 1–4.
2. National Research Council, *Preservation of Historical Records* (Washington: National Academy Press, 1986), 5.
3. Commission on Preservation and Access, *Brittle Books: Report of the Committee on Preservation and Access* (Washington: Council on Library Resources, 1986), 22.
4. National Association of Government Archives and Records Administrators, *Warning: We Are Losing Our Past* (Lexington, Ky.: Council of State Governments, 1986). Pamphlet
5. [Library of Congress and National Archives and Records Administration], *Materials at Risk: The Preservation Challenge* (Washington, 1990). Transcript to accompany slide show.
6. "Joint Resolution to Establish a National Policy on Permanent Papers," 101st Congress, Public Law no. 101-423, October 12, 1990.
7. National Research Council, *Preservation of Historical Records,* 12–16.
8. Mary Lynn Ritzenthaler, *Archives and Manuscripts: Conservation* (Chicago: Society of American Archivists, 1983), 26–27; Norvell M. M. Jones and Mary Lynn Ritzenthaler, "Implementing an Archival Preservation Program," in James Gregory Bradsher, ed., *Managing Archives and Archival Institutions* (Chicago: University of Chicago Press, 1989), 188–190.
9. Pamela W. Darling and Duane E. Webster, *Preservation Planning Program: An Assisted Self-Study Manual for Libraries* (Washington: Association of Research Libraries, 1982), 63.
10. Ibid., 53–54; Paul H. McCarthy, ed., *Archives Assessment and Planning Workbook* (Chicago: Society of American Archivists, 1989), 35–38.
11. Jones and Ritzenthaler, "Implementing an Archival Preservation Program," 185.
12. See Ritzenthaler, *Archives and Manuscripts: Conservation,* 64–65.
13. National Archives and Records Administration, *Twenty Year Preservation Plan* (n.p., 1984).
14. Paul N. Banks, "Environmental Standards for Storage of Books and Manuscripts," *Library Journal* (February 1, 1974), reprinted in Wesley L. Boomgaarden, ed., *Preservation Planning Program Resource Notebook* (Washington: Association of Research Libraries, 1987), 41–45.
15. Jones and Ritzenthaler, "Implementing an Archival Preservation Program," 191; Ritzenthaler, *Archives and Manuscripts: Conservation,* 30–33.
16. Bruce W. Dearstyne, "Microfilming Historical Records: An Introduction," American Association for State and Local History *Technical Leaflet* 32 (June 1977):2.

17. Carolyn Hoover Sung, *Archives and Manuscripts: Reprography* (Chicago: Society of American Archivists, 1982), is an excellent source of information on the technical aspects of archival microfilming.

18. William Saffady, *Optical Disk Systems for Records Management* (Prairie Village, Kans.: Association of Records Managers and Administrators, 1988), 1.

19. Ibid., 18.

20. Ritzenthaler, *Archives and Manuscripts: Conservation,* 73; Jones and Ritzenthaler, "Implementing an Archival Preservation Program," 205.

21. Ritzenthaler, *Archives and Manuscripts: Conservation,* 78.

22. George Martin Cunha and Dorothy Grant Cunha, *Library and Archives Conservation: 1980's and Beyond,* 2 vols. (Metuchen, N.J.: Scarecrow Press, 1983), I, 97–98.

23. John P. Barton et al., eds., *An Ounce of Prevention: A Handbook on Disaster Contingency Planning for Archives, Libraries, and Record Centres* (Toronto: Toronto Area Archivists Group, 1985), 1.

24. Ibid., 171–173; Cunha and Cunha, *Library and Archives Conservation,* I, 171–173.

9 Researcher Services

"The use of archival records is the ultimate purpose of identification and administration. . . . Promoting the use of these materials is a fundamental goal of the archival community," says the Society of American Archivists' statement on goals and priorities. "This commitment rests on a belief that the access to information contributes to the strength and well-being of a democratic society, and that knowledge of the past contributes to a better future."[1]

Archivists see the benefits of research in historical records every day: information is discovered, research advanced, students' questions answered, and individuals' curiosity satisfied. Research use has a broad, cumulative effect, in terms of individuals' enlightenment and understanding of their place in the flow of time and history, solution of practical problems, and scholarly advances. On an even grander scale, research in historical records contributes to growing human self understanding and the increasing sum total of human knowledge. There is no practical benefit to saving records if they are never perused by researchers who extract useful information from them and limited benefit if they are rarely used. Historical records are an asset and a resource whose use their custodians—archivists— have a positive duty to promote.

Archival services to researchers are sometimes grouped under the heading of reference, but that term, associated with library service, is actually too narrow and confining. *Researcher services* is a broader term that is better suited to the range of assistance that archivists should provide, including encouraging research use of their holdings, actively counselling and assisting researchers, making records available, and analyzing and measuring research use to help determine future program directions and priorities. In providing these services, the archivist attempts to satisfy three sets of obligations: to the records themselves, in promoting their use; to the archivist's institution, in furthering its mission and goals; and to researchers, in assisting their research efforts. If use of records is the ultimate goal of all archival work, then researcher services are the essential means to that end. Researcher services are closely related to historical records description (discussed in chapter 7) and to promotional marketing (covered in chapter 10).

Research Use: Direct, Indirect

The concept of research use is complex and measurement of use has significant implications for historical records programs. It is helpful to distinguish between two categories of users, direct and indirect. Direct users are "people who seek information in archival materials" and who have an "information need" that can be met through such research.[2] But not all of this use is the same or has the same significance. It depends in part on how much information is mined from the records, how imaginatively it is interpreted and used, how well it is integrated with other information, and whether it is disseminated for consideration by people beyond the researcher. These are matters of interest to archivists but beyond their ability to control.

People who draw on and benefit from work based on historical records might be called indirect users. For instance, students, lawyers, editors, and others draw on historical records for studies, reports, publications, and productions that eventually reach a broad array of people. Readers of books, viewers of certain television shows and movies, people affected by legal proceedings that draw on historical precedent, people whose health is protected through historical study of diseases that draws on historical records, may all be considered indirect users of these materials or benefactors from their use. Thus the ramifications of direct use—the activity where the archivist plays a leading role—may be broad, cumulative, and distanced in both time and space.[3] One study of research at the National Archives noted that:

> Interpreters—such as historians, film makers, journalists, public policy analysts, and biographers—pass on to the public information gleaned from the use of the records housed here. Their work serves as a multiplier effect, transmitting not only data from the National Archives holdings, but helping to provide the framework of understanding in which Americans see their country and its history. While it is useful in policy planning to analyze statistics on those who actually use the records, one must go beyond head counts to focus on the quality of services, especially to those who are transmitters of the American experience to the American public. Because most people are indirect and not direct users, the value of research conducted at the National Archives is frequently not fully appreciated.[4]

The Problem of Underutilization

"Archivists maintain and actively shape the record of the past and attempt to provide links with the needs of their research constituencies. . . . The cultural purpose [of archives] is realized in actively serving research use and in augmenting awareness of the collective memory."[5] But despite their potential value and the demonstrated importance of the research carried out in historical records, the fact is that they are underutilized. Many people with information needs that can and should be satisfied through use of historical records either do not know about them or, for one reason or another, do not use them. "The number of users of state archives is not particularly large," notes one report. "The overwhelming percentage of these users are genealogists. . . . The posture of state archives toward . . . researchers is generally passive."[6] An SAA study found that historical records programs as a whole average 1,400 researchers per program per year, but about half have fewer than 325 per year—less than one per day.[7] Practically all the state historical records program assessment reports also document the pattern of low use.

Why aren't historical records used more extensively? Part of the explanation lies with the way many archivists approach researcher services. They conceive their appropriate role as serving people who happen to visit, phone, or write, rather than actively interesting and attracting researchers and ratcheting up research use. According to this interpretation, it's up to the researcher to find his or her way to the repository, via phone, letter, or in person. Programs to reach out to researchers and promote use are therefore lacking or underdeveloped. Many archivists feel this approach is justified because they are already overwhelmed with work and feel the last thing their program needs is more researcher traffic to handle. Underutilization of historical records may prevent an overload on the reference or researcher service archivist, but it frustrates research and harms the program in the long run. A low incidence of research use undercuts the program's claim that it is performing an important information service and cultural function and contributing to the parent institution's mission. Limited reportable use thereby makes it difficult for the program to lay claim to the resources it needs to carry out and expand its work.

Another reason for low incidence of use is that many materials are inadequately maintained or not yet arranged and described, placing them in a sort of archival abeyance—they exist but they are virtually inaccessible. The state assessment projects revealed that a significant portion of the nation's historical records in repositories has not been adequately arranged and described. The quantity is probably growing as new materials are accessioned and consigned to already overcrowded holding areas. Older accessions may get shoved further back in the stacks, and further down the list of processing priorities. Lack of finding aids makes it difficult or impossible for researchers—and in some cases, archivists as well—to identify relevant holdings. Lack of arrangement discourages perusal of the materials. Researchers who are used to having material presented in an orderly way through books, or who lack patience or time to wade through volumes of material, are likely to simply bypass historical records that are difficult to use.

Few educational institutions—elementary and high schools, colleges and universities, and even graduate schools—have courses that introduce students to research in historical records. There is little published material on how to do research in archives; the only manual on the topic is more than twenty years old and badly outdated.[8] Even graduate history research seminars seldom stress archival records and students with advanced degrees may never encounter historical records other than indirectly, through footnote citations in historical literature. In part due to lack of training, many researchers simply lack familiarity with historical records, are unaware of potential information that might be gleaned from them, and do not even know where to find them.

Ironically, even advanced scholars may overlook national databases, directories of repositories, and published finding aids and learn of the existence of historical records by "serendipity and word of mouth" or just plain chance.[9] They ask fellow researchers, librarians, and others or follow up on footnotes in published works. When they finally discover important archival sources, they may express frustration at the perceived lack of means of learning about them. Many an archivist has given a sigh of disappointment at reading the newest article or book on a topic that is well documented in his or her repository's holdings but that did not draw on those holdings.

Historical records programs should reach out to researchers. A repository's mission statement should reflect a conscious decision to give priority to use. It should indicate the types of research and research use that should receive priority based on the institution's mission and the strengths of its holdings. Such a statement provides guidance for setting direction and priorities, for instance in deciding which records will receive priority for arrangement and description, and which will receive the most extensive publicity and other outreach activities. Long-term strategic and annual workplans should follow through with attention to use.

A proactive approach is needed, in line with the repository's mission statement and goals, and suited to the strengths of its holdings and researcher audiences it has defined as priorities. For instance, archivists need to become directly involved with researchers' associations and groups. They should promptly report new accessions available for research to appropriate databases, journals, and newsletters that researchers are likely to encounter. They should consider writing articles for journals and newsletters on the nature, content, and research potential of holdings, especially rich materials that are underutilized. As an example, archivists at our Madison University might write for the university newsletter and for newsletters and journals or associations interested in agriculture, public administration, and public policy.

Such writing requires knowledge of the records, understanding of the researcher groups' interests, and an ability to write interesting material that researchers will want to read. Finely developed literary skills may be needed to bring to light interesting information in seemingly dull old records. Sometimes this can be done through citing examples or quoting actual passages from particularly interesting items. Archivists can call on such things as revealing diary entries, poignant letters, eyewitness accounts, colorful reports, and interesting photographs to make the case that records can be exciting. This may be a new experience for archivists who are accustomed to writing mainly for archival journals or publications in closely allied fields such as librarianship and records management. The writing must be informative, interesting, and tailored to the needs of the research audience.

Archivists should propose and participate in sessions at professional meetings to emphasize the research potential of the materials they hold. The presentations should be tailored to the audience, which will be interested in the potential use of historical records for their research but will become bored or weary if presented with a lecture on the fine points of archival techniques. Archivists should also organize and hold conferences, seminars, workshops, and other training forums on how to do research in archival material and on the particular value of the materials in their own institutions. The National Archives and Records Administration, for instance, organizes "Primarily Teaching" institutes for educators that introduce the Archives' holdings, show teachers how to make effective use of historical records as teaching tools, and provide opportunities for teachers to make copies to take back for classroom use. A bank archives could sponsor a conference on banking history, featuring presentations on source material; a corporate archives could do the same for some aspect of business history; a program that collects the papers of literary figures could organize lectures on the creative process for fine literature. A slightly different approach is to seek cosponsorship with other institutions and organizations, a means of sharing the work, ensuring a responsive program, and increasing participation. The general strategy of outreach to researchers can work even for a small repository, which can cooperate with appropriate organizations in its region or in specialty areas represented by its holdings.

As discussed in chapter 7, a repository's finding aids program should also be in part outreach-oriented. Finding aids are by definition and nature records-oriented and reflect archivists' reliance on provenance and function as central organizing tenets. However, researchers approach sources from a different perspective, and are usually interested in whether the records contain information on their subjects. Much research, especially modern social history research, tends to explore diverse, complex topics drawing on multiple sources. Researchers may be unaware of the principle of provenance and impatient with archivists' clinging to records-focused approaches that seem to run against researchers' need for subject information retrieval.

Three features are needed to transcend this dichotomy and ensure that finding aids bridge the gap between records and researchers. First, lengthy finding aids should include "a sensitive, perceptive, provocative essay on the strengths and weaknesses of records for research use" that stresses "areas of study" that could be supported through use of the records. This approach requires familiarity with research interests and trends as well as with the content of the records. It goes beyond the traditional scope and content note that describes the extent and nature of the materials but does not always make explicit how they can and should be used for research.[10]

Second, where possible the finding aids should include subject-indexing or references to subjects covered. This feature helps researchers determine quickly the relevance of records for their research topic. It preserves the traditional archival approaches to description related to the organic nature and organization of the records but, at the same time, provides a shortcut for the researcher.

A third strategy is to issue "finding aids" that do not describe particular collections or series in detail but, instead, feature general descriptions of records pertaining to certain subjects. A county historical society might, for instance, issue a brochure that calls attention to its holdings on the business history of the county; a university archives might issue a booklet on its holdings related to campus architecture and construction if that is regarded as a strength of the collection and an important research topic. The objective is to attract attention, provide enough information that a researcher can decide whether the historical records warrant further attention and, if they do, to convince the researcher to contact the historical records program for more information or more detailed records descriptions.

Access: A Question of Balance

The issue of access to historical records in a repository is complicated, and, like other important aspects of archival programming, should be addressed in the program's written policies which are shared with all researchers before their research begins. This ensures fair, evenhanded treatment of all researchers and guarantees that researchers understand the ground rules before they begin examining finding aids and requesting materials from the stacks.

In general, all historical records held by a repository should be accessible to all researchers on an equal basis. Free, open access is a fundamental tenet of most archival programs and widely endorsed within the profession. For instance, records should be available to all researchers, not just those of the archivist's home institution, and all should be treated equally in the sense of sharing finding aids and providing advice and information on how to use the records. Privileged approaches and exclusivity run against this ingrained archival tradition.

However, archivists need to deal sensitively with the issue of researchers' right to know *vs.* individuals' right to privacy and other factors necessitating restricted access or closure of records. "It is the tension between these two ideas—to provide access to research materials and to protect confidentiality—that creates the frustration archivists feel when confronted with access problems," says the Society of American Archivists' manual on legal issues.[11] That manual should be perused by anyone collecting, or contemplating collecting, historical records. In recent decades, historians have given greater emphasis to studying historical topics from the relatively immediate past and the historical day-to-day experiences of ordinary citizens. This has led to reexamination of the issue of access.

At the national level, and in most of the states, "freedom of information" laws have been enacted to govern public access to all government records; in many instances, they also cover government archival records. These laws usually close or restrict certain categories of information where disclosure would compromise national security, provide an unfair advantage in the marketplace, compromise police invetigatory methods, or constitute an unwarranted invasion of personal privacy. The issue of privacy is particularly complicated; in general, the term refers to a person's right to be left alone and not to have embarrassing information made public. In some statutes, these restrictions expire a set number of years after creation of the record; if this is not the case, the archivist may need to decide on a series-by-series or record-by-record basis, whether to make materials available.[12]

Freedom of information laws usually apply only to government records, but there are comparable challenges for nongovernment historical records. Donors may require certain types of information to be withheld from research, as a condition of transferring the historical records to the repository. A church, for instance, may be sensitive about information on relationships between clergy and church members; a company may worry about unflattering information on trade practices; associations may not want their membership lists disclosed, even if they are quite old; or an individual may not want information gained in confidence to be disclosed. In these and other cases, the material may be offered to the program with a proviso that certain parts be restricted or closed for a period of time, for instance, until some years after the death of the person who created the records. The records may be of sufficient value that the archivist is grateful to get them, restrictions and all. But acceptance of such a condition requires the archivist to carefully go through the materials and pull out and set aside particular series or items, or to store the materials for many years before they can be used for research. Materials may not be researched prior to the expiration of the restriction without violating—or renegotiating—the agreement.

Some programs deal with restrictions by excising sensitive information. For instance, government archives holding sensitive records may copy the material, cut out names and other identifying information, then copy the copies and make the new copies available to researchers. Such elaborate, time-consuming work may be warranted for a small amount of material with exceptional research value. If the quantities are sizeable, however, the work will try the patience of most archivists and exceed the resources of most programs. Some repositories permit access to sensitive information on the condition, which the researcher must accept in writing, that individuals' names or other specified information not be published.

A much different strategy for dealing with difficult access restrictions may be to consider whether the records are really worth having. Clearly, for instance, a collection with severe restrictions of long duration is less desirable than one that is unrestricted, if the informational content and research use potential are approximately equal. The voluminous collection of a marginal literary figure, for instance, may have to be refused if her heirs require that it be closed for half a century. The potential research value is simply not worth the resources to store the closed materials for that long.

Another set of considerations, the physical status of the records, may make it appropriate to temporarily restrict access. Materials that have not yet been arranged or described may be withheld because the repository does not know their order or content. Materials in need of conservation treatment or copying may also be held back, on the reasoning that it is better to withhold records now than to lose them to deterioration later. Early twentieth-century letterbooks on thin tissue paper that literally crumbles when touched are good examples of records that should be held away from researchers until something can be done.

It may also be appropriate to temporarily limit access because materials have not yet been arranged and described. These appropriate concerns must not, however, become an excuse for indefinitely barring access to materials. The restriction should be of limited duration—only until the program, in line with a planned approach to arrangement, description, or preservation, can appropriately deal with the materials. Otherwise, concern for the physical well-being of the records becomes the justification, or excuse, for keeping them from researchers indefinitely. The repository's restrictions and closure policy should be clearly spelled out in its written materials presented to researchers so there is no question about what is being restricted, and why.

Researcher Services: Policies

Historical records programs need settled policies to deal consistently with researchers, to facilitate research, and, at the same time, to protect their holdings. These policies should be produced in written form and given to researchers. Some programs go a step further and require researchers to read the policy and sign a statement that they will agree to abide by it. The policies should cover several areas and should be reviewed periodically to determine their effectiveness.

The program needs a policy that all researchers must fill out a standard registration form that includes their name, address, institutional affiliation, and research topic or purpose of their research. As discussed below, it is desirable to include space for other information, e.g., how the person found out about the repository and the records, for tracking and reporting purposes. Repositories should require researchers to produce an acceptable form of identification when they fill out the form. There should be a requirement for researchers to sign in each day they return to do research. These requirements are advantageous as security provisions as well as useful for tracking and monitoring.

The policy should govern the quantity of material a researcher may request and peruse at one time. Limiting the quantity is one way of reducing the possibility of theft or getting the material out of order. There should be a requirement that researchers leave the material in the order in which it is presented to them. Most repositories forbid the use of pens since ink could damage the paper. Provision

Rules For the Research Room

Historical records programs should have written requirements and guidelines for the use of historical records in the search room. Researchers should be required as a condition of using the materials to read the rules and indicate through their signature that they will abide by them. The following example illustrates the areas that should be covered.

Madison University Department of Special Collections
Rules for Use of University Archives and Manuscripts

The University Archives and Manuscripts research room is open to researchers from 9:00 AM to 5:00 PM Monday through Friday and 9:00 AM to 12:00 noon on Saturday whenever the university is officially open. These historical records are maintained by the university for research regardless of purpose and it is the university's policy to make them easily accessible and to encourage and assist use. However, these materials are unique and some require special restrictions because of their origin, the nature of the information they contain, or their physical condition. In order to ensure the safekeeping of these materials for continued use, the following rules apply in the research room.

1. Researchers must fill out forms that provide identifying information, including their name, address, phone number, institutional affiliation if any, and research topic. The university requests, but does not require, that they also provide additional information needed by the university for analysis of researcher traffic and topics. Researchers must also show an appropriate form of identification.

2. Researchers are required to deposit all coats, hats, pocketbooks, briefcases, and other personal property not required for their research in the lockers down the hall from the research room.

3. Pens may not be used in the research room. Pencils may be used; the researcher services desk will loan pencils if needed.

4. Researchers may use typewriters, computers, tape recorders, and cameras, but only in the specially designated area of the research room, with permission of a researcher services archivist.

5. Eating, drinking, smoking and unnecessary or loud talking are prohibited.

6. Researchers must request records by filling out the request form provided by the archivists. No more than three boxes at a time will be provided. As research concludes in these records, they must be returned to the archivist and additional material may be requested. No records will be retrieved after a half hour before closing time.

7. Only limited quantities of records will be retrieved and provided to researchers at one time.

8. Historical records may not be borrowed or taken from the research room under any circumstances.

9. Many of the historical records are old and fragile, and all are unique and irreplaceable. Researchers must be careful in handling material, turn pages gently and slowly, ensure that fragile material stays intact, and maintain records in the order in which they are received. Researchers should report torn or damaged material, or material that is out of order, to the archivist.

10. In some instances, copies of the records, e.g., microfilm, rather than the original records, will be made available to researchers.

11. Certain records are not open to use, their use is restricted, or only copies are available with certain information deleted. Researchers must agree to these conditions in order to use the records.

12. Special Collections staff will make copies of records for posted fees where the physical condition of the records permits. Copying is governed by any restrictions that may exist for the materials and by provisions of the U.S. Copyright Law (Title 17, United States Code).

13. In cases where two researchers are working on topics that significantly overlap with or seemingly duplicate each other, Archives and Manuscripts staff will inform both researchers if they agree to such disclosure of their research topics.

I have read and agree to abide by these research room rules.

Name _____

Date _____

---

must be made for the use of tape recorders, typewriters, computers, and cameras and microfilm equipment, sometimes by setting aside a part of the research room or a separate area so that use of this equipment does not disturb other researchers. Food, drink, and smoking should be banned from the research room. Unnecessary conversation which disturbs other researchers should be discouraged.

Security is a major concern, central to the archivist's responsibility to ensure the protection of materials against damage or loss through mishandling or theft. Several elements of a comprehensive preservation and security program impact on researchers' use of the material, as discussed in chapter 8. It is advisable to make copies of particularly valuable materials that seem especially susceptible to theft and offer the copies, rather than the originals, for research. Stack areas where records are stored should be closed to researchers. Personal effects, such as coats, briefcases, and pocketbooks, should be checked or left outside the search room, in a secure area designated by the program, to reduce chances of theft of records. An archivist or other staff person should be present in the research room at all times for surveillance (as well as to assist researchers as needed). Surveillance cameras are a significant deterrent to theft, but they are expensive and their use requires someone to watch a monitor in order for them to be effective.

The program's copying policy should be clear to researchers and should indicate which materials may be copied; whether the researcher or an archivist is to do the copying; and the costs involved. Some repositories permit researchers to make their own copies, but only with the approval of, and under the surveillance of, an archivist or other staff person. If the repository holds copyrighted material, it

Security in the Research Room

Every year, significant historical records are harmed or stolen from historical records repositories. Historical records programs need to include provision for security in their operating manuals and in training they provide for their personnel. Researchers should not feel uncomfortable but they should be aware of a high degree of vigilance on the part of the program's staff. Here are a few provisions that should be applied in the research room to reduce the chance that historical records will be damaged or stolen.

- Include in overall program planning some provision for copying (e.g., photocopying, microfilming) selected materials that seem particularly susceptible to theft, for instance, letters with signatures of famous people that might conceivably be stolen and illegally sold. Consider making the copies rather than the originals available to researchers.

- Require that researchers identify themselves, provide addresses, and present some form of identification before they use any historical records, and that they sign in and sign out each day.

- Maintain historical records in secure stack areas clearly separate from the search room, and ensure that researchers and other nonstaff members do not enter those areas.

- Insist that researchers leave pocketbooks, briefcases, overcoats, and other potential receptacles for concealing documents outside the research room. Provide lockers or a special room where these materials can be left.

- Limit the quantity of records that a researcher may have at his or her table at one time.

- Never leave the search room unattended. The best practice is to assign someone to search room surveillance. A reasonable compromise, given staffing limitations, may be to have the researcher service archivist perform the surveillance responsibility while greeting and assisting researchers. Installation and use of a surveillance camera system may supplement direct oversight by a staff member but should not be substituted for it.

- Make sure that the staff member assigned to search room security can see all researchers at all times. This may necessitate arrangement of tables to ensure clear lines-of-sight and asking researchers not to pile materials high on the tables so as to restrict surveillance.

- Train staff members in security procedures and include those procedures in the program's administrative manual or other guidelines. Include search room security in the performance plans of appropriate staff.

- Develop a policy on how to react if a theft is suspected or spotted. This should be done in consultation with the institution's security personnel or local police and with the program's legal counsel to ensure that repository staff are on firm legal ground when they act.

should also have a clear statement on the restrictions of the federal Copyright Law that defines rights and responsibilities for making copies. The revised Copyright Law of 1976 (Title 17, United States Code) provides copyright protection to literary, musical, pictorial, graphic, and other creative works.[13] In general, the law provides that any work created is automatically copyrighted at the time of creation and the protection continues for the life of the author plus fifty years.

The law poses at least two sets of issues for archivists. First, who holds copyright when records are transferred from their point of origin, for instance an individual, to a repository, for instance a library? There is no simple answer, but the transfer or transmittal document should provide for transfer of copyright if possible. Second, may copyrighted records be copied by a repository or by researchers? In general, the law seems to proscribe copying by other than the copyright holder. However, it also provides for two exceptions: (1) under Section 107, "fair use" copying is permitted for purposes such as teaching, scholarship, and research. Repositories often assume that they may make copies requested by researchers under this "fair use" provision; and (2) under Section 108, archives and libraries can copy materials provided they are open to the public or specialized researchers, that the copying is not for commercial purposes, and that a notice of copyright is provided with the copies. These provisions are not simple or easy to apply. As Gary and Trudy Peterson point out, as a minimum, before copying a record, an institution should have a reasonable belief that the copy is to be used for private study, research, or scholarship. It is also highly desirable to consult with the parent institution's counsel in developing a policy. The notice below should be displayed where the repository accepts copying orders; it should also be on the order form:[14]

Notice
Warning Concerning Copyright Restrictions

The copyright law of the United States (Title 17, United States Code) governs the making of photocopies or other reproductions of copyrighted material. Under certain conditions specified in the law, libraries and archives are authorized to furnish a photocopy or other reproduction. One of these specified conditions is that the photocopy or reproduction is not to be used for any purpose other than private study, scholarship, or research. If a user makes a request for, or later uses, a photocopy, or reproduction for purposes in excess of "fair use," that user may be liable for copyright infringement. The institution reserves the right to refuse to accept a copying order if, in its judgment, fulfillment of the order would involve violation of the copyright law.

The historical records program's policies should cover other operating aspects of the repository's services that may be of interest or concern to users. For instance, does the repository inform researchers about other people pursuing the same topic? The SAA's "Code of Ethics" provides that it is appropriate for archivists to inform researchers of parallel projects using common materials and, if both parties agree, to exchange the names of the researchers.[15] This policy gives researchers the opportunity for discussions that may prevent duplicative research projects and publications. If a repository follows this policy, researchers should be so informed before their work begins. Researchers should also be informed of the repository's policies for eliciting information from and on its researchers through entrance and exit interviews, questionnaires, and in other ways.

Researcher Services: The Concept of Mediation

Archivists serving researchers interact between their materials and the researchers. They ought to be as helpful as possible in assisting researchers. This requires the archivist to have command of the finding aids and/or other access tools and general familiarity with the records themselves, including their origin, the function that produced them or resulted in their creation, the state of their arrangement and usability, and the information they contain. It also requires an ability to understand researchers and their needs and an ability to deal patiently, politely, and effectively with people.

For many researchers, archival records are encountered through chance, as noted above. Researchers may assume that historical records resemble more familiar sources that they use, such as books, which are easily accessible by topic and present focused, unified information in a systematic way. They may assume that a historical records program will have finding aids that set forth in simple fashion a description of the materials. This leads to initial disorientation and need for assistance, since records are organic and not always topic-specific, are arranged according to provenance and original order rather than by topic, and are described in finding aids that vary from library patterns. Researchers used to library card catalogs or indexes may be perplexed by even the most straightforward archival finding aid unless the introduction to the finding aid explains its makeup, or unless an archivist does so.

Researchers may at first be wary about telling the archivist their research needs. They may not understand the archivist's reasons for seeking information, may feel that their privacy is being challenged, or may find it difficult to formulate and articulate their actual research questions. Often, they state the research topic broadly out of concern that they will miss something or because the topic is still being precisely identified and the research project formulated. The researcher who writes on the registration form that he is interested in nineteenth-century politics may actually be researching a particular governor. The researcher who tells the archivist that she is researching a specific city may actually be working on a particular ethnic group or neighborhood. The researcher who insists he is interested in passenger ships entering a port in a specified range of years may actually be looking for an obscure ancestor as part of a genealogical or family history project.

Archivists who work with researchers have as an initial challenge zeroing in on the topic and determining what information the researcher actually needs. In effect, the archivist becomes the go-between or mediator between the researcher, on the one hand, and the repository's finding aid system and its holdings, on the other.

The first step is soliciting information on the registration form, but an oral discussion process, often referred to as an entrance interview, should also be carried out. The archivist, through questions and answers at the interview, elicits information, in some cases through an interrogatory process that includes helping researchers formulate or reformulate their research topics so as to define the information need with precision. This process is sometimes called question negotiation—"the process in which a reference specialist communicates with the patron in a manner designed to clarify the patron's initial question and to identify the patron's exact information need." This back-and-forth negotiation process permits the researcher to define his or her information need more precisely and enables the archivist to match that need with the repository's finding aids and holdings.[16] This requires tact and helpful but probing questions and making sure the researcher understands the purposes of the interview process.

The second part of the challenge is familiarizing the researcher with holdings and finding aids. The questions are: "How can an archivist best assist researchers in translating their questions into the language of the finding aids and in identifying promising sources? How can archivists best raise issues and assist in the development of a research strategy based on the identified sources and users' capabilities and time constraints?"[17] The archivist should discuss appropriate finding aids, make sure that the researcher understands how to use them, and suggest records that are likely to be of particular interest. If the repository holds records not yet described in the finding aids but nevertheless available for research, the archivist should bring them to the researcher's attention. Archivists point out material and describe how it may be helpful and they retrieve material requested by the researcher. They stop short, however, of perusing the material themselves or of actually doing any of the research. The archivist's job is to counsel, advise, and retrieve; then, the researcher's work begins.

The archivist's service does not end when the first box of material is delivered to the researcher, however. Without being too persistent or interrupting the research, the archivist should check to see if further assistance is needed. For instance, does the researcher have questions about the records that the archivist can answer? Did the researcher encounter references to other records that the repository might hold that might be germane to the topic? At the end of the research, the archivist should elicit from the researcher information needed to track and measure research use, as discussed below. This may be accomplished via a questionnaire, a brief oral exit interview, or some combination of the two.

Tracking, Measuring, Reporting

Archivists need to maximize use of the materials they so carefully identify and save, and to engender support for their programs by demonstrating the importance of that use. "Archivists do not know who their users are and, moreover, do not seem to be trying to count them," according to the 1985 SAA census of historical records programs, where only two thirds of respondents could even provide information on the number of research visits.[18] Many programs simply count researchers or research visits but do not systematically gather, analyze, or use information on actual research use. The archival community as a whole needs to achieve an adequate understanding of "who uses archives, for what purposes, and . . . which theories and techniques are most suited to facilitating use and satisfying most users over time."[19] As one archivist put it:

> The identity and the research habits of our users—who they are, how they think, how they learn, how they assemble information, to what uses they put it—must become as familiar a part of our thinking as the rules of order and practice (sometimes called principles) that govern acquisition, processing, description, and servicing of records. We must begin to learn systematically, not impressionistically as is our present tendency, who our users are, what kinds of projects they pursue, in what time frames and under what sponsorship; and, most importantly, how they approach records. Put another way, we must begin to think of archives administration as client-centered, not materials-centered.[20]

Several archivists, most notably Paul Conway of the National Archives and William Maher of the University of Illinois, have developed useful frameworks for tracking and measuring use.[21] The information needed can be gathered through forms that researchers fill out in part when they arrive and complete when they leave, through entrance and exit interviews, or through a combination of these information-gathering approaches. These questions need to be answered:

Who uses the records? The repository questionnaire should have standard categories, but these should be based on analysis of actual traffic rather than arbitrarily designed to fit some preconceived pattern. William Maher suggests that a university archives might use categories of administrative staff, faculty, graduate students, undergraduate students, people from other universities, and the general public.

How do researchers learn about the existence of the repository and its holdings? Do they use databases, directories, published guides, and other reference and access tools developed by the repository for their use? Or, do they find out about the program and its holdings through more indirect means: citations in publications, sessions at meetings, word-of-mouth advice from colleagues, referrals by librarians, or other means? What could be done to let more researchers know about the program and its holdings?

What are the purposes of use? Again, there need to be fixed categories based on researcher traffic. A listing of purposes might include: academic requirements; genealogy; publication (of a book or article, for instance); background information for newspaper, magazine article, or advertising; exhibit; background for radio, TV, or film; government research; personal interest or hobby; and other (this category should not become a large catch-all).

What specific subjects are being researched? As noted above, under the discussion of the archivist's mediatory role, some discussion may be required to focus on the precise topic. The objective here is to develop a list of categories or types of research and then keep count within those categories, for reporting purposes, to analyze patterns, and to track changes over time.

What records are used? There should be provision for recording the information at the series level or at more detail, such as box or folder, in order to track use.

What is the intensity of use—the time spent in research use in relation to the quantity of records used? This is an indirect measure of how compact and useful the researcher found the information. Long periods of time spent with small quantities of information usually indicate a high degree of interest in the material and usefulness; short periods spent going through significant volumes of information may indicate only passing interest or limited relevant information being discovered.

How rich and significant was the information gleaned from the record? This is a subjective measurement, dependent on the researcher's impression after the research concludes. Did the information cast new light on the subject, lead to new interpretations, suggest new avenues to pursue, suggest new sources that might be helpful? How successful did the researcher rate the research in the records?

How will the information be disseminated? For instance, will it be used only for the individual's own edification, or will it be used as part of a publication or in some other way that disseminates the information? This is a way of determining whether the information will benefit "indirect" users, as discussed above.

If the information is disseminated, what type of impact can it be expected to have? This question is speculative and anticipatory since it is impossible to foresee precisely how information will be used, who will use it, and what influence it will have. But some key questions include: are there legal ramifications to the research findings? Will the welfare of an individual, a group, or an institution be affected? Will important institutional or public undertakings be substantially affected or redirected? Will broadscale attention be drawn to the topic, thereby leading to further discussion, research, publications, or other results?

How helpful are the repository's finding aids and other services? The intention of these questions is to obtain suggestions for improving services.

Figure 4 shows an example of an information gathering form, developed by Paul Conway.

Researchers should be requested to furnish to the repository a copy of any written product based on their research that is available to the public. This would include in particular copies of articles, theses, dissertations, books, and newspaper and magazine articles. This is another means of measuring and documenting the impact of the research use of the materials in the repository. Some historical records programs feature such products in exhibits as a way of graphically demonstrating the research potential of their holdings.

Research reporting forms can be used to generate reports and track trends over time. These reports have two types of uses. First, they are useful for internal planning, management, and allocation of resources. They provide information for adjusting collecting policies and appraisal in light of actual requests for material and research use made of it. Research use is actually a key reality check on the effectiveness of the entire selection process. Reports on use help establish priorities for arrangement, description, and preservation that will fit researcher demands for the material. The reports reveal areas where improved researcher services are needed. They help identify needs for heightened outreach and public educational efforts to bring important, but underutilized, collections to the attention of researchers.

Reports on use should also be packaged as part of the program's regular reporting to its supervisors and resource allocators, provided that researchers agree to have their research topics disclosed. Publicity of the actual use made of historical records is one of the most

REFERENCE LOG

Information in this box is required to use the research room facilities. The principal purpose of this form is to identify and record individuals who use materials at the archives, to help us identify which materials may be most useful, and to permit later contact with researchers as part of more detailed studies of research use.

APPLICANT'S NAME (Last, First, Middle Initial)	PERMANENT PHONE NO.	OCCUPATION (please be as specific as possible)

PERMANENT ADDRESS (Stret, City, State, ZIP)	INSTITUTION	WHAT WORK BROUGHT YOU TO THE ARCHIVES?

DESCRIPTION OF RESEARCH PROJECT (Include subject, dates, important names, type of material needed)

☐
☐
☐
☐
☐
☐
☐

MAY WE ADVISE OTHER INDIVIDUALS OF THE SUBJECT OF YOUR RESEARCH? ☐ YES ☐ NO	MAY WE ADVISE OTHER INDIVIDUALS WHICH ITEMS WERE SERVED TO YOU? ☐ YES ☐ NO

I HAVE READ "REGULATIONS FOR THE PUBLIC USE OF RECORDS" AND I WILL COMPLY WITH THE RULES. Applicant's Signature　　　　　　　Date	MAY WE CONTACT YOU BY MAIL OR TELEPHONE AS PART OF A FUTURE USER STUDY? ☐ YES ☐ NO

Orientation

Your answers to questions in this section of the form will help the reference archivist orient you to using the archives' holdings. Together with answers from other researchers, the information you provide will enable archivists to assess the overall use of the archives.

What is the purpose of your current research project that involves using the archives' holdings or services (circle all that apply)

1. Academic requirements
2. Genealogy
3. Publication (book, article)
4. Background information for newspaper, magazine article, advertising
5. Exhibition
6. Film, radio, television program
7. Government research
8. Professional research (for individual, group, association)
9. Personal interest/hobby
10. Other _____

Some researchers prefer to rely on their background preparation or the finding aid system in the research room. Others feel most comfortable if reference archivists guide their searchers of the holdings.

Please mark the scale below to show your personal preference for doing archival research.

```
1        |2       |3       |4       |5
rely on      archivist and        rely on
finding aids  finding aids        archivist
```

Before your first visit on this project, did you write or telephone to get information on holdings or services?

☐ YES   ☐ NO   ☐ DON'T KNOW

Excluding writing or telephoning the archives directly, which of the following sources did you most rely on to identify the holdings or services of use in your research. (Circle the best choice)

1. References, citations in published works
2. Published guides to archives, primary sources, bibliographies
3. Teacher, professor, colleagues
4. Archivist/librarian at other institutions
5. Information from historical, professional or genealogical organizations
6. Television, radio, newspaper
7. Presentation by archives staff
8. Visit to museum exhibition
9. General knowledge, assumptions
10. Other_____

If you have done archival research in the last five years, please write the name of the archives in which you have most recently worked.

Figure 4. Sample information gathering form.

An example of a form that can be used by researcher services archivists to gather information on researchers and research use. From Paul Conway, "Facts and Frameworks: An Approach to Studying the Users of Archives," *American Archivist* 49 (Fall 1986): 402–403. Reprinted with permission of The Society of American Archivists

Search Report

The reference archivist should note the first ten collections consulted by the researcher, the source of the recommendation, and whether the researcher located information of use in the research project. Data for this section is obtained from paging slips, photocopy request forms, observation, and if necessary, by questioning researcher.

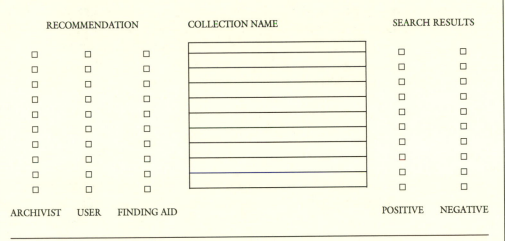

RECOMMENDATION   COLLECTION NAME   SEARCH RESULTS

ARCHIVIST   USER   FINDING AID   POSITIVE   NEGATIVE

Follow Up

The information you provide in this section will assist archivists to understand how archival research is carried out, and how archival information may be used.

Please provide an approximate breakdown of the total time you spent at the archives during this research project across each of the activities listed below. (Make sure the total equals 100%)

Orienting yourself to the archives' services and facilities ——%

Searching through finding aids and collections to locate documents ——%

Actually reading/viewing/studying documents ——%

Discussing research project with archivists or other researchers ——%

TOTAL   100%

If you expect to share the information you find at the archives, please describe below in what ways the information will be used. Please use this opportunity to name the title of a proposed publication, describe the group that may benefit from your archival research, or describe the results of your research in more detail.

What portion of your research project will be based on archival materials located at this archives or other archives?

1. I hope to use primarily archival sources of information.
2. I hope to use archival sources and other sources about equally.
3. I hope to use other sources of information primarily.
4. I don't know yet.

On the line below, please write the name of the collection in which you located the most useful information.

☐ no useful information located

effective means of boosting regard and consideration for archivists and archival programs. "The purposes, uses, and contributions of the archives have to be made more vivid, more concrete, and reported in various ways [through] communication of a steady flow of examples to heighten awareness and appreciation of what is being gotten for the money."[22] Reporting on use "can counteract substantially the stereotypical view of squirrel-like archivists lurking in basements, moving dusty boxes from shelf to table and back again."[23]

The reports should include statistics on numbers of researchers, volume of records used, and topics being pursued. But they should also include analytical narrative that draws attention to certain aspects of use. The reports should highlight use that relates to and advances the program's central mission. For instance, if a government archives has defined legal research by government or on government policies and issues as its top priority, then reports highlighting this type of research are likely to get attention. A medical archives in a research and teaching hospital that specializes in a particular disease would do well to feature in its reports research in that area. The reports should also attempt to draw attention to other significant research use, particularly examples where the results are expected to be disseminated and to have a substantial impact.

Archivists and Researchers: Common Agendas?

For the most part, archivists serve and assist researchers as part of their programs' mission to encourage use of their holdings and facilitate research. The relationship can and should have another dimension: engaging the user community as allies and colleagues in approaching difficult archival issues and needs. The people who use archival records may be in a good position to advise archivists in several areas. For instance, researchers can assist in the development of documentation strategies, as discussed in chapter 6. Experts may assist archivists in evaluating records, provide information on their relationship with other records and other resources, and discuss their potential usefulness for active areas of research. It is advisable to involve researchers when planning automated systems, which offer the potential for user-oriented access to historical records that are arranged according to traditional archival precepts. Archivists need to improve automated descriptive practices by "constructing information systems that relate to user needs rather than those that reflect traditional practices of doubtful utility for archivist and researcher alike."[24]

Finally, users can become advocates for strong archival programs. As people who have actually made use of the materials and services, they know firsthand and can attest to both the value of the records and the importance of the programs and their services. If their experiences as researchers have been positive, they can testify to the quality of the service and the helpfulness of the staff in particularly repositories. Archivists need to educate the researcher community about program issues and resource needs, as part of promotional work described in chapter 11. The local historian who appears before the county commissioners' budget hearing and lauds the county historical society, the faculty member who mentions to the university's dean or president how much she appreciates the archives' work, the prominent historian who writes the governor or testifies at a legislative hearing, the genealogist who tells how the local library's historical records program assisted his family research—all are advocates for stronger historical records programs. Cultivating researchers as supporters and advocates requires tact and patience, but it can be done, and it is another benefit of sound, helpful, responsive researcher services.

NOTES

1. Society of American Archivists, Task Force on Goals and Priorities, *Planning for the Archival Profession* (Chicago: Society of American Archivists, 1986), 22.

2. Paul Conway, "Facts and Frameworks: An Approach to Studying the Users of Archives," *American Archivist* 49 (Fall 1986):395. For a discussion of the significance of research use of historical records, see Bruce W. Dearstyne, "What Is the *Use* of Archives? A Challenge for the Profession," *American Archivist* 50 (Winter 1987):76–87.

3. Conway, "Facts and Frameworks: An Approach to Studying the Users of Archives, 395.

4. Page Putnam Miller, *Developing a Premier National Institution: A Report from the User Community to the National Archives* (Washington; National Coordinating Committee for the Promotion of History, 1989), 23.

5. William L. Joyce, "Archivists and Research Use," *American Archivist* 47 (Spring 1984):125.

6. Edwin C. Bridges, "Consultant Report: State Government Records Programs," in Lisa Weber, ed., *Documenting America: Assessing the Condition of Historical Records in the States* (Albany: National Association of State Archives and Records Administrators, 1984), 8.

7. Paul Conway, "Perspectives on Archival Resources: The 1985 Census of Archival Institutions," *American Archivist* 50 (Spring 1987):186–190.

8. Philip C. Brooks, *Research in Archives: The Use of Unpublished Primary Sources* (Chicago: University of Chicago Press, 1969).

9. Leon J. Stout, *Historical Records in Pennsylvania: An Assessment Report for the State Historical Records Advisory Board* (Harrisburg: Pennsylvania Historical and Museum Commission, 1983), 173.

10. Mary Jo Pugh, "The Illusion of Omniscience: Subject Access and the Reference Archivist," *American Archivist* 45 (Winter 1982):42.

11. Gary M. Peterson and Trudy Huskamp Peterson, *Archives and Manuscripts: Law* (Chicago: Society of American Archivists, 1985), 39.

12. David R. Kepley, "Reference Service and Access," in James G. Bradsher, ed., *Managing Archives and Archival Institutions* (Chicago: University of Chicago Press, 1989), 166–167.

13. The following discussion of copyright is based on the discussion in Peterson and Peterson, *Archives and Manuscripts: Law*, 81–89. Anyone interested in this topic should consult that manual.

14. Ibid., 83–84.

15. Karen Benedict, "Archival Ethics," in Bradsher, ed., *Managing Archives and Archival Institutions*, 182.

16. Linda J. Long, "Question Negotiation in the Archival Setting: The Use of Interpersonal Communication Techniques in the Reference Interview," *American Archivist* 52 (Winter 1989):41–43.

17. Page Putnam Miller, *Developing a Premier National Institution: A Report from the User Community to the National Archives*, 20.

18. Conway, "Perspectives on Archival Resources: The 1985 SAA Survey of Archival Institutions," 187.

19. Lawrence Dowler, "The Role of Use in Defining Archival Practice and Principles: A Research Agenda for the Availability and Use of Records," *American Archivist* 51 (Winter and Spring, 1988):75.

20. Elsie Freeman, "In the Eye of the Beholder: Archives Administration from the User's Standpoint," *American Archivist* 47 (Spring 1984):112.

21. Conway, "Facts and Frameworks: An Approach to Studying the Users of Archives"; William Maher, "The Use of User Studies," *Midwestern Archivist* 11 (1986):15–26.

22. Social Research, Inc., *The Image of Archivists: Resource Allocators' Perceptions* (Chicago: Society of American Archivists, 1984), 4.

23. Maher, "The Use of User Studies," 16.

24. Nancy Sahli, "National Information Systems and Strategies for Research Use," *Midwestern Archivist* 9 (1984):11.

10 Promotional Marketing

Historical records are firsthand accounts of human experience; evidence of personal, social, and institutional endeavor; direct, unfiltered connections with past thoughts and actions, now lost in time but captured in documents. Their human origins make them intriguing, engaging, even fascinating. They appeal to our natural curiosity about what people thought and how they acted and handled their affairs in the past. Reliable as sources for history, they also provide insights into the human condition. Presented and interpreted in the right way, historical records are of interest to a wide range of audiences, including but transcending researchers. Carrying the message to this broader public is the mission of what might be called *promotional marketing*—a continuing effort to encourage maximum use of holdings, explain and highlight work, and advance the general cause of historical records.

Promotional marketing may at first conjure up unsettling images of high-pressure salesmanship for products of dubious value or of self-serving tactics for financial gain. Some archivists are convinced that promotional work should be unnecessary; after all, shouldn't the value of historical records be evident to any thoughtful person, and shouldn't users be able to get to those materials on their own? Actually, promotional marketing, as described in this chapter, is useful, relevant—and respectable. Far from being commercial salesmanship, it is akin to marketing as practiced by enlightened non-profit institutions and associations. In that context, marketing is "a consumer-based activity designed to allow you to identify actual and potential customers; assess their needs, attitudes, and preferences; and address your plans to the realities determined by the investigation of your market. It is aimed at filling the needs of customers by offering them programs or services they will find attractive, beneficial, and useful."[1] It leads to interest, insight, appreciation, use—and program support. Promotional work requires imaginative interpretation and portrayal of historical records

197

and archival work to a largely uninformed audience. It is self-serving, in the sense that it has the program's own interests as one of its primary concerns.

Promotional activities of the type advocated here are sometimes referred to as outreach or public programs by archivists. A Society of American Archivists' manual defines public programming as "any activity that contributes to a greater awareness of archives and what they do . . . [and] encourages greater communication between archivists and the various institutional social, and professional communities to which they belong." The manual notes that:

> Public programs are tools that support and enhance other archival functions, including research, reference, preservation, and collecting. They can be highly educational, both for planners and participants; they can foster appreciation for history and historical records; and they help ensure firm and continuing support for future archival endeavors.[2]

The Problem of Image

The first promotional marketing challenge that archivists face is to improve the fuzzy but often unflattering impression that many people have of archival work. A public relations firm that analyzed the image of archivists pointed out the need for change:

> Traditionally, archivists point to the inscription on the National Archives Building—"The Past Is Prologue"—as *raison d'etre* for their existence. That's no longer sufficient. That hoary reference has little relevance to today, the here and now. Archivists must communicate specific values, particular benefits to make their records live—in short, provide information about archives that has a direct relevance to the lives of the American people.[3]

David B. Gracy II, president of the Society of American Archivists in 1983–1984, helped define and dramatize the issue of public misperception of archival work and sparked unprecedented interest and attention to the issue. He pointed out that some people have no image of archivists at all, some see them as having a "real but shabby grandeur," while others regard them as "permanently humped, moleish, aged creatures who shuffle dusty documents in dust-filled stacks for a purpose uncertain."[4] Lamenting public ignorance, Gracy quoted a journalist who, despite donating her own papers to a university historical records collection, wrote that "archivists are easy to please. . . . They find value beyond reckoning in what others discard."[5] Archivists may shudder at news media references to their work such as a *Chicago Tribune* article that was entitled: "The Archivist: A Keeper of Words and Doodles Who Dreams of the Ultimate Attic."[6]

As Gracy and others point out, mistaken images of archives as old records held in remote places by strange people hardly flatter a profession that is dynamic, highly motivated, and service oriented. The archival community, trying to advance its work, has become aware of how ignorance and misperceptions of archival work undermine what they are trying to accomplish. To gather more information, the SAA established a task force on "Archives and Society," which commissioned a study of the image problem close to home: the sponsors or resource allocators who control archival programs. The task force hired a professional public opinion firm, which interviewed dozens of administrators whose supervisory responsibilities included archival programs. Most understood their programs' work and claimed to be supportive. But their responses revealed two interrelated aspects of the image problem.

First, many of the people interviewed asserted that historical records program funding was adequate or stated frankly that they would not increase it. "It's a fairly low priority," said one business sector administrator. "They [the archives] are not a direct revenue department and that's why they don't have a high priority." Archives seem to "hark to the past, seem passive, stored [*sic*] compared to more current, ongoing, aggressive demands on the budget" and archivists were seen as content with "place and rewards"—a common impression that, the report concluded, "needs jarring so that the allocators can re-perceive archivists as deserving of greater support."[7]

Second, archivists were viewed as isolated professionals having little interest in the world around them. "I think most of them are bookworms," said one government administrator. An educational administrator claimed that archivists "are generally history buffs, somewhat introverted." Said another: "They have to like tedious tasks. They should be organized, patient, have a lot of stamina, and possess good management skills. They should have a flair for history and research and be able to deal with the public." According to another resource allocator, "Archivists are project-oriented people. They love to take a mess and make some order of it. They love the idea of the preservation of things."[8] Other responses conjured up images of solitude, confinement, and quiet. In some cases, their supervisors actually meant to compliment the archivists in their employment, but their comments provided important revelations about the need for information to present a more positive and engaging archival image. The report concluded:

> Summarizing the situation, it may be said that it is one weighted with "niceness"—the archivists having the impotence of virtue, which is expected to be its own reward, leaving the allocators to address themselves to more

pressing concerns. . . . Archivists are perceived as quiet professionals, carrying out an admired but comparatively subterranean activity. . . . Traditional stereotypes that linger on even among more knowledgeable resource allocators need to be counteracted. Making archives a more common and accessible concept, and doing more to open them to use and visiting, should diminish the various elements of dustiness and mustiness, sheer acquisitiveness, territoriality, and dead accumulation.[9]

A Promotional Orientation

The study's unsettling conclusions jolted archivists to unprecedented action in the area of promotion. The need for more assertive action was reinforced by the state assessment reports and other studies. "To improve the situation," the SAA report on the profession's goals and priorities recommended, "archivists need to define more coherent objectives and communicate greater freshness and distinctiveness in imagery by their training, programs, self-assertion, publicity, advertising, and relevance to modern life."[10]

Archival work is exciting and historical records are gold mines of useful information; getting the message across is the challenge. Using imaginative approaches, archivists need to explain their holdings and work in terms that appeal to, can be understood by, and are interesting to their customers or constituents, including sponsors, users, and the public. They need to demonstrate the ramifications of the work, including insights into current problems that continue from or are similar to those of the past and indirect contributions to social enlightenment.

It is important to weave promotional considerations into the entire program rather than developing them separately. Marketing should be based on the program's services and holdings and, in turn, it should contribute to other elements of the program. This is important so that archives staff realize that the marketing work is not just one more thing to do but, instead, a natural and essential part of a balanced archival program that supports, enhances, and extends other functions. Client-centered thinking and planning mean that some time and resources are naturally devoted to marketing and outreach work. Like other aspects of historical records programming, promotional marketing activities requires careful planning.

Promotional objectives should be defined in light of the program's mission statement and as part of a regular planning process. The objectives should be clearcut and should tie promotional marketing efforts to other aspects of the program. For instance, a series of exhibits on a particular theme, e.g., the history of architecture in a city, might encourage offers of additional records on that theme, perhaps from local architectural firms. A seminar or workshop for teachers on community history materials can be expected to result in students coming to the repository to use its records. Sponsoring a lecture series on a particular topic can demonstrate the potential usefulness of the repository's records.

In assessing program needs, the key question is: where can promotional efforts be of most assistance to the program? Answering this question may require considerable analysis of audience need and interest and extended internal discussion, preferably as part of the program's planning process. If a low level of research use is a problem, efforts that stress outreach to researchers may be the answer. If the repository wants to increase its visibility among resource allocators, users, or other segments of a defined public, an exhibit program may be the answer. An institutional archives might conclude that a modest, internal newsletter that stresses the program's contributions to the institution is the best approach.

To identify resources, determine the extent and level of staff interest and expertise and ascertain how much staff time is likely to be available for this effort. The findings may result in some trade-offs; for instance, resources devoted to promotional aspects of the program may mean that less resources are available for other efforts, such as arrangement and description of records.

Audiences for Promotional Efforts

Who are the users, participants, audiences? What central messages or themes need to be presented to them? These broad questions are at the heart of promotional marketing. Answering them may require some archival market analysis via a questionnaire or interviews. The objective is to determine how best to package and present information about the program. It may be useful to see the audience as having at least six elements.

The first, often overlooked or regarded as beyond the purview of promotion, is the group loosely defined as sponsors, supervisors, and "resource allocators"—people whose understanding, good will, and support help determine the success or failure of archival programs. "Managing the boss" is a part of good marketing and sound administration. Some useful approaches to convey information, promote involvement, and demonstrate program value are the following:

Participation in planning. Sponsors need to be involved in the planning process, hopefully as participants at least in the broad mission definition and goal identification aspects. Participation in the planning process lets the sponsor feel he or she is part of the process that defines where the program is heading, introduces the sponsor to issues and problems the program faces, provides a basis for the archivist to report and the sponsor to gauge what is being done, and makes the sponsor feel some stake in the program's welfare.

Regular reports. Informative reports are another aspect of sound management as well as marketing. Through regular reports, the archivist holds the sponsor's interest, keeps him or her apprised of progress and obstacles, highlights resource needs and problems, and showcases achievements that demonstrate the value of the program in terms the sponsor will understand.

Involvement in public presentations. It is wise to involve sponsors in presentations where they are identified with the program's achievements. Examples might include: giving a speech at the opening of a documents exhibit; preparing the preface for a document teaching packet; writing an editorial in the archives' newsletter; along with the archivist, meeting with the news media to discuss a particularly important document or new accession. The boss can take some credit for, and identify with, the work or document being unveiled, which leads to positive feelings about the value of the program.

Catering to institutional needs. Historical records programs, particularly institutional archives, should seek opportunities to contribute to the parent's institution's mission and needs (see figure 5). For instance, a corporate archivist may offer to assist the company's legal office in carrying out background research in archival materials for litigation. A city archivist may offer to provide historical material for the mayor's speech on urban problems. A state archives might extend an offer to legislators to assist in locating material on their home communities for use in speeches and commemorations. Archivists at Hallmark Cards, Coca-Cola, Wells Fargo, and other major companies, have cycled historical advertisements and other materials into their companies' advertising efforts.

A second audience group might be loosely defined as potential donors of historical records or, in the case of institutional and organizational archival programs, agencies and offices that need to schedule their records and work with the archival program. This audience is in effect the supplier of future accessions, so it is highly desirable to make a positive impression. Promotional activities with this group should include careful explanation of the program's documentation objectives, acquisitions policies, appraisal techniques, and services. The archivist needs to make the point that historical records will be well cared for and secure in the archival facility. The

The Archives

THE CHASE MANHATTAN Archives

What is it?

The Chase Manhattan Archives, established in 1975, is a secure central repository where records of Chase having permanent value are preserved, maintained and made available for research and reference use.

The Archives collection includes non-current records of The Chase Manhattan Corporation, The Chase Manhattan Bank, N.A., and their predecessors, that have lasting administrative, legal, or historical value.

Typical questions that might be answered using the Chase Archives include:

- How long has Chase provided trust services for its customers?
- What was the nature of banking in the early 19th century?
- Trace the history and development of the Chase Global Network.
- How did Chase contribute to the revitalization of Lower Manhattan?

Chase recognizes that the records housed in the Archives are an important management resource and a valuable corporate asset. Many of the records have significant research value and are vital to the documentation of the history of Chase and its relationship with and contributions to business, society and world affairs.

The Archives is part of the Public Affairs Division of Corporate Communications. The full-time staff includes two professional archivists. The Archives Council helps to create and review policy for the department and makes recommendations regarding appropriate documentation for inclusion in the collection.

Who uses it?

Researchers who frequently use the Archives include:

- Chase employees seeking information for their work
- Communicators and media representatives
- Scholarly researchers
- General public

Access to the records in the archives is governed by the policy set forth in the Chase Organization and Policy Guide. Most records are open to employees for business-related research. Some records are available for outside researchers.

All materials must be used in the Archives under supervision and in accordance with the regulations of the department.

Individuals interested in using the Archives may make an appointment by contacting:

**The Chase Manhattan Archives
One Chase Manhattan Plaza
23rd floor
New York, New York 10081**

(212) 552-6658

Figure 5. This introductory brochure notes first in the list of researchers who frequently use the archives: "Chase employees seeking information for their work." It discusses the value of the archival program to the company as well as to scholarly researchers. (*Courtesy of Chase Manhattan Bank Archives*)

program should stress its work in arranging, describing, and making available the records. Good finding aids and guides, and publicity on the extent and seriousness of research use, are ways of demonstrating that historical records receive active use.

A third element of the audience is the user community. Here, the objective is to encourage maximum use of holdings, especially by those parts of the total user community that have been identified as priorities. This has two benefits: it puts records to good use and builds constituent support. As discussed in chapter 9, among the best approaches are speeches and publications for particular groups, promotional descriptive publications, and classes, tours, and seminars on the value of records and on how to do research in them.

A fourth part of the audience might be educators and their students, at all levels. Working with elementary and high schools won't appeal to every historical records program, but it certainly makes sense for those in library, historical society, and other settings whose business is education and service to the public. Almost every historical records program has some materials that can be used by imaginative social studies and history teachers, with some assistance from archivists (see figure 6). The educational community's increasing emphasis on interdisciplinary studies may suggest possible applications for language arts, science, environmental studies, and other courses. Study of historical records shows students the value of historical source material. It provides an exciting introduction to the primary material of history, shows students how history is recovered and represented from historical records, and shows them that history may be unclear and has to be derived and interpreted from incomplete and sometimes inconsistent or contradictory sources. Study of historical records also improves reading, analytical, and writing and presentation skills.

Study of historical records is helpful to students, but it can also have benefits for the repositories. Today's elementary and high school students are tomorrow's scholarly researchers and day-after-tomorrow's institutional administrators, legislators, and taxpayers. An early appreciation of the usefulness and fascination of historical records will give them an affinity for historical records later in their lives.

At the college and graduate school level, the challenge is to reach professors and students and to make both groups aware of the information available in historical records. Archivists need to demonstrate the relevance of their holdings to the interests of the academicians. They also need to cooperate with professors on showing students how to do research in historical records, which involves skills and experience that many students lack, even at the graduate level. In order to reach college and university students, archivists need to visit their campuses, meet with classes, discuss holdings, and invite visitations to carry out research.

DIVERSITY IN DOCUMENTS

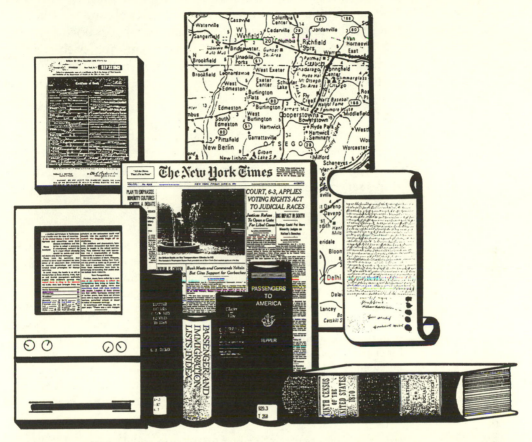

A SUMMER INSTITUTE FOR EDUCATORS
July 7 - 12, 1991   Cooperstown, N.Y.

Figure 6. Advertisement for seminar on archival materials for educators.

Seminars and workshops can demonstrate to both archivists and educators the techniques of teaching with historical records. The New York State Historical Association's summer institutes also tie use of documents to state curricular requirements. (*Courtesy of New York State Historical Association, Cooperstown, N.Y.*)

A fifth group might be loosely defined as the concerned public—people interested in cultural affairs, libraries, history, and information. Perhaps the best examples of appropriate programs for their benefit are exhibits that showcase choice materials and also educate the viewer about the historical topics that the records document and about archival techniques and procedures. This approach requires considerable planning and imaginative interpretation to bring the records to life and make sure the viewers understand how historical records present history.

A final group might be defined as the public as a whole. At first, this may seem far too diffuse to be helpful. After all, most citizens will never make a research visit or even come to the institution for a document display. But it is important to reach them with a generalized message nevertheless. That message might be summarized as follows:

> Citizens, you may not know it, but historical records are important to you! Historical records document the development and progress of our institutions and civilization and therefore constitute a general, collective record of our progress as a people. They are among the most important evidence from the past that we have. Archivists and archival programs perform an important public service by identifying, caring for, and making available these materials. And, finally, every day, people use these materials for research with direct or indirect consequence for the public as a whole. This is true, for instance, of research use of government archives to check legislative intent and legal issues; for institutions using their archives to ensure administrative continuity; and for research with important ramifications into environmental, legal, social, and other issues. Some of *your* history is here in our keeping, and we're keeping it for *you*.

Distilling this message is easier than getting it delivered. The natural approach to the citizenry as a whole is through the mass media, including newspapers, television and radio, and popular magazines and other publications, but that is a difficult path for something that appears to be as unnewsworthy as historical records. Several approaches to the media are discussed below.

Six Basic Promotional Tools

Not every historical records program can mount a full-scale promotional marketing campaign. Even programs with limited resources, however, should consider at least some promotional efforts, using relatively modest resources to reach significant, broad-scale audiences. There are at least six potentially useful tools: a program brochure, newsletter, promotional publications and productions, the program's own staff, open houses or tours, and the news media.

Careful planning is needed so that the commitments of time and resources reinforce other program objectives.

The first tool is a general program brochure. The brochure is the lead item in introducing and representing the program, no matter what the occasion or audience. It should be useful with everyone from school groups to media representatives to the trustees of the institutions that sponsor the historical records program. The basic brochure should be short, easy to read, free of jargon, illustrated if possible, and aimed at a broad range of readers (see figure 7). While format and content may vary, the brochure should at least cover:

History and mission of the program and its relationship to its parent institution and its mission.

Types of material that the program collects and topics that it aims to cover.

Types of research it is best equipped to support.

Examples or generalizations about research carried out in the recent past.

Services available to researchers and others.

Researcher policies, e.g., restrictions on research.

Information on location and how to reach the facility, hours of operation, etc.

Information on whom to contact before coming to the repository to discuss research needs, relevant holdings, availability of those holdings, and other issues pertaining to research.

A second basic tool is a regularly issued newsletter. A newsletter updates all concerned and interested parties on major program developments, important new accessions, records arranged and available for use, patterns of research and upcoming public events. By listing new accessions or records available for research, it becomes an adjunct finding aid and encourages research inquiries. A newsletter should carry news of the program's progress and accomplishments and, occasionally, information on its future plans. It should convey a fresh, attractive image but it need not be ostentatious, expensive, or lengthy.

Since newsletters must reach well beyond specialists and people who are well informed about archival affairs, design and writing style are important. A clean, inviting design is essential to encourage people to pick it up and look through it; clear, crisp, nontechnical, jargon-free writing is essential to induce them to read it. With the advent of desktop publishing, program staff may be able to produce an attractive and informative newsletter in relatively short order, in-house and on a modest budget. At the other end of the spectrum are

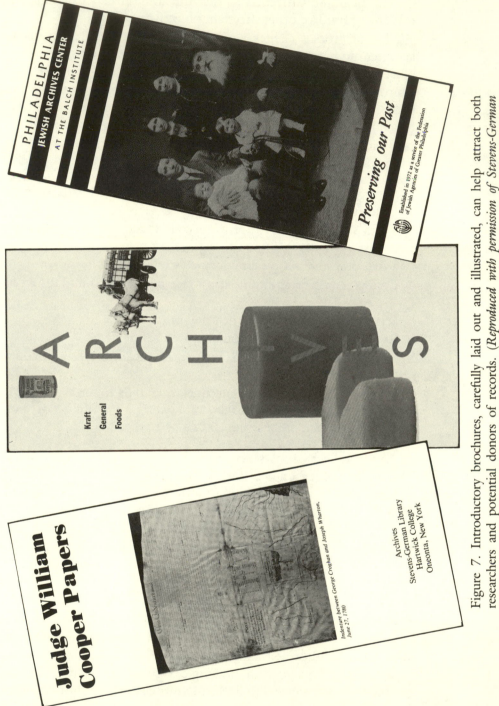

Figure 7. Introductory brochures, carefully laid out and illustrated, can help attract both researchers and potential donors of records. *(Reproduced with permission of Stevens-German Library, Hartwick College; Kraft General Foods, Inc. [© 1990]; and the Philadelphia Jewish Archives Center at the Balch Institute)*

professionally designed newsletters on slick paper and replete with photographs. These newsletters represent their programs, their services, and their holdings, to advantage. Any newsletter should appear on a regular, predictable basis, and carry news that is not outdated (see figure 8).

A third type of tool is the promotional publication or audiovisual production that touts the value and importance of historical records (see figure 9). Increasingly, archives are considering slide/tape or videotape presentations that appeal to a generation that is accustomed to getting its news and entertainment from television and videocassettes. The New York State Archives and Records Administration, for example, has produced a brochure, *Archives and You: The Benefits of Historical Records* and a companion slide-tape and videotape show, *Let the Record Show: Practical Uses for Historical Documents*. The brochure has a catchy design and features interesting photographs of people making use of records; the audiovisual production is lively and fast-paced and is also focused on people using records as well as on the records themselves. Both make the basic point that "historical records contribute valuable information to our lives, information which helps us address contemporary issues and solve current problems."

Historical records help institutions and organizations improve their administration, document and protect legal rights, enhance education, protect the ownership of property, help in the study of environmental issues, and assist in analysis of bridges, roads, water and sewer lines, and other components of the infrastructure. The brochure and show present actual examples with real people: a homeowner's association uses historical records to document its case for a new bridge; a research botanist uses historical records for a survey as part of a study to determine the future use of Goat Island, Niagara Falls; a Saratoga teacher's class studies the 1842 diary of a child their age to understand what life was like in the past. The brochure and the slide production then move to brief discussions of what archivists do. Both conclude with sections on what viewers can and should do to improve the management of historical records in their own communities:

> You can take action to make sure that the historical records in your community receive the attention they deserve. Find out the status of historical records in your community. Support your local historical society, library, or other institution that cares for historical records. Become an advocate for historical records. Help others to understand the value of historical records and encourage them to support the historical records programs in their community.[11]

Rockefeller
Archive
Center

Newsletter

FALL 1991

Grant-in-Aid Program

The Rockefeller Archive Center's Grant-in-Aid Program was established to provide support for scholars whose projects require substantive research in the collections housed at the Center. From an annual pool of $40,000, the competitive program makes grants of not more than $1,500 to scholars in any discipline engaged in research that requires extensive use of these collections. The deadline for applications is December 31, 1991 and grantees will be announced in March 1992. Requests for application forms and any of the Center's guides and surveys (see page 16) should be addressed to the Director, Darwin H. Stapleton.

Scholar-in-Residence Program

The next two resident scholars at the Rockefeller Archive Center have been chosen by the Center's search committee. Dr. Theresa Richardson will hold the appointment from January through August 1992, and Dr. John B. Sharpless will serve as the Center's resident scholar for 1992-1993.

Dr. Theresa Richardson, the author of *The Century of the Child: The Mental Hygiene Movement and Social Policy in the United States and Canada* (1989), received her doctorate from the University of British Columbia in 1987. She is currently Visiting Professor in the Department of Communications and Social Foundations, Faculty
(continued on page 13)

Additional Nelson A. Rockefeller Papers Opened for Research

Nelson A. Rockefeller, center, touring the MINIMAX supermarket in Valencia, Venezuela, ca. 1947.

Two more series of Nelson A. Rockefeller's papers were recently deeded to the Rockefeller Archive Center and are now available for scholarly research. These series include Rockefeller's files on the American International Association for Economic and Social Development (AIA) and the International Basic Economy Corporation (IBEC), and a collection of gubernatorial press releases issued primarily during his last two terms as governor of New York.

The twenty-eight cubic feet of press releases cover February to April 1961 and December 1967 to December 1973. Topics covered include legislation; budget summaries; appointments; transcripts of speeches, news conferences, and

interviews; the Governor's itineraries; and official proclamations. The releases are arranged chronologically and are currently not indexed.

The AIA-IBEC series includes sixteen cubic feet of correspondence, reports and publications.
(continued on page 9)

Figure 8. Newsletters inform a variety of audiences about the historical records program's accessions, holdings, and services. (*Courtesy of Rockefeller Archive Center*)

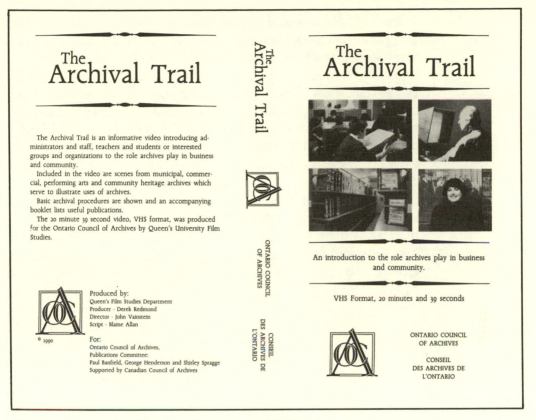

The
Archival Trail

The Archival Trail is an informative video introducing administrators and staff, teachers and students or interested groups and organizations to the role archives play in business and community.

Included in the video are scenes from municipal, commercial, performing arts and community heritage archives which serve to illustrate uses of archives.

Basic archival procedures are shown and an accompanying booklet lists useful publications.

The 20 minute 39 second video, VHS format, was produced for the Ontario Council of Archives by Queen's University Film Studies.

© 1990

Produced by:
Queen's Film Studies Department
Producer · Derek Redmond
Director · John Vainstein
Script · Blaine Allan

For:
Ontario Council of Archives,
Publications Committee:
Paul Banfield, George Henderson and Shirley Spragge
Supported by Canadian Council of Archives

The
Archival Trail

ONTARIO COUNCIL
OF ARCHIVES

CONSEIL
DES ARCHIVES DE
L'ONTARIO

The
Archival Trail

An introduction to the role archives play in business and community.

VHS Format, 20 minutes and 39 seconds

ONTARIO COUNCIL
OF ARCHIVES

CONSEIL
DES ARCHIVES DE
L'ONTARIO

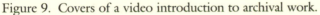

Figure 9. Covers of a video introduction to archival work.

The Ontario Council of Archives produced a lively and informative video to introduce administrators and staff, teachers, students, and interested citizens to the role archives play in communities and in business. Through the use of actual examples of research uses of archives, it makes the case for their importance. An accompanying booklet includes a list of readings. (*Courtesy of Ontario Council of Archives*)

Members of the archival staff can bring the personal touch to marketing efforts. Archivists should spend some time as marketing agents—addressing researcher groups and the public, giving interviews, writing news releases, working with the news media, giving interviews, and writing articles on services and holdings. The archivist is the program's best ambassador to the outside world. Often, the archivist's own enthusiasm and expertise are enough by themselves to garner attention and engender interest. Time spent in preparing articles and other materials for publications of the parent organization or of researcher groups is a good investment in getting support and researchers for the program.

This activity requires archivists to explain their work and services in terms that appeal to their audiences, not just to fellow archivists (see figure 10). How to discuss appraisal in a way the local

Rotary will appreciate? How to dramatize the tragic toll that high-acid paper deterioration is taking on our archives? How to get local social studies teachers excited about the historical gems the archivist holds? How to answer the person who asks the archivist on a radio call-in "talk show" where he can find records on his immigrant ancestors? How to convince the City Council that the city's bicentennial is an opportune time to start an archival program and launch a documentary exhibit program in the rotunda of City Hall? Challenges of these types are exciting and require development of top notch interpretive, organizational, and communication skills.

A fifth type of tool is open houses and tours of the archival facility. These need careful planning and preparation and must be more than mere walk-throughs with informal commentary. They cater to people's curiosity about old records and what may seem esoteric and mysterious work and they have a degree of excitement by being "behind the scenes" and in the inner sanctums of archival work. Tours must not just show the physical surroundings; viewing row after row of bound volumes and cartons on shelves is unlikely to stir the interest or engage the intellect of many people. Instead, the tours should illustrate the richness of the records and explain the range of archival work. Well-planned and organized tours should cover at least the following:

> What services does this program provide? What is its mission? What are its top priorities?
> What are the most important records that are held? Why are they considered most important? People on the tour should be able to see, read, and even handle them.
> What are the most interesting records? What makes them so interesting? Again, there is no substitute for letting people see, read, and peruse the records.
> What kinds of research are carried out here? How do archivists assist researchers?
> How are records physically preserved? What types of conservation work are carried out by the program?
> What do archivists do? What are the most interesting and exciting aspects of their work? What do they find most rewarding? Especially important are the themes of records appraisal to identify those of continuing value, and service to researchers.
> What kind of training and experience are required to become a proficient archivist?

A sixth tool is the news media. News articles and feature articles are likely to reach a far broader audience than archival newsletters, brochures, tours, or any other activity that the historical records

Figure 10. To commemorate the 50th anniversary of America's entry into World War II, the New York State Archives and Records Administration mounted an exhibit to illustrate conditions on the Home Front, showed films from the 1940s, and offered tours and workshops. (*Courtesy New York State Archives and Records Administration*)

program undertakes solely with its own resources. Archivists need to send the media information and press releases on important new accessions, public events such as the opening of a new exhibit or a seminar in the archives, and other newsworthy developments. These materials should be written in plain language and should demystify archival work by explaining it in terms that can be understood and appreciated. These are legitimate "news items" and some of them, at least, should be of interest to the press. It pays for the archivist to get to know editorial staff at local newspapers and TV and radio stations and to convince them that the items really are newsworthy and that readers and viewers would be interested in them.

However, there is a second, and potentially more rewarding, approach to the media: "to cultivate reporters with historical and cultural interests and furnish them with ideas and visual materials for stories about archival programs and collections."[12] This strategy assumes that the program's holdings are of potential usefulness to media representatives for background material on current news items and for interesting feature articles.

The archivist needs to relate records to current affairs and events in the news that the media is interested in. Historical records may yield useful background information, provide the basis for comparing present day situations to the past, furnish the potential for historical analysis, and, in general, assist the news media representative's work. The news article on the current political campaign could be enriched by a historical comparison of candidates and issues a century ago; the current debate over educational standards has historical roots in school board minutes and records from decades ago; the article on an oil spill or sanitary landfill issue could be accompanied by a sidebar based on archival research into pollution concerns at the turn of the century. The possibilities of archives-*cum*-news are fascinating and require a good working relationship between the archivist and reporters, feature writers, and radio and television personnel. Such a relationship can be built up over time through inviting media representatives to tours and open houses, sending them descriptions of particularly appealing and interesting records, calling them with suggestions for background research, and assisting them in use of finding aids.

Exhibits: Records Appearing on Their Own Behalf

Exhibits of historical records can serve a variety of audiences and needs through direct presentation of the repository's most interesting or important documents. The records appear on their own behalf and "speak" for themselves. Exhibits attract attention, introduce people to historical records as sources of history and are useful in advancing archival programs:

> Archival exhibits are mounted to interest, inform, stimulate, entertain, and educate viewers. Well-planned exhibits designed to meet these goals can be an important tool in encouraging public appreciation and use of archives and archival institutions, and an understanding of historical events. Exhibits . . . are useful in drawing attention to the resources available in archival institutions and serve as an invitation to further research. . . . Exhibits can encourage people to study the past; donate records, money, or services to the institution; and even stimulate civic pride.[13]

Exhibits engage the attention of members of the public who will never visit a historical records program or be concerned with archival techniques or issues. When imaginatively presented, exhibits can be engaging, exciting, and even entertaining. Like other promotional efforts, exhibits require careful planning and integration with other program efforts to ensure that they reinforce and contribute to other program objectives. Exhibit planning should include an analysis of audiences that the program desires to reach, identification of potential themes or topics for exhibitions, identification of records that would illustrate the themes or topics, and an assessment of resources available for exhibit-related work.

It is useful to consider three types of exhibits: educational or thematic, those that show the contribution of the program, and those that present the archival function.[14] Exhibits focus on selected historical events, activities, and topics, and serve to introduce viewers to the raw materials of history. They enlighten, illustrate, and explain history through direct presentation and imaginative interpretation of the evidence. Often, these exhibits are tied to commemorations or anniversaries (e.g., the bicentennial of the town, the bank's golden anniversary) or historical perspectives on current events (e.g., an exhibit on crime in the 1920s, documents on the Home Front during past wars) (see figure 11). They may also relate to accomplishments of families or individuals (e.g., a prominent professor whose work is documented in the university archives) or to themes in institutional development (e.g., advertising and public relations material from a corporate archives). These ties give the exhibits relevance and attract viewers who are interested in the exhibit theme and curious about the evidence that the exhibit has to offer.

A second type of exhibit shows the contribution of the historical records program. These exhibits usually concentrate on how records have been used for research, for instance, by displaying records juxtaposed with passages from new publications that drew on or

Figure 11. The Chicago Historical Society's "We The People" exhibit is a good example of using manuscripts, maps, and pamphlets to supplement a variety of artifacts. The artifacts and documents are displayed together to present varying perspectives on how people lived during the colonial and early national periods. The New-York Historical Society Library's exhibit "Markers of Change: Documents of American History" includes newspapers and publications as well as historical records. (*Used with permission of the Chicago Historical Society, © 1987, all rights reserved; and the New-York Historical Society*)

footnoted the records, by showing photographs depicting research activities that have benefitted from historical records use, or by otherwise showing how records have contributed to research. Some exhibits feature photographs of archivists assisting researchers, groups of researchers at work in the historical records program's search room, and brief commentary on researcher services available, along with examples of completed research. The objective of such exhibits, of course, is to call attention to past research as well as to engender new research.

A third category of exhibit might be called documenting the archival function. These exhibits focus on archival functions and services, such as appraisal, reference services, preservation work, or new accessions. Exhibits on archival work are challenging to develop because they can easily be uninteresting or appear self-serving. An exhibit on appraisal would need to show the archivist at work, illustrate the analytical and decision-making process, and also provide examples of the records being appraised. One on preservation might feature records illustrating the condition before and after and showing the actual work in between. One on reference would highlight the program's services and also convey to researchers an impression of available finding aids and search room rules.

Experts in the field of archival exhibits stress the need to identify a target audience or audiences and tailor the exhibit program to their interests and needs. The defined role of exhibits in the overall promotional marketing scheme is also a fundamental consideration in deciding which exhibits to develop. Selection of appropriate documents requires time and careful judgment. The items selected should have "strong documentary value and visual impact"; as a rule, it is better to select a few outstanding items rather than a larger number of less interesting ones.[15] Usually historical records are not particularly visually interesting and should, therefore, have a dramatic, engaging informational message. Archival exhibits must compete with museum exhibits and other presentations that are more attention-grabbing. In addition, it is important to realize that even the most dedicated visitors to exhibits will eventually tire from fatigue after walking and standing for too long.

Recognizing that viewers' attention spans may be relatively short, archivists should try to choose a variety of formats, for instance, letters, maps, photographs, posters, advertisements, drawings, and other historical record material and, if possible, to include three-dimensional artifacts that are related to the records. The objective is to create an exhibit that is interesting, that will catch and hold attention, and that is compact enough that people will consider all of it and not become fatigued or bored. If the exhibit has several cases, each one should present a distinct subtheme, but it should be clear how they all relate together and convey the total theme. Preparation of attractive and informative signs and captions will require considerable time and care. The captions must be concise but, at the same time, identify the document, explain its significance, interpret its message, and tie it to the rest of the exhibit.

The impact of a good exhibit can be enhanced and extended through the development of companion publications, which may range all the way from a simple listing of the documents on display to an extensive publication which reprints all the documents and explains them. The publications help interpret the exhibit, and viewers take the publications with them when they leave, continuing and extending their educational impact. Many historical records programs have also linked exhibits to other promotional efforts, such as media initiatives, open houses and tours, seminars, workshops, and lectures by experts in the fields covered by the exhibits. An exhibit, by itself or with accompanying activities, is a significant event for any historical records program. It should, therefore, be preceded by a press release and other attempts to gain media attention.

Exhibits that involve original records present conservation and security issues. Documents should be evaluated to make sure that they will not be harmed by being exhibited. Where necessary, basic conservation work, such as cleaning, mending, reinforcement, and other activities, must be carried out before the documents are exhibited. Documents should be placed in specially constructed or purchased secure cases with pick-resistant locks, and there should be adequate security, such as an alarm system or on-site guards. If security cannot be provided at an appropriate level, or if the exhibit will travel, the best approach may be to use facsimiles rather than actual documents. Facsimiles have additional advantages: they can be blown up in size for emphasis or backdrops, or they can highlight only selected excerpts from documents.

To further protect documents, air conditioning or other ventilation systems that keep relative humidity and temperature at appropriate levels are highly desirable. Significant fluctuations should be avoided if possible. Lighting is an important factor: documents should be kept out of direct sunlight or light from fluorescent lights, both of which contain ultraviolet rays that damage documents. Low levels of light are generally desirable. Some programs provide light switches that come on automatically when a viewer nears a case, or that viewers can switch on, and that go off when the viewer departs.

Special Opportunities: Working with Teachers and Students

As noted above, teachers and students should be considered as an important potential part of a historical records program's audience. There should be natural opportunities to encourage the use of historical records in connection with social studies and history courses which are part of the curriculum in most states. Archivists interested in this field may begin by reviewing educational publications and state education departments' course curricula and attending meetings of professional educational associations to learn first-hand about teachers' educational backgrounds and needs. This should be followed by meetings with local educational administrators and teachers to explore course needs and the possibilities of cooperative efforts. Archivists should not be surprised to find that teachers are busy, curricular requirements leave little time for extras, and even arranging for bus transportation from a school to a historical records program site may be a significant undertaking.

There are at least four types of potential programs that have worked well with students and teachers. The first is programs aimed at teachers themselves, to apprise them of the benefits of teaching with historical records, to demonstrate to them how to use this teaching method, and to introduce them to particular series of records that can be of most use to them. Some archival programs accomplish this through publications or special seminars or summer institutes for teachers where archivists work closely with the teachers and the teachers become familiar with the materials that are available, concentrate on sources for particular historical themes, and demonstrate how to successfully integrate historical records, and the information they contain, into classroom teaching.

A second approach is in-the-repository activities for students. These activities need to be carefully planned and organized by the teacher and the students so that they are more than field trips with little lasting impact. Worthwhile activities can include tours and presentations to the students on interesting records and on archivists' work. Students may also be given opportunities to actually study selected historical records, take notes, and extract information from them. This introduces students to the repository and its search room rules and procedures and also eases them into historical research methodology. The result may be a written student research paper, a debate among students on the conclusions that should be drawn from the historical evidence mined from the records, or a comparison of how the same event or development is presented by more than one source.

A variation on this approach would be needed in case lack of transportation funds or other factors made it impossible for students to come to the repository, or the repository could not accommodate them because of size, security, or other considerations. In these cases, the archivist might arrange to take records—or copies—to the school for study in the classroom.

A fourth approach is development of historical records packets. This involves more time, expense, and planning than other approaches, but it may have more lasting value in the sense that the packets can be used over and over. A typical packet is focused on a particular theme or event. It includes copies of documents, typescript versions of the documents to facilitate reading and discussion, presentation of themes that the documents illustrate, and activities or questions for the teachers. Document packets should be accompanied by teachers' guides that explain the background and purposes of the packet, provide historical context and background for the documents, explain why these particular items were selected, and provide advice on how to make the best use of the packets.

NOTES

1. Siri N. Espy, *Handbook of Strategic Planning for Nonprofit Organizations* (New York: Praeger, 1986), 60.
2. Ann E. Pederson and Gail Farr Casterline, *Archives and Manuscripts: Public Programs* (Chicago: Society of American Archivists, 1982).
3. Society of American Archivists, Task Force on Archives and Society, "Public Relations and the Society of American Archivists: A Report and Proposal," (n.p., typed report, January 9, 1987).
4. David B. Gracy II, "Archives and Society: The First Archival Revolution," *American Archivist* 47 (Winter 1984):7–10.
5. David B. Gracy II, "Archivists, You Are What People Think You Keep," *American Archivist* 52 (Winter 1989):73, 77.
6. Jon Anderson, "The Archivist: A Keeper of Words and Doodles Who Dreams of the Ultimate Attic," undated clipping from *Chicago Tribune* (ca. December 1986).
7. Social Research, Inc., *The Image of Archivists: Resource Allocators' Perceptions* (Chicago: Society of American Archivists, 1984), 27, ii.
8. Ibid., 45.
9. Ibid., ii, vi, v.
10. Society of American Archivists, Task Force on Goals and Priorities, *Planning for the Archival Profession* (Chicago: Society of American Archivists, 1986), v.
11. *Let the Record Show: Practical Uses for Historical Documents,* slide-tape and videotape (Albany: New York State Education Department, 1989); *Archives and You: The Benefits of Historical Records,* booklet (Albany: New York State Education Department, 1990). Both of these items were developed primarily by Judy P. Hohmann, Associate Public and Educational Programs Specialist, New York State Archives and Records Administration.

12. Pederson and Casterline, *Archives and Manuscripts: Public Programs,* 57.
13. James Gregory Bradsher and Mary Lynn Ritzenthaler, "Archival Exhibits," in Bradsher, ed., *Managing Archives and Archival Institutions* (Chicago: University of Chicago Press, 1989), 228.
14. Ibid., 230; Pederson and Casterline, *Archives and Manuscripts: Public Programs,* 10–11.
15. Bradsher and Ritzenthaler, "Archival Exhibits," 233.

11 Electronic Records: A Challenge for Archivists

Until recently, archival work concentrated mainly on paper records and other materials that could be handled and read without reliance on equipment (except in the case of microfilm, where the equipment merely magnified and projected an image). The finality of records—the fact that they represent information that is set down for a settled purpose and survives unchanged for later study—has been at the heart of archivists' claims that records reliably document the past. People act, events occur, information is fixed, recorded, and made manifest in records, and, later, the most important records are identified by archivists for continuing preservation. The process implies a sense of order, continuity, and reliability.

The volume of paper records continues to increase. As noted earlier, the United States alone each year turns out enough paper records to wallpaper the Grand Canyon more than one hundred times.[1] Use of computers has added to the avalanche of paper, confounding predictions from a few years ago about the advent of the "paperless office" era. The body of archival theory and practice described in earlier chapters in this book was developed primarily to fit records with information that is fixed and unalterable in tangible form. Archivists will continue to apply and refine their traditional approaches to fit these records. But new challenges are clearly at hand.

An Information Revolution

Modern information technology has radically altered the seemingly orderly, settled pattern of traditional recordation. During the past generation, a virtual electronic revolution has occurred with the advent and increasing use of computers and related information creation and interchange technology and telecommunications systems. The electronic representation of information has in part displaced the recording of information on paper. Archivists are swept up in one of the most fundamental changes in the creation, manipulation, and interchange of information since the invention of the printing press.

Computers are the key generators of the change; during the past decades, they have shrunk in size, increased in capacity to generate, store, and transmit information, and increased vastly in numbers. A growing variety of software has increased computers' versatility and usefulness. The capacity of personal computers has continually increased, providing for widespread dispersion of computing power to more people. On the other hand, computers can be linked together, increasing their information generating, manipulating, and sharing capacities. Office automation systems and local area networks featuring linked-together computers provide unprecedented capacity to generate and share information in electronic form. These and other technological developments have helped escalate the importance of information. So important has information become to our businesses and society as a whole that it is recognized as a commodity and strategic asset to be managed.

Management expert Peter F. Drucker has described the arrival of "the information based organization" where production workers are supplanted by "knowledge workers," information is central to corporate operations, and information managers are essential to the enterprise.[2] The book *Infotrends* asserts that information resources now rank with labor, technology, and capital as a strategic asset to be managed and deployed, that information is a "transforming resource" and an "engine of productivity improvement," and that companies need information officers to ensure its sound management.[3] The federal government, responding to the need for a changed approach, in the Paperwork Reduction Act some years ago advanced the notion of information resources management and required every federal agency to appoint an official to coordinate it. A new professional field called information management or information resources management has emerged and is expanding and becoming more specialized.

Information specialists predict that information will become even more central to Americans. "The information age will be a period in human history when information and knowledge directly shape the fabric of society. . . . Possession and control over information and knowledge will form the basis of social power and dictate the social structure."[4] Futurist Alvin Toffler has heralded the arrival of the "electronic infrastructure" in the advanced economies of the world. The new order will feature increasing numbers of people interacting with computers, more mobile computer and telecommunications devices, capacity to transform information from one medium to another (for instance, oral messages to printed form), and "the systematic spread of the new media system around the world and down through every economic layer of society." Electronic information will become central to creating wealth, controlling productivity, and to everyday work and daily life.[5]

The revolutionary changes are most evident in government and other institutions. For instance, there are now reportedly more than a million microcomputers in the federal government alone and a study in New York identified more than a thousand separate state government "information systems" (a term that is defined below).[6]

The Challenge for Archivists

Where do archivists fit in? They are trying to cope with *electronic records*—a term that lacks a settled definition but "is meant to broadly include data and information input to, manipulated by, or output from computers or computerized systems and not readable without mechanical aid." Alternate terms used include computer records, electronic data, and machine-readable records. Instead of dealing with familiar record groups and series, archivists recognize a need to deal with information systems—another term seeking a settled definition but meaning "the organized collection, processing, transmission, and dissemination of information in accordance with defined procedures, whether automated or manual."[7] An information system might include both paper based records and electronic records. A university financial information system, for instance, might include fiscal information on-line in the computer and also periodic paper-based reports.

The electronic generation of information poses many advantages from an archival and research standpoint. The information is compact, it can be readily accessed, manipulated, and used if the appropriate equipment and software are available, and it can be easily and inexpensively duplicated and disseminated. It can be queried and analyzed in ways beyond what its creators envisioned, inviting creative and imaginative research uses. Multiple users can draw simultaneously on the information and analyze and manipulate it for their own purposes. They can combine electronic information from several sources to study correlations, identify patterns, and reach statistically supported inferences that would have been impossible with traditional research in paper-based records. For instance, social security numbers are now used as a common identifier for individuals, and through that identifier it is possible to locate, link, and analyze information on individuals that appears in several databases.

But the gradual increase in the use of computers and modern information technology also poses unprecedented challenges which concern—even alarm—many archivists and researchers. A report issued by a number of national scholarly associations concluded that "the United States is in danger of losing its memory. . . . Potentially precious documents disappear as word processors erase old texts and substitute new ones with no human saying 'Stop.'" The report noted that by the mid-1970s, when computer tapes from the 1960 census first came to the attention of archivists, there were only two machines left that could read them; one was in the Smithsonian Institution and the other was in Japan! It predicted that future researchers would have disappointingly thin documentation for their studies and called for action by the National Archives and the archival profession in general to develop approaches to deal with electronic records.[8]

Archivists are searching for ways to cope with these changes. In the 1960s and 1970s, most of the electronic records consisted of computer-generated scientific and technical data. The essential challenge seemed to be appraisal, preservation, and provision for accessing these machine-readable records—primarily computer tapes and disks. Other than the complications presented by the requirements for maintaining hardware (computers) and software (the instructions to operate them) to "read" these records, archivists' approaches were similar to those used for many years for paper records. But later the level and complexities of computer and telecommunication technologies increased significantly.

Grappling with complex information systems has proven far more difficult than dealing with comparably simple early machine-readable data files. Archivists are now faced with preserving and managing complicated databases and compound documents composed of text, images, sound, graphics, and data.[9] In the government arena, state and federal agencies are placing increasing reliance on computers and electronic information systems for things like cartographic systems to produce maps, geographic information systems, legal documents, and computer systems to help forecast change and help decision makers assess policy options.[10]

Indeed, information has become so volatile and constantly changing that the traditional concept of "record" needs revision. In an electronic environment, information displayed on a screen or printed out on a form may in fact be spread over different files, databases, or even over several organizations and different locations.[11] "An electronic document is not so much a 'thing' as it is a set of relationships," one study concluded. "It is this characteristic of electronic documents that challenges traditional information science. No longer are archivists and historians working with objects but with processes. The new 'documents' are more malleable and complex than the familiar documents of the past."[12]

Beyond the increasing pervasiveness and complexity of electronic records, archivists face other issues and problems. Electronic records are essentially patterned electronic impulses with no meaning or comprehensibility unless transformed into human-readable form by equipment and software. It is these intermediary, interpretive devices and material that transform electronic impulses into understandable text, images, sound, or graphics. Therefore, archivists—and researchers who use the electronic records they collect—are dependent on the hardware and the software for the electronic records to be usable. However, technological advances and commercial considerations, not archival concerns, determine the direction and rate of information technology change, and there have been rapid and continual advances in both hardware and software. There has been some movement toward more standardization in computer systems. But the changes are not fast enough to rescue archivists from the dilemma of having to preserve, and ensure future access to, electronic information that depends on technology over which archivists have very little control.[13]

The related issue of access has many dimensions. Without appropriate hardware and software, access is impossible. While modern information technology makes it possible to manipulate and disseminate information easily, it may also increase the barriers to using it. As one expert put it,

> The more sophisticated technologies become, the more educated the accessor of the technology will have to be. . . . Paper history requires literacy. To find your history on a disk or tape requires yet another form of literacy. Today, almost anyone can read Civil War rolls in the [National] Archives; but they will not be able to access the information about our army in Grenada. We are indirectly creating a class of people who will not have access to their history.[14]

The access issue also includes concern over confidentiality of sensitive personal information, trade secrets, information that is restricted because of government security reasons, and other information that, for one reason or another, should not be disclosed. Restricting access is relatively easy for paper files; they can simply be withheld from researchers, or personally identifying information or other confidential information physically blocked out. Such work is often labor intensive, but it can be carried out with assurance that the information restriction will be effective. Restricting and monitoring access becomes much more difficult in an electronic environment. This stems in part from the ability of computers to link data from two or more databases, thereby compiling what amounts to a new record. This ability is a boon for the researcher who, for instance, wishes to link census data with educational and welfare information for a study of the connections among demographics, education, and poverty.

But the same ability can also serve the person who is intent on electronic snooping or compiling information for proscribed commercial gain or personal reasons. Many of the confidentiality and access issues need to be confronted before the archivist accessions the records. In some cases, it is possible to use the computer to suppress or delete particular identifying information. But in many cases, the solutions are not that clearcut, and archivists of the future may be torn between guiding researchers to electronic information and fulfilling an obligation to prevent disclosure of some of it.

Unless preventative safeguards are built into the system, information in electronic form can be easily changed without leaving any trace of what came before. This permits easy destruction of documentation, making it difficult or impossible later on to analyze the developments, processes, and steps to a final product, for instance, the drafts that led up to a final policy document. In a setting of "electronic pathways of information exchange . . . the documentary history of . . . policy formulation vanishes with the push of a button."[15]

Electronic information flows instantaneously from one computer system to another. For instance, social services data generated in a Pennsylvania county yesterday may be in the state's central database today, tomorrow be combined with information from other counties for transmission to Washington, and next week may form part of the basis for Federal policy analysis and formulation. Where and how will the "archival record" be collected and preserved? The challenge for archivists is to find ways to collect drafts or retain a semblance of a documentation trail, in paper or electronic form, and to develop strategies for capturing the most revealing and usable information from a complex electronic flow.

Electronic information is stored in a variety of formats that are temporary and fragile. Computer floppy disks, hard disks, and magnetic tape all use technology that magnetizes particles and that requires specific equipment to interpret the magnetic configuration and present the information in an intelligible way. None of this media is considered archival in the sense that it can be expected to endure for a long period of time; most of it is regarded as being reliable for the retention of information for only twenty-five years or less under the best of conditions. This means that information on magnetic media must be checked repeatedly and transferred to new media periodically to ensure its survival.

This media is also sensitive to dirt, external magnetic interference, and physical contact that can obliterate information. Some newer technologies, such as optical disks, use different information recording and retrieval approaches and have attractive features of relatively low-cost, high-density storage and ready access. But none of the new media can be counted upon to last for the long periods of time associated with archival preservation. Furthermore, of course, all of it requires appropriate equipment, storage, and handling.

The Archival Response

Archivists have studied the implications of electronic records through committees, task forces, and special projects, and have begun to evolve a series of responses. Their emphasis on careful appraisal and systematic management of information with continuing value may seem out of place or incompatible with information specialists whose watchwords seem to be: create, transmit, and expunge. In a paper-based environment, people seemed more likely to keep and file documents; in an electronics-based environment, there may be less inclination to save.

Archivists are developing a new style and role as advocates or ombudsmen for information of continuing value. They are reexamining some fundamental archival principles. For instance, the concept of record as something that embodies fixed and recorded information is difficult to apply where information is modified again and again without residual evidence of the changes. As Charles Dollar of the National Archives and Records Administration has pointed out, this concept seems outmoded in light of

> relational databases, geographic information systems, and hypermedia where bits and pieces of information may be selected from an organization-wide database and incorporated into an electronic document sent to someone. This electronic document represents only a partial view of the database. In fact, it may exist only as a set of retrieval instructions that a computer generated in response to the person preparing the document.

An emerging redefinition of record avoids this problem by shifting the emphasis from physical form or content to transaction—any electronic activity which documents an official transaction should be considered to be a record. This promising proposal needs further study and elaboration to determine whether this new definition can and should supplant the traditional one.[16]

Likewise, "original order" ceases to have coherent meaning in an electronic environment. Charles Dollar points out that "because electronic records do not exist as discrete physical entities and because the actual storage of the electronic signals that comprise a record seldom bear any relationship to a record that is displayed on a monitor or printed out, the physical location of the bits and pieces of electronic records neither requires not carries intellectual content." Dollar adds, however, that it is possible to determine and document logical relations within information systems. The concept of provenance, another fundamental archival precept, is also undermined. Users may retrieve information from a consolidated database without knowing where the information originated, where it is stored, who created it, or when it was most recently modified or updated. Provenance becomes even murkier when the information is continually updated or when several databases are linked together. Archivists have not yet developed a substitute for the concept of provenance in an electronic setting.[17]

Some archivists advocate a far-reaching approach that involves a fundamental transformation of their profession to that of a species of information manager or at least a reorientation that would make archivists and information managers close working partners.

> We must cease to act as archivists in the traditional sense; we must become information specialists, drawing upon a wide array of automated tools and analytical techniques in serving our constituents. [Archivists must] move from acting as the passive recipients of documents to a more active role in the creation, distribution, and preservation of information.[18]

Says another change advocate:

> Information cries out to be moved and merged, and the popular emphasis is no longer on history but on heritage with all its multi-media applications. . . . We must be prepared to abandon the concept of archives as bodies of "historical" records over against the so-called active records which are put to sleep during their dormant years prior to salvation or extinction. . . . The archivist as intermediary, preparing intractable historical records, long since abandoned by administrators, for painstaking and protracted research by the scholar with the help of manual retrieval systems, is no longer needed for the automated record. . . Now is the time for archivists to be present at the creation of documents, to ensure that they are designed not only to serve immediate administrative ends but also administrative/historical research for policy planning and development.[19]

This type of advocacy for a significantly revised role has brought counter appeals for caution and adherence to traditional missions involving historical documentation. Some archivists fear loss of identity and sense of mission if the archival profession is merged into an undifferentiated information management field. Archivists' role as guardians of culture and agents of history will diminish if the archival function is relegated to a corner of the large and growing information world. In the end, archivists will need to reach a compromise that retains their role as appraisers and identifiers of important information and, at the same time, makes them more active partners in the creation and management of information.

Archivists are also trying to participate in and encourage the development of organization or institution-wide policies that takes archival considerations and concerns into account. Policy declarations are needed with the force of top administration behind them that carefully define records and information and assign responsibility for the identification of that with continuing value—in effect, the equivalent of archival records. One of the best is the government-wide policy framework developed for the Canadian government by the Treasury Board of Canada. It is the government's policy to:

> Manage all information as a corporate resource to support effective decision-making, meet operational requirements, and protect the legal, financial, and other interests of the government and the public; make the widest possible use of information within the government by ensuring that it is organized to facilitate access by those who require it [and] . . . identify and conserve information holdings that serve to reconstruct the evolution of policy and program decisions or have historical or archival importance and to ensure that such information is organized in a manner to be readily available for the study of decision-making in government and other educational purposes which explain the historical role of the federal government in Canadian society.

Governmental agencies are further charged to "ensure that records of enduring value which document the evolution of government policies, programs, and major decisions, are maintained; and identify and document projects, programs, and policies sufficiently to ensure continuity in the management of government institutions and the preservation of a historical record." The National Archives of Canada has statutory power to control "the destruction and disposal of the information holdings of government institutions . . . and the transfer of information of historic or archival importance to the National Archives."[20] Several states in the United States have begun moving toward comprehensive information policy statements that will, it is hoped, take archival needs into account.

One other strategic approach under development is what might be called early intervention. In a paper-based environment, archivists were largely unconcerned with creation of records; they appraised them later in their life cycle or even at the end of that cycle. In an electronic records environment, records created on tapes or disks are often lost or erased before anyone can intervene to appraise or save them.

Under the emerging strategy, archivists would assert an interest in working with the originators of electronic information systems.

This unprecedented role requires archivists to possess basic computer literacy skills and an understanding of information system design. The archivist participates in system development and ensures that appropriate standards are met and that the capacity to create and retain particular information for historical and other research purposes is included. For instance, office automation systems with likely long-term value should include needed documentation, i.e., name of creator, date of creation and transmission, office of origin, filing codes, document identification, security/access classification, links to previous documents and systems, and subject keywords.[21]

Archivists would reach beyond their roles as curators and custodians and begin to play "quasi-archival functions within administrative departments" to identify information of continuing value.[22] Put another way, archivists would in effect represent future users and would specify user requirements that would be addressed by systems designers. This bold new approach assumes that archivists can assert enough influence to get themselves included in information system development. In order to do this, they need to advance arguments that their role is beneficial for the documentation purposes of the parent institution, not just that it serves the long-term cause of history.

Archivists are also developing a related notion that is variously called information accountability or information stewardship. According to this emerging concept, people who create information using computers and other advanced technology are, to a significant degree, responsible for its management, including identifying that with enduring value and ensuring that it is maintained in accord with archival appraisal decisions. Such an approach, in effect, makes all information creators into adjunct archivists, and provides for sharing of responsibility for ensuring the survival of important information. It recognizes the fact that archivists can't be everywhere at once and that their influence is limited. By the time archivists have the opportunity to appraise complicated information systems, it may be too late because the most desirable information from an archival standpoint has already been deleted or changed, or the essential documentation needed to make sense of the system is lost. Development of a sense of corporate responsibility would help meet this problem.

Some archivists are ready to go further and conclude that the best approach is to convince the automated data processing departments of originating offices and agencies to themselves retain invaluable electronic information, since they have the expertise, and presumably can and will maintain the necessary hardware and software needed to do so. In this scenario, the archivist's role as custodian of electronic archives would be transformed to that of advisor, standard setter, and ombudsman. Under this scenario, Madison University's financial management office might retain information identified as having continuing value, but it would follow recommendations or requirements from the university archives. Archivists might also concentrate on cooperative development of "metadata" systems—sophisticated resource directories that describe information systems in order to facilitate access and use. They would become the guides through electronic pathways to desired information. The traditional notion of the archives as a repository gives way to a new service function.

Archivists are also turning to the development of necessary standards. The National Archives and Records Administration is attempting to encourage agencies to transfer permanent computer files in a hardware and software independent format in the hope of being able to maintain and access them in the future with a minimum of new hardware and software.[23] But some experts question whether that can be done as a practical matter and they are concerned that it will become increasingly difficult in the future. The challenge is to "be able to transfer electronic records from the hardware and software systems that are in use today to new computing environments as they are developed."[24] This requires the development of standards and protocols, something that archivists certainly cannot do by fiat. It will take concerted action via professional associations and involving government, manufacturers, vendors, and users. The processes are lengthy, intensive, and costly, and thus far the interests of archivists and the research community they serve and to a degree represent, have not been sufficiently articulated or heeded.

Identifying Electronic Records with Continuing Value

There is no surefire approach to identifying electronic records with continuing value. The most advanced archival approaches fall under three headings: consider electronic records as part of information systems whenever possible; carefully appraise them for informational and evidential value; and consider technical characteristics that affect the usability of the information.

Archival proponents of early intervention believe archivists can assist with design of information systems. At the same time, as a leading expert in the field of appraisal of electronic records has pointed out, archivists can and should appraise electronic

A Checklist of Considerations for the Preservation
of Archival Records in Electronic Formats

There are several considerations that need to be taken into account in planning to preserve archival records in electronic formats. They are summarized below. The list was developed for electronic information systems in governmental settings, but it has wider applicability to electronic records in general. From National Association of Government Archives and Records Administrators, A New Age: Electronic Information Systems, State Governments, and the Preservation of the Archival Record (*Lexington, Ky.: Council of State Governments, 1991*), 10.

Representation for archival concerns on a state information policy coordinating body.

An information directory or locator system that provides a full picture of state information systems and information holdings.

Clear guidelines about the legal status of public records in electronic formats.

Adequate legal authority for the archival agency to set standards and requirements for the preservation of archival records, regardless of format.

Incorporation of archival concerns in government-wide standards for information systems.

Program manager involvement in the development and implementation of records disposition decisions.

Early consideration of archival requirements in system planning, design, and evaluation to ensure identification and preservation of archival records.

Early transfer to appropriate, secure storage of records of long-term value.

Complete and accurate documentation of systems that produce archival records.

Archival storage conditions appropriate for the particular medium on which information is recorded.

Periodic testing of stored records to guard against deterioration.

Timely migration of archival records to new systems or new formats to ensure that records are readable with available hardware and software.

Accessibility for research (unless restricted), regardless of where or how the records are stored.

High priority consideration for electronic records concerns by the administrators of archival programs.

Archival capability to identify, describe, preserve, and make assessible electronic records.

records as part of information systems. "Systems designs, diagrams of information flows, system specifications, and other documentation of information systems are rich sources for archivists to begin to understand the background, purposes, and organization of modern records."[25] Information systems may contain enough information that they constitute a sizeable portion of the documentation of a given topic or development, enabling appraisal decisions to be made in a broad context.

Electronic records appraisal involves a search for informational and evidential values and anticipation of research uses. It is preferable for appraisal to take place within the contexts of documentation strategies and in light of a sound collections policy, just as it is for records in older formats. Therefore, in assessing the importance of electronic records, archivists particularly consider the informational content of the records and the probability of their use by researchers. One key question is whether researchers will want to manipulate the data in ways not already carried out by the people who produced it in the first place. If the answer is no, then it may suffice to preserve printouts, reports, and other outputs of the electronic system. But if the answer is yes or probably, then archivists are likely to decide to save the detailed electronic records. The National Archives and Records Administration suggests that electronic records that document significant agency missions and programs warrant permanent preservation. A NARA publication provides these examples:

Electronic records that replace records scheduled as permanent in another medium.

Automated indexes to permanent records.

Unique and important scientific and technical data resulting from observations of natural events or phenomena or from controlled laboratory or field experiments.

Management data that have government-wide coverage or significance.

Socioeconomic data on such topics as trade, education, health, or behavior.

Natural resources data related to land, water, minerals, or wildlife.

Data that document military or civilian operations during times of war, civil emergency, or natural disaster.

Political or judicial data related to such topics as elections, special investigations, or court proceedings.

Cartographic data used to map the earth's surface, other planetary bodies, or the atmosphere.

National security and international relations data that document such activities as strategic or foreign policy assessments, foreign public opinion, or international negotiations.[26]

There are several technical concerns and considerations that affect the selection of electronic records:

Readability and usability. The records must be in good enough physical condition that they can be accessed and used. Determining this may require actually using a computer to read the tape or disk.

Software dependence. If the records require particular software to be used and read, then that software must be transferred with the records or made available at the archival program, or else the records must be transferred to a format that does not require special software.

Hardware dependence. Some electronic records require particular computer equipment in order to be read and used. If this equipment is obsolete or unavailable, then the records must be reformatted so that they can be read and used with available equipment.

Access provisions and restrictions. Access may need to be restricted when personal identifying information, such as names, addresses, or numbers associated with individuals, are included. It may be possible to obtain a "disclosure-free" version of the records which suppresses the personal identifiers or which summarizes the information from a given subgroup within the records. A second type of access complication may occur with records produced as part of a grant or contract or purchased in the course of normal business. The actual data in the records may remain the property of someone else unless clear title is obtained. Another access issue may arise when information is available only through a proprietary software package. Reformatting the information into a software-independent version overcomes this restriction.[27]

Documentation of the records. Two types of documentation are essential if the electronic records are to be appropriately described and serviced by archivists, and accessed and used by researchers. The first type of documentation includes record layout and record code books, which have technical data on the layout of information in the records. The second type of information is more descriptive, and includes such information as the purpose of the system that produced the records, data input and sources, output (reports, tables, correspondence, and other items that the system produced), informational content, hardware and software used, restrictions on access, if any, and other information that will be helpful in interpreting and using the records.[28]

Costs and resources. Costs may include the expense of the tape or other format for storage and for creating a back-up file. Staff time and technical expertise may be needed to reformat the records, to locate, correct, or reconstruct needed documentation, or to salvage deteriorated or damaged media. In addition, as discussed below, programs need appropriate storage environments for continued preservation of electronic records.

Applying the approaches outlined above is not an easy matter. One example that has received widespread attention is a case study of New York State criminal history records.[29] The Division of Criminal Justice Services maintains a central computerized criminal history system with information on criminal offenders, and one of its offices uses the information in the system to produce data files for

Optical Media Technology: An Emerging Challenge for Archivists

Optical imaging technology is becoming an increasingly important means of generating, storing, and transmitting information. As noted in chapter 8, this technology is not yet suitable for copying archival records because its longevity cannot be predicted with certainty. However, archivists recognize a need to develop approaches to deal with this increasingly popular technology. A study by the National Archives and Records Administration recommended five objectives for government officials who are contemplating use of optical media systems and are concerned with long-term longevity and access of information. Much of the advice in the report is general rather than detailed and prescriptive, which is typical of archival approaches to emerging technological issues. It also recognizes that custodians of information must anticipate and prepare for further technological developments. Adapted from National Archives and Records Administration and National Association of Government Archives and Records Administrators, Digital Imaging and Optical Media Storage Systems: Guidelines for State and Local Government Agencies *(Albany: National Association of Government Archives and Records Administrators, 1991), Executive Summary.*

Maintain the long-term usability of digitally stored information. Long-term usability of digitally stored information, including both scanned document images and descriptive index data, will be achieved by implementing a sound policy for migrating data to future technology generations, adhering to well-documented image file header formats, and monitoring media degradation through the use of disk error detections and correction codes. System managers should create the technical and administrative infrastructure required to implement relevant technology standards as they are developed.

Ensure the quality of digital images captured through an electronic conversion process. Ensuring the quality of digital images means exercising continuous control over three processes: conversion of the original image to digital data; enhancement of the digital image, if necessary; and compression/decompression of the digital data for storage and retrieval. Quality inspection, either at the scanner workstation or as a follow-up task, should compare the original documents to the captured electronic images. A density of 200 dots per inch (dpi) should be employed for office documents; higher densities, between 300 and 600 dpi, should be used for more detailed information. The

chosen density should be validated with tests on actual documents.

Provide for the ongoing functionality of system hardware and software components. Ensuring that digital image data stored on optical media continues to serve the functions for which they were intended involves a long-term commitment to an open systems architecture and an approach to component upgrading and data transfer that guarantees the interoperability of current technologies with those yet to be developed. Administrators should require the use of Write-Once-Read-Many (WORM) times technology for records of long-term value or ensure that read/write privileges are carefully controlled and that an audit trail of rewrites is maintained. Unless there are program reasons for high density on a single disk, administrators should follow market trends, which now point toward a preference for 5.25 inch disks.

Limit the deterioration of optical storage media. Ensuring the long-term stability of optical media is a matter of specifying a storage/recording technology and protecting the media to minimize damage and abuse from handling and adverse environmental conditions. Although optical media appear to be more durable and stable than the hardware and software required to maintain access, vendor claims regarding durability must be carefully examined; a pre-write shelf life of at least five years and a minimum post-write life of twenty years should be required. Since optical media are not immune to hostile storage environments, it is prudent to store them in areas with stable room temperatures and relative humidity. In addition, optical media drive systems should not be located in environments with high levels of airborne particulate matter.

Anticipate and plan for further technological developments. Digital imaging and optical media applications cannot solve access problems stemming from inefficient manual or computerized information systems and practices; indeed, these applications may exacerbate existing deficiencies. Administrators who have taken advantage of a newly introduced optical media technology to reassess office operating procedures appear more likely to maximize the benefits of increased access while reducing administrative disruptions and subsequent costs.

Ensuring long-term access to records of enduring value stored on optical media systems involves more, however, than image quality, system functionality, and media stability. A commitment to digital imaging of information and its storage on optical disk links the agency to a technological evolution that it does not control. Administrators must monitor technological trends; plan for systematic maintenance, upgrade, and eventual migration to newer technologies; use existing and emerging standards; support the development of data interchange standards; and adopt prudent preservation measures in the interim.

It is the responsibility of agency administrators, archivists, and records managers, working together, rather than manufacturers and vendors, to ensure that policies and procedures governing the care of records of long-term value are created and consistently implemented.

---

research and statistical analysis. The project explored the issues of collection of data from multiple sources and the interrelationships among information systems, preservation of and access to information that is closed or restricted, software dependence, costs, and other technical considerations. The analysis began with an examination of the historical development and objectives of the system and proceeded with detailed analysis of data acquisition, data processing, information dissemination, the handling of sealed cases and juveniles, technical facets, including the hardware and software environment, and the relationship between information maintained in electronic form and that available in paper records. The archivist also considered research use by the creating agency and potential use by outside researchers, with the attendant issues of confidentiality. He recommended the downloading of selected data to a software-independent tape file and transfer to the State Archives after a set number of years, further discussions to deal with appraisal of other information and issues of confidentiality and access, discussion of how to improve documentation in the future, and design of a new

Looking to the Future: Research Issues in Electronic Records

Archival approaches to electronic records are unsettled because many issues need further research and analysis. Until that research and analysis is completed, archivists will need to continue to modify traditional practices, improvise, and adapt to changing technologies as best they can. A report issued by the National Historical Publications and Records Commission, based on a conference of nationally recognized experts, identified ten research issues in the area of electronic records.

1. What functions and data are required to manage electronic records in order to meet archival requirements? Do data requirements and functions vary for different types of automated applications?

2. What are the technological, conceptual, and economic implications of capturing and retaining data, descriptive information, and contextual information in electronic form from a variety of applications?

3. How can software-dependent data objects be retained for future use?

4. How can data dictionaries, information resource directory systems, and other metadata systems be used to support electronic records management and archival requirements?

5. What archival requirements have been addressed in major systems development projects, and why?

6. What policies best address archival concerns for the identification, retention, preservation, and research use of electronic records?

7. What functions and activities should be present in electronic records programs and how should they be evaluated?

8. What incentives can contribute to creator and user support for electronic records management concerns?

9. What barriers have prevented archivists from developing and implementing archival electronic records programs?

10. What do archivists need to know about electronic records?

The report noted that the order in which the questions are addressed is important. Specifically, progress on the first three questions should precede major projects to address the last seven questions. This is because the first three project categories will define the requirements of archival electronic records programs; explore the conceptual, economic, and technological constraints on the long-term retention of electronic records; and establish criteria against which to measure the effectiveness of policies, methods, and programs.

The report also identified three other categories of activities that the archival community needs to undertake in order to successfully address archival issues in the area of electronic records, and where the Commission would be interested in providing grant support:

Analysis. Projects that analyze the nature and significance of electronic records management problems, especially to determine how these problems affect specific constituencies (e.g., historians, the press, scientists) and the general public. Such projects could result in white papers and other products intended to increase awareness of electronic records problems and build support for effective programs.

Advocacy. Projects that would result in initiatives for organizing, coordinating, attracting, funding, and providing leadership for electronic records management research and program development. Projects might include a feasibility study for a national institution or development of effective mechanisms to raise general awareness about electronic records issues.

Action. Challenge grants to institutions to establish basic archival electronic records capabilities and to launch programs for effective management of archival electronic records in their jurisdictions. A greater number of archivists need to gain experience in preserving archival information in electronic form for the profession to go forward in developing more sophisticated methods to handle increasingly complex technologies. Moreover, there is a pressing need for the preservation of electronic data that archivists already know how to preserve. . . .

From *Research Issues in Electronic Records* (St. Paul, Minn.: Minnesota Historical Society for the National Historical Publications and Records Commission, 1991), v, 6.

---

system for creation of criminal history files. This short vignette provides some notion of the complexities of appraising information systems that include significant information in electronic form.

Preserving Electronic Records

Many of the general preservation practices discussed in chapter 8 pertain to electronic records. Computer tapes and disks are not regarded as long-term storage media. There are no generally recognized industry standards that guarantee their durability or lifespan. Therefore, it is necessary to periodically inspect the media to identify any deterioration and to copy electronic records at least once a decade, or more frequently if necessary, to prevent the physical loss of information. Computer tapes should be stored under secure conditions with carefully controlled temperatures (60 to 70 degree Fahrenheit range) and relative humidity (35 to 45 percent range). Fluctuations in either temperature or humidity should be avoided if possible. The storage area should be clean and free from dust and dirt and, for obvious reasons, magnetic media should be insulated against strong electric or magnetic fields. Archivists must be particularly careful to keep food and drink away from electronic records; one spill can wipe out much information. Unauthorized access to electronic records should not be allowed because people can enter commands that can change or delete information.[30]

NOTES

1. Alvin Toffler, *Power Shift: Knowledge, Wealth, and Violence at the Edge of the 21st Century* (New York: Bantam Books, 1990), 88.
2. Peter F. Drucker, "The Coming of the New Organization," *Harvard Business Review* 66 (January/February 1988):45–53.

3. Donald A. Marchand and F. Woody Horton, *Infotrends* (New York: John Wiley, 1986), 1–27.

4. Richard A. V. Diener, "Information Management: An Application for Information Science," *Journal of the American Society for Information Science* 15 (August/September 1989):17.

5. Toffler, *Power Shift,* chapter 23 and passim.

6. *Federal Computer News* 4 (September 17, 1990):1; New York State Archives and Records Administration, *A Strategic Plan for Managing and Preserving Electronic Records in New York State Government: Final Report of the Special Media Records Project* (Albany: New York State Education Department, 1988), 5.

7. Wisconsin Public Records and Forms Board, "Statewide Information Records Policy," October 23, 1989, 1; National Archives and Records Administration, *Managing Electronic Records* (Washington: National Archives and Records Administration, 1990), G-9.

8. Committee on the Records of Government, *Report* (Washington, 1985), 9–10.

9. National Historical Publications and Records Commission, *Electronic Records Issues: A Report to the Commission* (Washington: National Archives and Records Administration, 1990), 5.

10. Margaret Hedstrom and Alan S. Kowlowitz, "Meeting the Challenge of Machine-Readable Records: A State Archives Perspective," *Reference Services Review* 1–2 (1988):32.

11. Charles M. Dollar and Thomas E. Weir, "Archival Administration, Records Management, and Computer Data Exchange Standards: An Intersection of Practices," unpublished paper, 1989, 3.

12. Panel of the National Academy of Public Administration, *The Effects of Electronic Recordkeeping on the Historical Record of the U.S. Government* (Washington: National Academy of Public Administration, 1989), 31.

13. National Historical Publications and Records Commission, *Electronic Records Issues,* 3.

14. Panel of the National Academy of Public Administration, *The Effects of Electronic Recordkeeping on the Historical Record of the U.S. Government,* 44.

15. Richard Kesner, "Automated Information Management: Is There a Role for the Archivist in the Office of the Future?" *Archivaria* 19 (Winter 1984–1985):166.

16. Charles M. Dollar, "The Impact of Information Technologies on Archival Principles and Practices: Some Considerations," unpublished paper delivered at the University of Macerata, Macerata, Italy, September 5, 1990, 12–13.

17. Ibid., 14–18.

18. Kesner, "Automated Information Management," 164.

19. Hugh Taylor, "Information Ecology and the Archives of the 1980s," *Archivaria* 18 (Summer 1984):30.

20. Treasury Board of Canada, *Management of Government Information Holdings* (Ottawa: Treasury Board of Canada, 1989), 3, 7, and 18.

21. National Archives and Records Administration, "Managing Electronic Records: An Information Package," unpublished draft paper, 1989.

22. Taylor, "Information Ecology," 30.

23. National Archives and Records Administration, "Managing Electronic Records," 26.

24. Hedstrom and Kowlowitz, "Meeting the Challenge of Machine Readable Records," 34.

25. Margaret Hedstrom, "New Appraisal Techniques: The Effect of Theory on Practice," *Provenance* 7 (Fall 1989):17.

26. National Archives and Records Administration, "Managing Electronic Records," 23–25.

27. Bruce I. Ambacher, "Managing Machine Readable Archives," in James Gregory Bradsher, ed., *Managing Archives and Archival Institutions* (Chicago: University of Chicago Press, 1989), 130–131.

28. National Archives and Records Administration, "Managing Electronic Records," 15–17.

29. Alan Kowlowitz, *Archival Appraisal of Online Information Systems* v. 2, no. 3 (Pittsburgh: Archival and Museum Informatics, 1988).

30. National Archives and Records Administration, "Managing Electronic Records", 30–31; Sidney B. Geller, *Care and Handling of Computer Magnetic Storage Media* (Washington: National Bureau of Standards, 1983), passim.

Delineation of Archival Roles

Archivists play several interrelated roles as they carry out their work of identifying, preserving, arranging, describing, and making available records of enduring value. In preparation for the examination for Certified Archivist, a group of experienced archivists developed a statement of the "domains" of archival work, an indication of the tasks involved for each domain, and a description of the types and levels of knowledge that archivists need to carry out the work. While the statement is not an official or definitive statement of "professional archivist," it is an excellent overview of the nature of modern archival work.

The statement, reprinted below, is from Society of American Archivists *Newsletter* (January 1989): 6–8 (© 1989, reprinted with permission from The Society of American Archivists).

Society of American Archivists
Role Delineation

PREAMBLE

These test specifications outline seven major domains of archival practice, as well as a more detailed series of task and knowledge statements. Together these elements delineate commonly accepted duties and responsibilities that professional archivists perform as a part of their work. This document assumes that individuals seeking certification recognize that (a) their professional practice is performed within the context of an institutional mission and is directed to the achievement of goals consistent with that mission, and (b) their professional practice has an ongoing effect on the emergence and evolution of that overall mission and its associated goals.

In addition, although those seeking certification do not necessarily control how archival policies relating to activities such as acquisition, access, preservation, and security are set, it is also assumed that archivists have an understanding of how the elements contained in such policies are important in carrying out in a professional manner the tasks specified below.

Each of the seven major domains is comprised of task statements that outline the duties included within each domain, as well as knowledge statements that describe generally what archivists need to know in order to complete each of the tasks. Preceding the domains is a listing of General Knowledge Statements that are applicable to several or all of the seven areas.

As it is used hereafter, the term "document(s)" means personal papers, manuscripts, organizational records (current and noncurrent), and government archives, and refers to all the various media (ie. print, electronic, photographic) on which information is preserved.

The percentage appearing in the title line of each domain represents the relative importance, as ranked by the role delineation working group, of that domain within the broader scope of archival work. The parenthetical figure following each task statement relates to the above percentage, and represents the group's ranking of that task's relative importance within the domain.

GENERAL KNOWLEDGE STATEMENTS

Archivists know and can apply knowledge about:

K-1 ● the impact of cultural, economic, political, and technological factors on the evolution and characteristics of documents and their management;

K-2 ● trends in the nature of current research in archives;

K-3 ● the origins, development, and current definitions of archival principles, methods, terminology, and institutions;

K-4 ● similarities and differences between the organization and administration of archives and manuscript collections;

K-5 ● the physical characteristics of documentary media and how these characteristics influence the content of documents;

K-6 ● archival functions and standard archival practices appropriate for different forms of documentary media;

K-7 ● standards and accepted professional practices that apply to archival work, including their rationalimplications;

K-8 ● the concept of the life cycle of records ;

K-9 ● the relationship between accepted professional practices and institutional applications of these practices;

K-10 ● the interrelationships among such core archival functions such as appraisal, description, preservation, and reference and how these influence the administration of document collections;

K-11 ● the different institutional settings in which archives may exist, and the implications of where an archives is placed within a particular institution.

Domain 1 - SELECTION OF DOCUMENTS (17%)

Task 1
● Identify sources of documents by researching subjects, individuals, organizations, and such activities as may produce or provide documents appropriate for acquisition. (2.7)

Task 2
● Establish, maintain, and keep a record of communication(s) with creators and/or potential donors of documents. (2.3)

Task 3
● Determine by survey and eaxamination those characteristics pertinent to the acquisition of documents, such as form, quantity, availability, and informational content of documents. (3.1)

Task 4
● Make retention recommendations concerning documents by appraising such characteristics as legal, fiscal, administrative, evidential, and informational value. (5.8)

Task 5
● Implement disposition recommendations through such legal instruments of transfer as schedules, deeds of gift, purchase, and deposit agreements. (3.1)

KNOWLEDGE STATEMENTS

Archivists know and can apply knowledge about:

K-12 ● how information about the holdings and acquisition policies of archival repositories relates to the selection of documents;

K-13 ● techniques for surveying and conducting research about the location of possible archival documents;

SAA Role Delineation

K-14 ● the nature of record-keeping practices for public, private, and individual archival documents;

K-15 ● how to find information pertaining to the role and history of document-creating sources;

K-16 ● factors that should be considered when defining collecting areas and developing an institutional collection policy;

K-17 ● solicitation and negotiation techniques, as well as ways of educating records creators about the importance of preserving archival documents;

K-18 ● policies, regulations, procedures, and legal instruments relating to accessioning and other forms of records transfer;

K-19 ● the archival concept of multiple values, including evidential, informational, legal, and monetary values;

K-20 ● the past and potential uses of records.

K-21 ● sampling and scheduling techniques;

Domain 2 - ARRANGEMENT and DESCRIPTION OF DOCUMENTS (17%)

Task 1
● Analyze the existing arrangement and description of documents and plan for any further arrangement and description that may be necessary. (5.0)

Task 2
● Implement an arrangement plan to either establish or perfect the manner in which documents are arranged. (3.8)

Task 3
● Implement a description plan that includes (a.) creating such appropriate finding aids as guides, inventories, registers, series descriptions, folder lists, and calendars, and (b.) disseminating descriptive information in reading rooms, through publications, and by using electronic data bases. (8.2)

KNOWLEDGE STATEMENTS
Archivists know and can apply knowledge about:

K-22 ● the corollary principles of provenance and original order

K-23 ● the history and range of filing practices;

K-24 ● the importance of access and retrieval when making arrangement and description decisions;

K-25 ● the concept of five levels of arrangement;

K-26 ● the impact of technology on archival descriptive practices;

K-27 ● levels, types, and components of finding aids;

K-28 ● such standards as the MARC format, Anglo American Cataloging Rules--Second Edition (AACR2), and Library of Congress Subject Headings (LCSH).

Domain 3 - REFERENCE SERVICES AND ACCESS TO DOCUMENTS (17%)

Task 1
● Define the informational needs of users by analyzing their requests and providing consultation. (5.1)

Task 2
● Determine appropriate action(s) regarding user requests by relating them to available resources, access policies, and other pertinent factors. (6.4)

Task 3
● Make an appropriate response to user requests by providing access to or- iginal documents, making copies, supplying information, making referrals, or denying the request for information. (5.5)

KNOWLEDGE STATEMENTS
Archivists know and can apply knowledge about:

K-29 ● the issues and components of archival reference services, including policies and procedures governing access, reading room policies, appropriate equipment, and user services;

K-30 ● laws and ethical principles governing access and confidentiality;

K-31 ● research strategies of historians, social scientists, genealogists, and other major users of archives and manuscripts in order to assist these user groups;

K-32 ● appropriate reference strategies based upon holdings, format, and user needs;

K-33 ● the subject areas documented by their institution's holdings;

K-34 ● accepted practices for safeguarding archival documents while they are being used.

Domain 4 - PRESERVATION AND PROTECTION OF DOCUMENTS (17%)

Task 1
● Analyze the current physical condition of documents and determine appropriate preservation actions and priorities. (3.7)

Task 2
● Make and implement decisions about reformatting, handling techniques, appropriate laboratory treatments, phased conservation, and referral to technical experts. (3.7)

Task 3
● Ensure correct storage of documents through such means as using proper containers and shelving, and by maintaining acceptable environmental controls (3.9)

Task 4
● Ensure the security of documents from damage, destruction, theft, and other forms of loss. (3.6)

Task 5
● Prepare and implement procedures for disaster prevention, reaction, and recovery. (2.1)

KNOWLEDGE STATEMENTS
An archivist knows and can apply knowledge about:

K-35 ● supplies, storage equipment, and environment standards;

K-36 ● the causes and consequences of the deterioration of paper

SAA Role Delineation

and other forms of documents;

K-37 ● the elements of preservation management and the components of a preservation plan for an archival repository, including disaster preparedness, feasible in-house operations, and services available through outside vendors;

K-38 ● when to preserve archival documents in their original form and when to replace the originals with microform reproductions, with photocopies, or by using some other reformatting medium;

K-39 ● the range of preservation actions and the application of each for different documentary media.

Domain 5 -
OUTREACH AND PROMOTION OF DOCUMENTARY COLLECTIONS (10%)

Task 1
● Promote the use of documents by identifying potential users and uses, by analyzing and describing the benefits of use, and by utilizing public and educational programs. (3.4)
Task 2
● Develop an understanding of and support for the archival program among resource allocators, key constituents, and allied professional groups. (3.6)
Task 3
● Participate in interpretive programs that draw directly on records to support such activities as exhibitions, conferences, publications, and editorial projects. (3.0)

KNOWLEDGE STATEMENTS

An archivist knows and can apply knowledge about:

K-40 ● the range of uses for archival documents, as well as the benefits of such use, and can express this information to potential users;

K-41 ● the different means, such as publicity, educational programs, exhibitions, publications, and public presentation, that can be employed to communicate with potential users supporters, collaborators, resource allocators, and the public;

K-42 ● the potentially important sources of influence whose support may benefit the archival program;

K-43 ● how to interpret or obtain expertise to interpret information in documents for the enlightment of different audiences through exhibitions, publications, and similar programs.

Domain 6 -
PROGRAM ASSESSMENT OF ARCHIVES (6%)

Task 1
● Participate in assessing one's own program by (a.) measuring and evaluating archival activities in order to identify patterns, and (b.) comparing the results with other programs so that the institution can justify program and budget needs and make any appropriate adjustments to its priorities, procedures and resources. (6.0)

KNOWLEDGE STATEMENTS

Archivists know and can apply knowledge about:

K-44 ● the methodologies for gathering data about archival functions within one's own institution, at other institutions, and through multi-institutional surveys;

K-45 ● sources of professional and technical advice, assistance, internal and external funding agencies, and other forms of potential program assistance.

Domain 7 -
PROFESSIONAL, ETHICAL, AND LEGAL ISSUES (16%)

Task 1
● Keep up to date on current issues in the field of archival theory and practice through such activities as reading professional literature and attending conferences. (4.5)
Task 2
● Contribute to the development of archival interests through oral presentations, by writing for publications, and by participating in professional organizations. (3.6)
Task 3
● Respect such rights as copyright, freedom of information, and right to privacy, and adhere to such legal requirements as disposition statutes. (4.5)
Task 4
● Conform to professional ethical standards. (3.4)

KNOWLEDGE STATEMENTS

An archivist knows and can apply knowledge about:

K-46 ● the variety of international, national, regional, and local organizations whose activities include archival concerns;

K-47 ● important American and international literature relating to archival theory and practice;

K-48 ● laws and regulations governing loans, deposits, exchanges, and gifts of property to institutions, including tax consequences, copyright, privacy, and freedom of information;

K-49 ● the Society of American Archivists' Code of Ethics;

K-50 ● the requirements of documents used as legal evidence in courts;

K-51 ● laws governing the definition of public records, their retention, and their proper disposition;

K-52 ● the SAA/ALA joint statement on Standards for Access to Research Materials In Archival and Manuscript Repositories.

A Sample Long-Range Plan and A Sample Annual Plan

Even small- to modest-sized historical records programs should develop both long term plans and annual work plans. The plans presented here, for our model Salem Public Library, are intended to provide samples that may assist historical records programs, regardless of setting, in developing their own plans.

The long-range plan is short and general; it does not need the level of operational detail that is exhibited in the annual plan, which guides day-to-day operations. The plan does not go to the activities level. The strategies—broad statements of how to reach goals and objectives—are also general, and strategies have not been identified for every goal. The long-range plan is like a general road map that provides an overview and points along the way to a desired destination, but does not provide much detail.

The annual plan is tied to the long-range plan, but it is more specific because it must guide the operations of the library's historical records program during the year. It has more concrete expectations and is more product-oriented. It includes information on activities as well as on goals and objectives. Where appropriate, it includes target dates by which selected work should be accomplished.

Long-Range Plan for the Historical Records Program, Salem Public Library, 1993–1997

Introduction. This plan covers five years, 1993–1997. It is intended to establish expectations for program direction, performance, and achievement; serve as a basis for long-term estimates of financial, space, and other resources; and provide a basis for annual workplans. This plan was developed by the library's Historical Records

Program Division and reviewed and approved by the director of the library and the library's board of trustees. The plan will be revisited, discussed, and possibly revised, each year. Annual workplans will be based on and derived from it.

Mission. The Salem Public Library's Historical Records Program exists to collect, preserve, and make available records that document the historical development of Salem's people, groups, organizations, institutions, and physical infrastructure. Its program, originated in 1990 and authorized in a resolution of the Board of Trustees, coordinates closely with the Salem Historical Society, Salem State College, and other programs that collect historical documentation on Salem and this region. According to a preliminary documentation plan worked out with these institutions and continually reviewed and refined, Salem Public Library concentrates on collecting business records, records of civic groups, and the papers of prominent civic and business leaders. Its work reinforces broader library priorities to serve civic and business groups as well as the general public.

Program Goals, Objectives, and Strategies, 1993–1997

I. *Continue the cooperative documentation and collecting program with Salem Historical Society, Salem State College, and other programs, and with creators and users of records, to improve the documentation of Salem's historical development. Salem Public Library will continue to act as the lead agency and secretariat for the Regional Documentation Planning Group.*

I.A.   Hold meetings at least annually to revisit, assess, and update the plan.

I.B.   Develop and implement general criteria to measure the success of the plan.

Strategies:

(a)   Organize a session at the Mid-Atlantic Regional Archives Conference to discuss approaches to documenting a city, and maintain informal contact with experts in this area.

(b)   Appeal to Salem's largest companies to create or strengthen their records management programs as a cost-and-space savings measure and counsel them to include an archival component and a documentation plan.

(c)   Work with Salem State College on development of an oral or video history program to create documentation to supplement historical records.

(d) Whenever possible, appeal for and receive funding from companies and institutions that agree to transfer historical records to the library, to pay for at least part of their processing and maintenance.

II. *Appraise and collect historical records with continuing research value, concentrating in the collecting areas mentioned in the mission statement.*

II.A.   Publicize the library's collecting policy and priorities in Salem, especially among groups and institutions that might have records to offer to the library.

II.B.   Carefully appraise records proposed for transfer to the library, selecting only those that clearly have continuing research value.

Strategies:

(a) Discuss and refine the program's collecting policies to achieve a tighter focus and develop means of interpreting and explaining the collecting policy to potential donors and others.

(b) Through conversations with business and civic leaders and others, and through formal and informal discussions and presentations, raise awareness of the importance of historical records and help clarify the library's collecting policy.

III. *Arrange and describe holdings in a timely fashion and in line with accepted archival guidelines to ensure that the holdings are accessible to researchers.*

III.A.   Arrange and describe the Donald Shultes Papers, the Annmarie Campanella Papers, the McAuliffe Family Records, the Salem Improvement Association records, the Salem Furniture Manufacturing Company Records, and the Mosher Photograph Collection on the box and folder levels.

III.B.   Develop at least summary guides to all new accessions within six months after they are received by the library.

III.C.   Ensure that descriptive information is entered into the regional library database and the state's historical records database in a timely fashion.

Strategies:

(a) Develop and implement a volunteer program for people to arrange and develop descriptions of historical records, with appropriate oversight and review.

    (b) Consult with Salem State College and other colleges and universities on the possibility of engaging student interns to help with arrangement and description work.

IV. *Carry out limited preservation work to ensure the preservation of the most important records and the information they contain.*

    IV.A. Carry out holdings maintenance work on backlog and on all new accessions within a year after they are received.

    IV.B. Develop and begin implementation of a plan to microfilm selected holdings, taking into account condition, research interest, and costs.

    IV.C. Ensure that records are stored in a secure and appropriate environment.

Strategies:

    (a) Urge Salem's companies, organizations, and groups to adopt and use acid-free paper for the creation of their records to ensure that future records have greater life expectancy.

    (b) Assess temperature and humidity and storage conditions in the stacks.

    (c) Develop a disaster prevention, preparedness, and response plan.

V. *Encourage the research use of historical records and serve and assist researchers who visit or contact the library.*

    V.A. Meet with history and other classes at Salem State College to apprise them of the library's holdings and encourage research use by students and faculty.

    V.B. Make a presentation on holdings and value at each annual meeting of the Southeast Regional Historical Association, the Association for Business History, the Civic History Research Association, and selected other meetings.

    V.C. Actively assist researchers who visit the library, including showing the use of finding aids, suggesting records for them to peruse, and answering their questions.

    V.D. Promptly respond to calls and letters with requested information on holdings and services.

VI. *Develop modest public programs to showcase selected holdings, encourage the educational use of historical records, and reach the general public with information about the records themselves and the historical information they contain.*

    VI.A. Hold at least one exhibit in the library each year.

VI.B. Organize at least one lecture, lecture series, or other discussion centering around topics covered by the library's historical records holdings.

VI.C. In consultation with Salem Central School's superintendent, Social Studies Department, and other interested departments and teachers, develop and implement initiatives for the educational uses of the library's historical records.

Strategies:

(a) So far as possible, tie exhibits and other public programs to anniversaries and other events that the community will be commemorating or celebrating.

(b) Explore the prospects for greater coverage in the city newspaper's Sunday magazine, *Salem Today*, and on public television.

(c) Work with and through the Salem Tourism Office and Salem Chamber of Commerce to tie public programs to other efforts designed to tout Salem's history and culture.

Annual Workplan for the Historical Records Program, Salem Public Library, 1993

Introduction. This annual workplan covers the year 1993. It is tied to and derived from the long-range plan for the Historical Records Program, Salem Public Library, which covers the years 1993–1997. This annual workplan was developed by the Historical Records Program and approved by the Library Director on November 1, 1992. It is intended to guide the Historical Records Program's operations, including providing background for the development of individual employees' workplans.

This annual workplan is accompanied by an program budget, which was approved by the library director on December 1, 1992.

Note: **long-range goals** are indicated in *italics* by Roman numerals; **annual goals** are indicated by arabic numbers; **objectives** by numbers and capital letters (e.g., 2-A), and **activities** by numbers, capital letters, and numbers (e.g., 2-A-1).

Long-Range Goal I. Continue the cooperative documentation and collecting program with Salem Historical Society, Salem State College, and other programs, and with creators and users of records, to improve the documentation of Salem's historical development. Salem Public Library will continue to act as the lead agency and secretariat for the Regional Documentation Planning Group.

1. Assess 1992 progress on the documentation plan through Regional Documentation Planning Group.

1-A.   Review and assess collecting reports from each of the cooperating collecting programs.

1-B.   Review and assess the development of new institutional archives programs in the Salem area.

1-B-1. Survey selected companies, churches, and other institutions for information on development of institutional archives.

1-B-2. Use results of the survey to develop and implement a proposal for the Working Group to work directly for more institutional archives.

2. Update documentation plan if necessary.

Long-Range Goal II. Appraise and collect historical records with continuing research value, concentrating in the collecting areas mentioned in the Mission Statement.

3. Improve understanding of the library's mission and collecting policies.

3-A.   Prepare and distribute a short (brochure length) publication on the library's historical records program by 9/30/93.

3-A-1. Prepare draft and list of proposed illustrations by 7/30/93.
3-A-2. Prepare distribution plan by 7/30/93.
3-A-3. Publish, distribute, and publicize the brochure.

3-B.   Make at least four public presentations on the library's historical records program.

3-B-1. Arrange for and plan presentations to ensure maximum attendance and to match the message to the audience's interests.

3-B-2. Arrange for one presentation to a business group; one to a civic or good government group; one to a group concerned with minorities' issues; and one to a group primarily made up of educators.

4. Appraise records that are proposed for accessioning and identify and accession those with continuing research value that fit the library's collecting policy.

4-A.   Develop a systematic approach to the appraisal of records.

4-A-1. Develop an appraisal manual that lays out criteria and procedures for appraising records by 12/31/93.

4-B.   Appraise records proposed for donation to the library, carefully considering values, research potential, and the library's financial and space resources, and identify and select those that clearly have continuing value and that are compatible with the library's mission and collecting policy.

4-B-1. Analyze and appraise an estimated 10–12 collections considered for acquisition by the library through offered donations or solicitations by the library. Prepare an appraisal report/recommendations for each.

4-B-2. Arrange for legal transfer and accession collections deemed to have sufficient continuing value.

Long-Range Goal III. Arrange and describe holdings in a timely fashion and in line with accepted archival guidelines to ensure that the holdings are accessible to researchers.

5. Arrange and prepare internal finding aids and summary finding aids for publication covering the Donald Shultes Papers and the Annmarie Campanella Papers.

   5-A. Arrange and describe the Shultes Papers by 6/30/93.
   5-B. Arrange and describe the Campanella Papers by 12/31/93.
   5-C. Prepare short summary finding aids for both collections by 12/31/93.

6. Develop summary finding aids to all new accessions within six months of receipt.

   6-A. Develop a standard format and approach for short, succinct summary finding aids that can serve in lieu of more detailed finding aids (or until such finding aids can be developed) by 6/30/93.
   6-B. Develop finding aids in format developed under 6-A by 12/31/93.

Long-Range Goal IV. Carry out limited preservation work to ensure the preservation of the most important records and the information they contain.

7. Carry out holdings maintenance work on all materials received during 1992.

8. Develop and begin implementation of an archival microfilming program.

   8-A. Develop a plan and procedures to ensure that microfilming is carried out systematically for selected records with high research importance and preservation problems, within available resources by 6/30/93.
   8-B. Microfilm at least 50 cubic feet of the Shultes Papers by 12/31/93.

Long-Range Goal V. Encourage the research use of historical records and serve and assist researchers who visit or contact the library.

9. Encourage broader use of historical records by college students and scholarly researchers.

   9-A.   Meet with at least two classes at Salem State College to discuss holdings and encourage research.

   9-B.   Make presentations at Southeast Regional Historical Association, Association for Business History, and Civic History Research Association.

10. Encourage broader awareness of the research value of historical records and enhance research use by researchers beyond the scholarly community.

   10-A.   Publish and distribute a short booklet, *Research in Historical Records at Salem Public Library*, by 12/31/93.

11. Facilitate research use of historical records held by the library.

   11-A.   Provide efficient, courteous, and helpful service to researchers on a continuing basis.

   11-B.   Provide accurate and timely responses to written and telephone inquiries.

Long-Range Goal VI. Develop modest public programs to showcase selected holdings, encourage the educational use of historical records, and reach the general public with information about the records themselves and the historical information they contain.

12. Develop public presentations which present selected records directly and also occasion discussion of the historical events and themes that they document.

   12-A.   Develop an exhibit making extensive use of historical records on the theme of "Images of Salem: Letters, Diaries, and Photographs, 1850–1900."

   12-B.   Organize and hold a lecture/public discussion on the topic "Company and Town: The Impact of Industrialization on Salem, 1820–1890."

13. Arrange for the educational use of historical records held by the library to enhance social studies and other courses.

   13-A.   Organize a meeting with Salem Central School personnel to discuss and develop a plan for collaborative efforts.

Examples of Records Descriptions and Finding Aids

This appendix provides five types of records descriptions from a variety of finding aids. They illustrate the diversity of finding aids, but they also illustrate emerging common approaches to descriptive practices.

They are as follows:

1. Series-Level Descriptions
2. Collection Level and Record Group Descriptions
3. Summary Description of a Repository's Holdings in a Multiple Repository Guide
4. Summary Guide
5. Records Inventory

1. Series-Level Descriptions

As discussed in chapter 7, description at the series level is probably the most practical approach for most historical records programs. The first two examples, from the Society of American Archivists' compendium of descriptive practices, show the information arrayed according to MARC/AMC (Machine Readable Cataloging for Archives and Manuscripts Control) tags. The last two examples show information arrayed according to MARC tags but also how it appears to the user with the tags not present. Both show extensive use of reference/indexing terms.

The first two examples are from Max. J. Evans and Lisa B. Weber, *MARC for Archives and Manuscripts: A Compendium of Practice* (Chicago: Society of American Archivists, 1985), Appendix B (© 1985, reprinted with permission from The Society of American Archivists); the last two examples are from Kathleen D. Roe, *Guidelines for Arrangement and Description of Archives and Manuscripts: A Manual for Historical Records Programs in New York State* (Albany: New York State Education Department, 1991), Appendix A (reprinted with permission of New York State Archives and Records Administration).

Hoover Institution - Archival Series Description

ID:CSUZ33005-A   RTYP:d   ST:p   NLR: MS: EL: AD:11-16-84
CC:9554 BLT:bc   DCF: CSC:d MOD: PROC: UD:11-19-84
PP:cau   L:rus   PC:i   PD:1897/1947   REP:
MMD: OR: POL: DM: RR: COL: EML: GEN: BSE:
040   CSt-H$cCSt-H$eappm
110 1   Russia.$bPosolstvo (United States)
245 00 $kRecords,$f1897-1947.
300      $f383 ms. boxes, 85 oversize boxes, 6 card file boxes, 6 envelopes.
545   Russian Imperial and Provisional Government Embassies in the U.S.
520   Correspondence, telegrams, memoranda, reports, agreements, minutes,
         histories, financial records, lists, and printed matter, relating to
         Russia's role in World War I, the Russian Revolution and Civil War,
         activities of the Russian Red Cross, Russian emigres in foreign
         countries, and operations of the embassy office. Includes files of the
         Russian Military, Naval, and Financial Attaches in the U.S.; the
         Russian State Control Office and the Russian Supply Committee Office in
         the U.S.; and the Consulate General in Montreal, Canada.
546   Mainly in Russian.
555   Register.
610 20   Rossiiskoe obshchestvo krasnogo kresta.
610 10   Russia.$bMinisterstvo inostrannykh del.
610 10   Russia (1917-1922. Civil War Governments)$bDobrovolcheskaia armiia.
610 10   Russia (1917-1922. Civil War Governments)$bVooruzhennyia Sily Iuga
         Rossii.
650 0   Russians in foreign countries.
650 0   World War, 1914-1918.
650 0   World War, 1914-1918$zSoviet Union.
650 0   World War, 1914-1918$xWar work.
651 0   Canada.
651 0   Canada$xForeign relations$zSoviet Union.
651 0   Siberia$xHistory$yRevolution, 1917-1921.
651 0   Soviet Union.
651 0   Soviet Union$xForeign relations$zCanada.
651 0   Soviet Union$xForeign relations$zUnited States.
651 0   Soviet Union$xHistory$yRevolution, 1917-1921.
651 0   United States.
651 0   United States$xForeign relations$zSoviet Union.
ACCN   33005
ACCD   09/21/77
SRCE   Ughet, Sergei
MTHD   Gift
PLOC   9.03/05, photo file, oversize photo file
ACT   Received
TAC   1933

Stanford University - Manuscript Collection Description


```
ID:CSUR84-A70        RTYP:d    ST:s          NLR:      MS:   EL:   AD:05-10-84
CC:9554  BLT:bc      DCF:    CSC:d   MOD:   PROC:b                 UD:06-13-84
PP:cau     L:eng     PC:i    PD:1902/1979   REP:
MMD:      OR:    POL:    DM:    RR:          COL:      EML:        GEN:  BSE:
```

```
040      CSt$cCSt$eappm
100 1    Steinbeck, John,$d1902-1968.
245 00   $kCollection,$f1902-1979.
300      7.5 linear ft. (including 2 oversize folders).
351      Series I. Correspondence (1928-1972), Series II. Literary manuscripts
         (1923-1975), Series III. Photographs, artwork and ephemera (1902-1979).
545      John Ernst Steinbeck was born in Salinas, California 27 February 1902.
         He was the author of short stories and novels, of which some became
         plays and films.  He died in New York City 20 December 1968.
520      The collection is primarily letters and documents written by Steinbeck
         to family, friends and business associates.  Also included are letters
         written to Steinbeck and letters written about him.  Includes
         manuscripts and typescripts of works by Steinbeck, proofs of books,
         tearsheets, and photocopies of published works by him.  Reviews of
         Steinbeck's work, articles about him, press coverage of his travels,
         memorabilia, photographs, and artwork complete the collection.
561      Gifts and purchases from various sources.
555      A Catalogue of the John Steinbeck Collection at Stanford University,
         comp. and ed. by Susan F. Riggs, 1980.$bAvailable for purchase.
600 10   Bailey, Margery.
600 10   Benchley, Nathaniel,$d1915-
600 10   Benchley, Margery.
600 10   Beswick, Katherine.
600 10   Cathcart, Robert S.
600 10   Conrad, Barnaby.
600 10   Dreiser, Theodore,$d1871-1945.
600 10   Fairbanks, Douglas,$d1909-
600 10   Fisher, W. K.
600 10   Goldberg, Rube,$d1883-1970.
600 10   Goldman, Eric.
600 10   Grabhorn, Jane Bissell.
600 10   Howell, Warren R.
600 10   McBride, Robert Martin,$d1918-
600 10   Noskowiak, Sonya,$dd. 1975.
600 10   Olson, Culbert Levy,$d1876-
600 10   Otis, Elizabeth.
600 10   Ricketts, Edward Flanders,$d1896-1948.
600 10   Sheffield, Carlton A.
600 10   Steinbeck, John,$d1902-1968.
600 10   Street, Webster F.
600 10   Valenti, Jack.
600 10   Vinaver, Eugene,$d1899.
600 10   Wagner, Jack.
600 10   Wagner, Max Leopold,$d1880-1962.
600 10   Wilhelmson, Carl.
```

Stanford University - Manuscript Collection Description - Continued

610 20 Stanford University Press.
610 20 Twentieth Century-Fox Film Corporation.
650 0 Authors, American.
655   Articles.
655   Manuscripts (literary)
655   Memorabilia.
655   Photoprints.
656   Authors.
851   Department of Special Collections,$bCecil H. Green Library,$cStanford
       CA 94305.
RPGN   M263
MATL   Entire collection.
PLOC   cc:13; mc:4/1, fc6c
ACT   Processed
AIDN   PCLS for individual gifts are included with appropriate series level
       description (Correspondence, Literary manuscripts, or Photographs,
       artwork and ephemera).
TAC   1980
AGT   sr
ACT   Project cataloged
TAC   01/06/84
AGT   mjk

Archival Series Descriptions

Cornell University. Crew.

Records, 1871-1973.

4.6 cubic ft., 1 phonograph record, 1 tape recording, 1 videocassette.

Summary: Includes varsity and freshman crew rosters; Coach Charles Courtney's diary and journals of distances rowed, weather conditions, and other information; regatta programs; scrapbook; map; correspondence with Todd Jessdale; minutes of the Sprague Boat Club; photographs, photograph albums, and glass negatives of crew events, Ithaca; New York views, and the Cayuga Lake Inlet; a phonograph record and cassette copy concerning a 1946 regatta at Lake Washington; material pertaining to John L. Collyer and Donald E. Maclay; and a videocassette of the 1957 Cornell crew victory at Henley.

Finding Aids: Box list.

Indexing terms:

Collyer, John L.

Courtney, Charles.

Jessdale, Todd.

Maclay, Donald E.

Cornell University - - Athletics.

Sprague Boat Club.

Regattas.

Rowing.

Ithaca (N.Y.)

Cayuga Lake.
Diaries.
Glass plate negatives.
Journals.
Maps.
Photoprints.
Scrapbooks.

MARC Record Version

110	2	≠aCornell University.≠bCrew.
245	00	≠kRecords,≠f1871-1973.
300		≠a4.6 cubic ft.,≠b1 phonograph record, 1 tape recording, 1 videocassette.
520		≠aIncludes varsity and freshman crew rosters; Coach Charles Courtney's diary and journals of distances rowed, weather conditions, and other information; regatta programs; scrapbook; map; correspondence with Todd Jessdale; minutes of the Sprague Boat Club; photographs, photograph albums, and glass negatives of crew events, Ithaca, New York views, and the Cayuga Lake Inlet; a phonograph record and cassette copy concerning a 1946 regatta at Lake Washington; Material pertaining to John L. Collyer and Donald E. Maclay; and a videocassette of the 1957 Cornell crew victory at Henley.
555	0	≠aBox list.

600	10	≠aCollyer, John L.
600	20	≠aCourtney, Charles.
600	10	≠aJessdale, Todd.
600	10	≠aMaclay, Donald E.
610	20	≠aCornell University≠xAthletics.
610	20	≠aSprague Boat Club.
650	0	≠aRegattas.
650	0	≠aRowing.
651	0	≠aIthaca (N.Y.)
651	0	≠aCayuga Lake.
655	7	≠aDiaries.≠2ftamc.
655	7	≠aGlass plate negatives.≠2ftamc.
655	7	≠aJournals.≠2ftamc.
655	7	≠aMaps.≠2ftamc.
655	7	≠aPhotoprints.≠2ftamc.
655	7	≠aScrapbooks.≠2ftamc.

Associated Colleges of Upper New York.

Records, 1946 – 1954.

2.3 linear ft.

Organized in two series as follows: I. Associated Colleges of Upper New York, 1946 – 1954; II. Metropolitan Survey, 1946 – 1949.

Historical note: To educators in New York State, the close of World War II heralded the return of an anticipated one hundred thousand veterans seeking the college level education provided by the G.I. Bill of Rights. To alleviate the overcrowded conditions facing colleges and universities, the State of New York created a temporary educational entity entitled Associated Colleges of Upper New York (ACUNY). ACUNY was chartered in 1946 by the Board of Regents of New York. Four temporary two – year colleges were established to absorb the influx of students and provide qualified veterans with the first two years of their college education. The colleges were Sampson College (1946, now known as SUNY at Champlain), and Middletown College.

The Board of Trustees of ACUNY consisted largely of presidents of private and public colleges in New York State. New York University was represented by Harold O. Voorhis, Vice President and Secretary. Voorhis acted as chairman of the Metropolitan Survey, 1946 – 1947, a study by ACUNY to determine the need of an emergency college to serve veterans in New York City.

Summary: The records consist of correspondence, minutes, reports, memoranda, financial records, surveys, press releases, and newspaper clippings relating to the administration of ACUNY. The Metropolitan Survey is well documented. Also included is printed matter such as administrative handbooks, facility bulletins, student handbooks, guidebooks, and brochures of the colleges of ACUNY.

Unpublished finding aid is available (folder level control).

Indexing terms:

Allen, John.

Chase, Harry Woodburn, 1883 – .

Day, Edmund Ezra, 1883 – .

Dewey, Thomas E. (Thomas Edmund), 1902 – 1971.

Gilbert, Amy.

Kastner, Elwood.

Knowles, Asa Smallidge, 1901 – 1956.

Louttit, Chauncey McKinley, 1901 – 1956.

Miller, J. Hillis (Joseph Hillis), 1928 –

Morse, Frederick A.

Rondileau, Adrian, 1912 –

Voorhis, Harold Oliver, 1896 –

Associated Colleges of Upper New York.

Cornell University.

New York University.

Rutgers University.

Mohawk College.

Sampson College.

Middletown College.

State University of New York -- Champlain.

Colleges and Universities -- Administration.

Higher education -- New York State.

Veterans -- Education -- New York State.

World War, 1939 – 1945 -- Veterans.

MARC Record Version

110	2	≠aAssociated Colleges of Upper New York.
245	00	≠aAdministrative subject and correspondence files,≠f1946 – 1954.
300		≠a2.3 linear ft.
351		≠aOrganized in two series as follows: I. Associated Colleges of Upper New York, 1946 – 1954; II. Metropolitan Survey, 1946 – 1949.
545		≠aTo educators in New York State, the close of World War II heralded the return of an anticipated one hundred thousand veterans seeking the college level education provided by the G.I. Bill of Rights. To alleviate the overcrowded conditions facing colleges and universities, the State of New York created a temporary educational entity entitled Associated Colleges of Upper New York (ACUNY). ACUNY was chartered in 1946 by the Board of Regents of New York. Four temporary two-year colleges were established to absorb the influx of students and provide qualified veterans with the first two years of their college education. The colleges were Sampson College (1946, now known as SUNY at Champlain), and Middletown College.
545		≠bThe Board of Trustees of ACUNY consisted largely of presidents of private and public colleges in New York State. New York University was represented by Harold O. Voorhis, Vice President and Secretary.

Voorhis acted as chairman of the Metropolitan Survey, 1946 – 1947, a study by ACUNY to determine the need for an emergency college to serve veterans in New York City.

520		≠aThe records consist of correspondence, minutes, reports, memoranda, financial records, surveys, press releases, and newspaper clippings relating to the administration of ACUNY. The Metropolitan Survey is well documented. Also included is printed matter such as administrative handbooks, facility bulletins, student handbooks, guidebooks, and brochures of the colleges of ACUNY.
541		≠aHarold O. Voorhis, ≠bOffice of the Vice President and Secretary, 16 College Lane, Poughkeepsie, NY ≠6cAdministrative transfer, ≠d1975.
555	8	≠aUnpublished finding aid is available≠c(folder level control).
600	10	≠aAllen, John.
600	10	≠aChase, Harry Woodburn,≠d1883 –
600	10	≠aDay, Edmund Ezra,≠d1883 –
600	10	≠aDewey, Thomas E.≠q(Thomas Edmund),≠d1902 – 1971.
600	10	≠aGilbert, Amy.
600	10	≠aKastner, Elwood.
600	10	≠aKnowles, Asa Smallidge,≠d1901 – 1956.
600	10	≠aLouttit, Chauncey McKinley,≠d1901 – 1956.
600	10	≠aMiller, J. Hillis≠q(Joseph Hillis),≠d1928 –
600	10	≠aMorse, Frederick A.
600	10	≠aRondileau, Adrian,≠d1912 –
600	10	≠aVoorhis, Harold Oliver,≠d1896 –
610	20	≠aAssociated Colleges of Upper New York.
610	20	≠aCornell University.
610	20	≠aNew York University.
610	20	≠aRutgers University.
610	20	≠aMohawk College.
610	20	≠aSampson College.
610	20	≠aMiddletown College.
610	20	≠aState University of New York≠zChamplain.
650		≠aColleges and Universities≠xAdministration.
650		≠aHigher education≠zNew York State.
650		≠aVeterans≠xEducation≠zNew York State.
650		≠aWorld War, 1939 – 1945≠xVeterans.

2. Collection Level and Record Group Descriptions

The first two examples are MARC/AMC records, one for a manuscript collection and the other for an archival record group. These are both examples presented by The Society of American Archivists' manual on MARC/AMC to illustrate the fields and subfields, but they also provide a good idea of the content of a description at the collection or record group level. The second two examples also show the information according to the MARC tags but also indicate how it might be presented to researchers without those tags. Like Example 1, both include numerous indexing terms.

The first two examples are from Nancy Sahli, *MARC for Archives and Manuscripts: The AMC Format* (Chicago: Society of American Archivists, 1985) (© 1985, reprinted with permission from The Society of American Archivists); the last two examples are from Kathleen D. Roe, *Guidelines for Arrangement and Description of Archives and Manuscripts: A Manual for Historical Records Programs in New York State* (Albany: New York State Education Department, 1991), Appendix A.

SAMPLE USMARC AMC FORMAT INPUT RECORD: MANUSCRIPT COLLECTION

NOTE: This hypothetical example does not display Leader or
Record Directory information. Such information, which is needed
only in automated implementations, can be assumed to be generated
and carried by the automated system being used. This sample also
does not reflect the full range of possible options for the use
of fields and subfields available to the AMC user. Its use of
thesaurus codes and Library of Congress Name Authority references
is conjectural. It is meant simply to show the type of record
that might be created using the format. Full record examples of
actual user practice may be found in Appendix B of MARC FOR
ARCHIVES AND MANUSCRIPTS: A COMPENDIUM OF PRACTICE.

001   NP0001-85
010   ƀƀ $amsƀ61003623ƀ
035   ƀƀ $a1939-0001
100   1ƀ $aProvenance, William Fonds,$d1897-1938.
245   00 $kPapers,$f[ca. 1917-1937].
300   ƀƀ $a15 cubic ft.
351   ƀƀ $aOrganized into four series: I. War Participation,
             1917-1919. II. College Years, 1920-1924.
             III. European Exile, 1925-1932. IV. Archival
             Career, 1933-1937.$bChronological arrangement.
506   ƀƀ $aAccess subject to donor restrictions.
510   4ƀ $aHollinger, Abraham. "W.F. Provenance and His
             Contribution to American Archives," Archives
             Description Quarterly,$cvol. 7, 1985, p. 187
520   ƀƀ $aIncludes cryptic diaries and illegible
             correspondence focusing on Provenance's unsuccessful
             literary endeavors and his development of the quark
             theory of archival description. Includes manuscript of
             his QUARKS: THE TAO OF ARCHIVES. Correspondents
             include Ernest Hemingway, Sigmund F. Groupie, and Ima
             Gusdorf.
524   ƀƀ $aWilliam Fonds Provenance. Papers. Department of
             Manuscripts and University Archives, Freen College.
540   ƀƀ $aLiterary rights of William Fonds Provenance have
             been dedicated to the public.
541   ƀƀ $aProvenance, Gertrude Thruxton$b122 East Stack
             Street, Arlenville, CA 93706$cgift$d1939 September 18
             $fWilliam Fonds Provenance Estate.
545   ƀƀ $aArchivist and literary gadfly. Born at Last Chance,
             Nevada, January 4, 1897. Served in World War I as
             ambulance driver. Following graduation from Freen
             College with a major in cryptogamic botany, he lived
             in Paris, where he tried, unsuccessfully, to attach
             himself to literary circles. To combat the depression

caused by this rejection he began to develop his quark
theory of archival description, published in his 1933
epic work QUARKS: THE TAO OF ARCHIVES. It was only
after the development of the USMARC Archival and
Manuscripts Control format that his ideas made any
sense to the American archival profession.

555	ƀƀ	Box listing.
583	ƀƀ	$3Diaries$1microfilmed$cOctober 1985
583	ƀƀ	$3Hemingway letter 1927 May 3$aexhibit$c1985 December 1 through 1986 April 30$jMuseum of Literary Lights
600	10	$aProvenance, William Fonds, $d1897-1938.$tQuarks: the tao of archives.
650	ƀ0	$aQuarks.
650	ƀ0	$aArchival description$xQuark theory.
650	ƀ0	$aLiterary communities$zFrance.
650	ƀ0	$aTaoism$xUnorthodox interpretations.
655	ƀ7	$aDiaries$2uraful
655	ƀ7	$aLetters$2uraful
700	12	$aHemingway, Ernest.
700	12	$aGroupie, Sigmund Freud.
700	12	$aGusdorf, Ima.
851	ƀƀ	$aFreen College$bDepartment of Manuscripts and University Archives$cProvenance Memorial Building, 727 Prologue Boulevard, History City, MA$dUSA$eRange 1, Shelves 3-7

SAMPLE USMARC AMC FORMAT INPUT RECORD: ARCHIVAL RECORD GROUP

Note: This hypothetical example does not display Leader or
Record Directory information. Such information, which is needed
only in automated implementations, can be assumed to be generated
and carried by the automated system being used. This sample also
does not reflect the full range of possible options for the use
of fields and subfields available to the AMC user. Its use of
thesaurus codes and Library of Congress Name Authority references
is conjectural. It is meant simply to show the type of record
that <u>might</u> be created using the format. Full record examples of
actual user practice may be found in Appendix B of MARC FOR
ARCHIVES AND MANUSCRIPTS: A COMPENDIUM OF PRACTICE.

```
001        NP0002-85
010   ϸϸ   $amsϸ61003624ϸ
035   ϸϸ   $a1985-0002
110   2ϸ   $aFreen College$bOffice of Federal Grants.
245   00   $kRecords,$f1972-1982.
300   ϸϸ   $a30 cubic ft.
340   ϸϸ   $3Financial reports data base$afloppy disk$b5 inch
           $iMS-DOS operating system microcomputer with Fugue
           software.
351   ϸϸ   $aOrganized into four series:  I.  Correspondence,
           1972-1982.  II.  Financial Reports, 1978-1982.  III.
           Narrative Reports, 1977-1982.  IV.  Annual Planning
           Meetings, 1972-1982.
506   ϸϸ   $3Financial reports$aNo one may examine these records
           or obtain information from them except by written
           permission$bComptroller of the College.
520   ϸϸ   $aDocuments relating to the administration of Federal
           government grants at Freen College.  Included is
           information regarding the development of the Provenance
           Center for Long-range Archival Planning, the Northeast
           Committee to Commemorate the Centenary of Milburn
           Freen, and the Freen College research program in
           cryptogamic botany.  Topics of general interest
           covered in the files include long-range planning,
           standard reporting practices, and the use of automated
           techniques in financial administration.
524   ϸϸ   $aFreen College, Office of Federal Grants.  Record
           Group 85-2, Department of Manuscripts and University
           Archives, Freen College.
540   ϸϸ   $3Financial reports$aCopying restricted:  information
           may be obtained from the Director of Archives.
541   ϸϸ   $aOffice of Federal Grants$ctransfer under schedule
           $d1985 March 1
545   ϸϸ   $aThe Office of Federal Grants was established in
           March 1972 to meet a growing need at Freen College for
```

administrative and financial services relating to
United States government grants.   It is
administratively responsible to the Comptroller of the
College.   Along with assistance to grant applicants
and recipients, the office has been instrumental in
introducing long-range archival planning to the nation
and was the first fully automated campus office.

555	₦₦	Folder listing.
583	₦₦	$aArrange$cJune 1985$1completed
583	₦₦	$aDescribe$cJune 1985$1completed
583	₦₦	$aMicrofilm$cOctober 1985$efollowing preservation needs assessment
610	20	$aFreen College.$bProvenance Center for Long-range Archival Planning.
610	20	$aFreen College.$bCryptogamic Botany Research Institute.
610	24	$aNortheast Committee to Commemorate the Centenary of Milburn Freen
650	₦0	$aGrants and grantsmanship$xGovernment programs
650	₦0	$aPlanning
650	₦0	$aStandards$xReporting practices
650	₦0	$aAutomation$xFinancial administration
655	₦7	$aLetters$2uraful
655	₦7	$aReports$2uraful
655	₦7	$aAccount books$2uraful
655	₦7	$aAudits$2uraful
851	₦₦	$aFreen College$bDepartment of Manuscripts and University Archives$cProvenance Memorial Building, 727 Prologue Boulevard, History City, MA$dUSA$eRange 7

Manuscript Collection Descriptions

Frederick A. DeZeng, 1756 – 1838.

Papers, 1781 – 1849.

.25 linear ft.

Baron DeZeng, a Hessian officer who became a naturalized American citizen, was the first manufacturer of window glass in the United States.

Summary: Letters and documents, 1781 – 1831, to, from, and about DeZeng, and letters, 1843 – 1849, to DeZeng's son, William Steuben DeZeng. Subjects include the Onondaga Nation, Shakers, the Ontario Glass Company, and personal and family matters. Correspondents include Governor George Clinton, General Philip Schuyler, and William H. Seward.

Use of this collection requires advance notice.

Inventory available.

Indexing terms:

DeZeng family.

Ontario Glass Company.

Onondaga Indians.

Windows.

Glass manufacture - - New York (State)

Glass manufacture -- Canada Ontario.

Hessians - - United States.

Shakers.

Ontario (Canada) Industries.

New York (State) Industries.

DeZeng, William Steuben, 1793 – 1844.

Clinton, George, 1739 – 1812.

Schuyler, Philip John, 1733 – 1804.

Seward, William Henry, 1801 – 1872.

MARC Record Version

100	1	≠aDeZeng, Frederick A.,≠d1756 – 1838.
245	00	≠a Baron Frederick DeZeng Papers,≠f1781 – 1849.
300		≠a.25 linear ft.
545		≠aBaron DeZeng, a Hessian officer who became a naturalized American citizen, was the first manufacturer of window glass in the United States.
520		≠aLetters and documents, 1781 – 1831, to, from, and about DeZeng, and letters, 1843 – 1849, to DeZeng's son, William Steuben DeZeng. Subjects include the Onondaga Nation, Shakers, the Ontario Glass Company, and personal and family matters. Correspondents include Governor George Clinton, General Philip Schuyler, and William H. Seward.
506		≠aUse of this collection requires advance notice.
555	0	≠aInventory available.
696	34	≠aDeZeng family.
610	10	≠aOntario Glass Company.
650	0	≠aOnondaga Indians.
650	0	≠aWindows.

650 0 ≠aGlass manufacture≠zNew York (State).

650 0 ≠aGlass manufacture≠zCanada≠zOntario.

650 0 ≠aHessians≠zUnited States.

650 0 ≠aShakers.

651 0 ≠aOntario (Canada)≠xIndustries.

651 0 ≠aNew York (State)≠xIndustries.

700 10 ≠aDeZeng, William Steuben,≠d1793 – 1844.

700 10 ≠aClinton, George,≠d1739 – 1812.

700 10 ≠aSchuyler, Philip John,≠d1733 – 1804.

700 10 ≠aSeward, William Henry,≠d1801 – 1872.

Metcalf, George R., 1914-

Papers, 1956 - 1971.

2 linear ft.

Writer, state senator, president of the National Committee Against Discrimination in Housing.

Summary: Collection comprises material for Metcalf's books, BLACK PROFILES (13 biographies of prominent black Americans living and deceased), and UP FROM WITHIN: TODAY'S BLACK LEADERS (a biographical sequence of emerging black personalities and their contributions to the "black revolution" in America). Material consists of clippings, correspondence, typescripts, transcribed interviews, notes and miscellaneous printed material, and one taped interview with Metcalf on a variety of topics including urban rehabilitation. Material in collection is about Martin Luther King, Jr., Malcolm X, Roy Wilkins, Shirley Chisolm, W.E.B. Du Bois, Rosa Parks, Thurgood Marshall, Medgar Evers, Jackie Robinson, Eldridge Cleaver, Whitney Young, Jr., Harriet Tubman, Edward Brooke, Julian Bond, James H. Meredith, Andrew Brimmer, and others.

Permission required to quote from transcribed interviews.

Finding aids: Partial inventory.

Indexing terms:

King, Martin Luther,Jr., 1929-1968.

X, Malcolm, 1925-1965.

Wilkins, Roy, 1901-

Chisolm, Shirley, 1913-

Du Bois, W. E. B. (William Edward Burghardt), 1868-1963.

Parks, Rosa, 1913-

Marshall, Thurgood, 1908-

Evers, Medgar Wiley, 1925-1963.

Robinson, Jackie, 1919-1972.

Cleaver, Eldridge, 1935-

Young, Whitney M.

Tubman, Harriet, 1820?-1913.

Brooke, Edward, 1919-

Bond, Julian, 1940-

Meredith, James Howard.

Black nationalism - - United States.

Afro-Americans - - Civil rights.

Afro-American athletes.

Afro-American judges.

Civil rights workers - - United States.

Interviews.

Afro-American authors.

MARC Record Version

100	1	≠aMetcalf, George R.,≠d1914-
245	00	≠kPapers,≠f1956 - 1971.
300		≠a2 linear ft.
545		≠aWriter, state senator, president of the National Committee Against Discrimination in Housing.
520		≠aCollection comprises material for Metcalf's books, BLACK PROFILES (13 biographies of prominent black Americans living and deceased), and UP FROM WITHIN: TODAY'S BLACK LEADERS (a biographical sequence of emerging black personalities and their contributions to the "black revolution" in America). Material consists of clippings, correspondence, typescripts, transcribed interviews, notes and miscellaneous printed material, and one taped interview with Metcalf on a variety of topics including urban rehabilitation. Material in collection is about Martin Luther King, Jr., Malcolm X, Roy Wilkins, Shirley Chisolm, W.E.B. Du Bois, Rosa Parks, Thurgood Marshall, Medgar Evers, Jackie Robinson, Eldridge Cleaver, Whitney Young, Jr., Harriet Tubman, Edward Brooke, Julian Bond, James H. Meredith, Andrew Brimmer, and others.
540		≠aPermission required to quote from transcribed interviews.
555	0	≠aPartial inventory.
600	10	≠aKing, Martin Luther,≠cJr.,≠d1929-1968.
600	10	≠aX, Malcolm,≠d1925-1965.
600	10	≠aWilkins, Roy,≠d1901-
600	10	≠aChisolm, Shirley,≠d1913-
600	10	≠aDu Bois, W. E. B.≠q(William Edward Burghardt),≠d1868-1963.
600	10	≠aParks, Rosa,≠d1913-
600	10	≠aMarshall, Thurgood,≠d1908-
600	10	≠aEvers, Medgar Wiley,≠d1925-1963.
600	10	≠aRobinson, Jackie,≠d1919-1972.
600	10	≠aCleaver, Eldridge,≠d1935-
600	10	≠aYoung, Whitney M.
600	10	≠aTubman, Harriet,≠d1820?-1913.
600	10	≠aBrooke, Edward,≠d1919-
600	10	≠aBond, Julian,≠d1940-
600	10	≠aMeredith, James Howard.
650	0	≠aBlack nationalism≠zUnited States.
650	0	≠aAfro-Americans≠xCivil rights.
650	0	≠aAfro-American athletes.
650	0	≠aAfro-American judges.
650	0	≠aCivil rights workers≠zUnited States.
655	7	≠aInterviews.≠2ftamc.
656	7	≠aAfro-American authors.≠21csh.

3. Summary Description of a Repository's Holdings in a Multiple Repository Guide

This example, from a county-level guide, provides an overview of some of the holdings of the Westchester County Archives and the Westchester County Historical Society in New York State. The descriptions are generally at the collection level.

From *Guide to Historical Resources in Westchester County, New York Repositories* (Ithaca, N.Y.: Cornell University Library, Division of Rare and Manuscript Collections, 1991), 41–43.

(NIC)NYWR276-880-0021
Westchester County (N.Y.). Archives.
  Miscellaneous records collection, 1795-1985.
  ca. 10 linear ft.
  Summary: Miscellaneous records which do not fall within the
scope of any particular county department including original
census rolls from New York State censuses of 1905, 1915, and
1925; reports, directories, travel guides, pamphlets, posters,
certificates, brochures, and bulletins, 1880-1985, concerning
government and local history; dues ledger of the Wood, Wire, and
Metal Lathers' Union, 1906-1928; appointments to county, state,
and federal offices made by New York State governors, 1795-1840;
and Historical Records Survey forms completed by Work Projects
Administration workers, 1936-1940, mostly concerning records in
the County Clerk's office.
  Finding aids: Item lists.
  Westchester County Archives, Elmsford, NY.

(NIC)NYWR276-880-0022
Westchester County (N.Y.). Archives.
  Photograph collection, [ca. 1870-1980]
  90 linear ft.
  Summary: Photoprints, film negatives, glass plate negatives,
and postcards of subjects including accidents, aerial views,
Afro-Americans, agriculture, airports, architecture, automobiles,
bridges, camping, cemeteries, children, churches, circus, clubs,
courthouses, ferries, fire departments, floods, Indians of North
America, lighthouses, police, postal service, railroads,
recreation, reservoirs, roads, schools, and women. Also includes
a series of glass plate negatives of the Bronx River Parkway,
1912-1924.
  Finding aids: Subject guide.
  Finding aids: List of Bronx River Parkway plates.
  Westchester County Archives, Elmsford, NY.

(NIC)NYWR276-880-0023
Westchester County Tricentennial Commission.
  Records, 1980-1983.
  2.5 linear ft.
  Summary: Memoranda, correspondence, clippings, booklets,
reports, minutes, resolutions, and other records concerning
planning and coordinating of activities in celebration of
Westchester County's tricentennial in 1983.
  Finding aids: Folder list.
  Westchester County Archives, Elmsford, NY.

(NIC)NYWR276-885
Westchester County Historical Society. Library.
  Repository description.
  162 v., 151 cubic ft., 21 linear ft.
  Collecting area: History of Westchester County, N.Y.
  Summary: Letters, diaries, legal and financial records,
minutes, and other papers and records of individuals, families,
businesses, churches, organizations, and government bodies in
(Continued next page)

(NIC)NYWR276-885 (CONTINUED)
Westchester County; and genealogy, photograph, map, scrapbook,
and vertical file collections pertaining to the history of
Westchester County.
  Finding aids: Card catalog with main entry and subject access.
  Hours: Tues., Wed. 9-4.
  Telephone: 914-592-4323.
  Copying facilities available.
  Westchester County Historical Society. Library, 2199 Saw Mill
River Road, Elmsford, NY 10523.

(NIC)NYWR276-885-0001
Amawalk Nursery (Amawalk, N.Y.).
  Records, 1909-1933.
  7 v.
  Summary: Records concerning orders, 1909-1911, 1914-1915, and
1933, and cash accounts, 1909-1925.
  Westchester County Historical Society. Library, Elmsford, NY.

(NIC)NYWR276-885-0002
Bolton, Reginald Pelham, 1856-1942.
  Papers, 1930.
  2 v.
  Summary: Notebook of clippings, notes, and other materials
regarding Ann Hutchinson, used in preparing his manuscript A
WOMAN MISUNDERSTOOD; and a typescript copy of the manuscript,
1930.
  Publications: Bolton, Reginald Pelham. A Woman Misunderstood;
Ann, wife of William Hutchinson. New York: Schoen Printing
Company, 1931.
  Westchester County Historical Society. Library, Elmsford, NY.

(NIC)NYWR276-885-0003
Christ Church (Pelham, N.Y.).
  Records, 1844-1893.
  5 v.
  Summary: Record books from the meetings of wardens and vestry,
1844-1893; cash account and receipts book, 1859-1875; and record
books from the Ladies' Missionary Association, 1875 and 1878.
  Westchester County Historical Society. Library, Elmsford, NY.

(NIC)NYWR276-885-0004
Cochran, Robert, 1826-
  Diary, 1850-1851.
  1 v.
  Cochran was a lawyer in White Plains, N.Y.
  Summary: Entries in this diary concern his reasons for keeping
a diary; recounting earlier events in his life such as his school
years, the death of his brother Charles while gold mining in
California, and friendships made at Yale University; his study
and reading of law; courtship of Eliza Jane Vanderbilt whom he
married in 1853; and social life and other ordinary activities,
including a religious camp meeting in White Plains.
  Westchester County Historical Society. Library, Elmsford, NY.

(NIC)NYWR276-885-0005
Ferris, John Mason.
    Sermons, 1852-1863.
    .5 cubic ft.
    Summary: Manuscript sermons from his pastorates in Dutch
Reformed Churches in Tarrytown, N.Y., 1852-1854, and in Chicago
and Grand Rapids, Mich., 1855-1863.
    Westchester County Historical Society. Library, Elmsford, NY.

(NIC)NYWR276-885-0006
French, Alvah P., 1867-1927.
    Scrapbooks, 1880-1925.
    42 v. on microfilm.
    Microfilm.
    French was the founder and editor of several Westchester County
newspapers and the author of the 5-volume HISTORY OF WESTCHESTER
COUNTY.
    Summary: Clippings, pamphlets, obituaries, marriage notices,
biographical sketches, and pictures relating to the history of
Westchester County and its townships. Subjects include churches,
schools, historic houses, government, politics, crime and
criminals, Indians, industry and commerce, newspapers, prisons,
railroads, water supply, and military history.
    Finding aids: People and subject index.
    Westchester County Historical Society. Library, Elmsford, NY.

(NIC)NYWR276-885-0007
Gedney, John.
    Diary, 1862-1864.
    1 v.
    Summary: Diary concerning his Civil War experiences in Company
B of the 6th New York Heavy Artillery, 1862-1864, with a
photograph of Gedney in his uniform and several clippings
concerning reunions of his unit and his obituary, undated.
    Westchester County Historical Society. Library, Elmsford, NY.

(NIC)NYWR276-885-0008
George Juengst & Sons (Croton Falls, N.Y.).
    Records, [ca. 1895]-1919.
    5 v.
    Electric light and power company in Croton Falls, N.Y.
    Summary: Record books of meter readings for Croton Falls,
Purdys Station, Katonay, and Goldens Bridge, 1907, 1918-1919, and
undated; account book with client directory, 1904; and an undated
book of work records.
    Westchester County Historical Society. Library, Elmsford, NY.

4. Summary Guide

A summary guide provides limited information on all of a repository's holdings. One approach is to include a historical essay on the person, group, or institution that produced the records and then simply list the series titles, inclusive dates, and approximate quantity. The addition of an index can help direct researchers to appropriate records. This type of summary guide is relatively easy to produce but it does not provide any information on the contents of the records. The example shows part of the summary description for one record group held by the New York State Archives.

From New York State Archives, *Guide to Records in the New York State Archives* (Albany: New York State Education Department, 1981), 67–68.

Banking Department

State banking policy began with a 1782 act prohibiting the operation of any bank within the state except for the federal Bank of North America. In 1791, the legislature authorized a charter for the first state bank, the Bank of New York, and thereafter chartered other banks by special acts. An 1829 (Ch. 94) law set up the Bank Fund, later renamed the Safety Fund, to guarantee the payment of debts of insolvent banks. All state-chartered banks were required to make an annual contribution to the fund, which was managed by the State Treasurer. The same law provided for the appointment of three bank commissioners to examine the financial status of banks and to report annually to the Legislature.

State regulation of banks was altered by the Banking Law of 1838 (Ch. 260), which required banks to file certificates of incorporation with the Secretary of State and report annually to the Comptroller. In 1843, the Safety Fund and the Office of Bank Commissioners were abolished, and bank examination responsibilities were transferred to the Comptroller. Bank regulatory functions of the Comptroller and Secretary of State were subsequently transferred to the Banking Department headed by a Superintendent of Banking, established in 1851 (Ch. 164). No major alteration of banking policy occurred for the next seventy-five years, and the Banking Department was continued (Ch. 352, L. 1926) after the 1925 constitutional reorganization of state government.

In 1932 (Ch. 118) the Banking Board was created to advise and cooperate with the Banking Department in the formulation of banking standards and to exercise power to approve or disapprove the issuance of bank charters and licenses and the establishment of branch banks. The Superintendent of Banking is chairman and ex officio member of the Board, which consists of twelve other members appointed by the Governor for three-year terms.

At present the Department is empowered to supervise and periodically examine state banks, trust companies, safe deposit companies, licensed lenders, credit unions, private bankers, sales finance companies, certain employee welfare funds, and licensed cashers of checks. It has broad powers to enforce sound policies of bank management. The Superintendent may issue orders to discontinue unlawful or unsafe practices and may remove directors, trustees, or officers of banking institutions from their posts for repeated violations of the law or unsound practices. Under certain conditions the Superintendent may take possession of a banking institution and liquidate it for the benefit of depositors and other creditors.

Records

Account Book relative to the Circulation of Bank Notes. 1835-1843. .5 cf.

Register of Bank Note Plates by Banks. 1838-1842. .5 cf.

Ledger of Paper Money in Circulation. 1838-1854. .5 cf.

Note Register (Securities deposited for circulation notes). 1838-1840. .5 cf.

Note Register (Received and Delivered). 1838-1842, 1848-1854. .5 cf.

Registry Ledger (Notes in Circulation). 1838-1846. .5 cf.

Note Register (Notes in Circulation). 1838-1851. .5 cf.

Note Register (Bank Certificates and Orders). 1838-1847. .5 cf.

Register's Receipts of Impressions. 1839-1866. 1 cf.

Book of Orders for Bank Notes. 1839-1849. .5 cf.

Roster of Corporations. ca. 1840-1930. .5 cf.

Ledger of Protested Bank Notes. 1840-1870. .5 cf.

Register of Bank Redemption Agents. 1840-1867. .5 cf.

Registers of Stock. 1841-1868. .5 cf.

Day Book of Interest on Stocks at Banks. 1843-1870. 4 cf.

Comptroller's Ledger (Incorporated Bank Department: Letters.) 1843-1847. .5 cf.

Comptroller's Ledger of General Transactions. 1843-1849. .5 cf.

Register of Plate. 1843-1844. .5 cf.

Ledger of Expenses for Examinations. 1844-1895. .5 cf.

Note Register (Notes Delivered). 1844-1847. .5 cf.

Note Register (Received and Disposed of). 1844. .5 cf.

Bank Note Circulation Ledger. 1844. .5 cf.

Circulation Journal. 1844-1850. .5 cf.

Daybooks Relating to Sealing and Burning of Notes. 1844-1881. 12 cf.

5. Records Inventory

Records inventories are one of the most common forms of archival finding aids. They provide enough detail about the records that researchers can determine with a reasonable degree of likelihood whether the records have information on their topic. Most provide descriptive information to the box level (some are even more detailed, down to the folder level), facilitating easy access and retrieval.

The example below has been invented to illustrate the features of an inventory. It covers the imaginary records of a fictitious character, Malcolm Hayden, and is related to the account of the appraisal of those records in chapter 6.

Auburn Research Library

INVENTORY OF THE MALCOLM HAYDEN RECORDS

1993

These records were created or received by Malcolm P. Hayden (1914-1991), an Auburn artist, teacher, writer, advocate for the arts, philanthropist, and prominent supporter of Republican party candidates. The records, referred to as the "Malcolm Hayden Records," cover the period 1960-1990. They are divided into eight series comprising in total approximately 50 cubic feet.

The records were donated to the Auburn Research Library in 1992 by Phyllis Hayden-Jones, Malcolm Hayden's daughter.

These records constitute most of the extant Malcolm Hayden records. Most earlier records are believed to have been destroyed in a fire in Hayden's home in 1959. The Auburn Arts Museum holds records from Hayden's tenure as the first Chairperson of its Board of Trustees, 1975-1980.

Malcolm Hayden's career

Malcolm Hayden, born in New York City to parents who had immigrated from Britain in 1905, attended public schools where his talent as an artist was first evidenced. He later attended the Sorbonne in Paris and received his bachelor's and master's degrees from the California State College of Fine Arts. He married Marilyn Reinholdt, who later achieved distinction as a history professor, in 1935, and they had one daughter, Phyllis. Hayden's career as an artist proceeded on two tracks. As a commercial artist, he specialized in artwork for newspaper and magazine advertising, commissioned work that made him comfortably wealthy. As a portrait artist, he specialized in painting people in suburban settings. Here he created a new genre, sometimes called the Hayden School, which emphasized the variety and drama of human life in modern day suburbia. His paintings appeared in galleries around the world and were reproduced in numerous publications.

Hayden also taught creative painting at Olympia University and later at Harper State College. A prolific writer, his most famous works were Commercial Painting and the Creative Spirit (1954), Suburbia on Canvas (1962), and Artists in America (1970), which is partly autobiographical. He was a staunch conservative and prominent benefactor of the Republican party, and was even mentioned as a possible U.S. senatorial candidate in 1964. Believing that the main purpose of amassing wealth was to assist others, he gave away most of his wealth to struggling young artists, art schools, and art galleries. Hayden drowned in 1991 after falling overboard from his yacht near San Francisco.

For more information, see Brenda Laurie, Malcolm Hayden and the Development of Modern Day Art in America (Chicago: American Art Association, 1982), and Todd Stevens, A Passion for Art: The Creative Spirit of Malcolm Hayden (New York: Lithgow Press, 1985).

Scope and Contents of the Records

Hayden's pre-1960 papers were lost in a fire in 1959. The records held by Auburn Research Library cover the three decades from 1960 to 1990, but the bulk date from the period up to 1980, the year Hayden retired from teaching. Hayden was a prolific letter-writer, and his location on the West Coast, away from many of his artist friends and colleagues in New York City, encouraged an extensive correspondence. It was not uncommon for Hayden to write two or three substantial letters in a day and to include comments on his work, his teaching and affairs at the universities where he taught, art issues, other artists, politics, government policy especially in the areas of arts and culture, and personal and business matters. Frequent correspondents included Mary Hills, administrator of the New York City Art Gallery and Museum, U.S. Senator William P. Bryan, Dean William Frear of the University of Albans, Marion White, the television talk show hostess, and Timothy Connors, the prominent publisher. Because Hayden was stimulating, provocative, and strong-willed, his letters often brought thoughtful, and sometimes spirited, responses. This makes the correspondence unusually rich on arts, education, politics, popular culture, literature, and commercial art.

Hayden also maintained a detailed diary during most of his adult life, where he recorded impressions of developments in the world of culture, observations about professional colleagues, and notes on the formulation of ideas for his paintings, writings, and lectures. The diaries provide a fascinating, ongoing insight into his thoughts and creativity.

Other records pertain to the commercial aspect of Mr. Hayden's work, including sale of commercial art, paintings, and his articles and books.

There is documentation of his charitable and philanthropic activities. Hayden's concern for fostering appreciation of art in his home town is documented in records on the founding of the Auburn Arts Museum, including planning, fundraising, and chartering of the Museum.

Record Series

The Hayden Records are comprised of the following eight series:

1. Personal and Miscellaneous Correspondence, 1960-1990.

This is the largest and most diverse series. Correspondents include professional and academic colleagues, art critics, galleries, museums, publishers, radio and television celebrities, government administrators, and political leaders, expecially in the Republican party. Topics covered include commercial and artistic painting, education (particularly in the arts), government policy toward the creative arts, publishing, the careers of various individual artists, issues pertaining to art museums and galleries, politics, social problems, the news and entertainment media, particularly television, and academic affairs, especially issues at Olympia University, Harper State College, and the National Association of Professors of Creative Artistry. This series also includes correspondence between Hayden and Art for Commerce, his agent for his commercial art work.

2. Correspondence on Paintings and Exhibitions, 1960-1985.

These letters document negotiations by Hayden and his agents to have his paintings appear in galleries, museums, traveling exhibits, and other locations. The correspondence covers such topics as the importance of the paintings, audiences to which they would appeal, publicity and promotion, security, and monetary compensation. Some of the correspondence covers the outreach activities of galleries, museums, and other institutions that sought and exhibited Hayden's works, organization of school tours and visits by local art students, and press reviews of the shows. Occasionally Hayden visited exhibitions of his own works and wrote curators about the methods of exhibit and promotion or wrote his agents about how to improve exhibits in the future; these letters are included in this series. There is extensive correspondence on the New York City Art Gallery and Museum, Artists' Haven Gallery in Philadelphia, the Center for Multicultural Studies in Los Angeles, and the Institute for Suburban Studies at Dearborn University.

3. Lecture Notes, 1960-1975.

These are Hayden's handwritten and typed notes for the art and art history courses he taught at Olympia University and Harper State College, and for his numerous public lectures. The notes are generally grouped into files by course name and number or by the date, location, and title of the lecture. Marginal annotations indicate last-minute changes and additions. The course notes show how Hayden systematically developed his topics, beginning with rationales for the importance of the course and its topic, covering definitions, reviewing the best writings on the topic, setting objectives, timetables, and requirements for the course, and then proceeding methodically to cover all aspects of the topic.

4. Diaries, 1960-1990.

Hayden's diaries include at least brief entries for most days during this entire three decade period, though the entries are more infrequent and shorter during the last five years, when Hayden's health began to fail. He records the origins and development of ideas that resulted in paintings, lectures, or publications. Particularly interesting are the notes made during the process of doing a painting, where the artist records his hopes for the painting and his own reactions, reservations, frustrations, and feelings of triumph as the work progresses and is finally finished. Hayden also recorded his frank impressions of professional colleagues, fellow academicians, students, political leaders, family members, and neighbors and sometimes jotted down reactions to news events.

5. Material on Articles, Books, and Media Appearances, 1960-1980.

This series consists mostly of research notes, jottings of ideas, outlines, drafts, and final manuscripts for more than two dozen articles and three books, Suburbia on Canvas (1962), Artists in America (1970), and the less well known Arts and Politics (1975). There are also transcripts for radio and television "talk shows" where Hayden was interviewed or was a featured guest. The series also includes several scrapbooks of newspaper and magazine clippings with information on Hayden and his career. Also included are notes Hayden made after each "talk show" appearance with his reflections on the questions that were asked and his critique of his presentation.

6. Philanthropic Activities and Donations, 1965-1985.

In 1965, Hayden began making donations to what he regarded as worthy causes. This series consists of letters from dozens of individuals and institutions seeking donations and assistance, Hayden's return letters (mostly denials), his correspondence to colleagues to help identify worthy causes, correspondence covering the making of grants and donations, information on income tax deductions for charitable contributions, political contributions, and account books documenting payments. Also included are thank-you letters from recipients of Hayden's support and a few reports on how the funds were used. There is extensive information on Hayden's relations with the Center for Struggling Artists in Atlanta, Art-To-The-People in St. Louis, and the National Coalition for Art Education in Washington.

7. Political Correspondence, 1960-1979.

This series includes letters to and from prominent Republican political leaders on the national, state, and local levels. Hayden was very interested in many aspects of political life, and his correspondence reflects this diversity of interests. There is extensive information on campaign strategies, national issues such as poverty, civil rights, women's rights, and the war in Vietnam; on state issues such as water management, highway construction, education, and medical care; and on local issues including transportation, parks, and cultural policy. There is also correspondence on fundraising and on Hayden's numerous donations to Republican candidates for office. The series also includes several files on the short-lived "Hayden for U.S. Senator" movement in 1964.

8. Records on Planning and Development of the Auburn Arts Museum, 1970-1975.

Hayden served as Chair of the Citizens' Committee that developed the proposal for creation of an Arts Museum in Auburn. Included are minutes of the Committee's meetings, information gathered on arts museums in other cities, transcripts of citizens' comments at several "town meetings" sponsored by the Committee, correspondence, records on fundraising and grants, and draft versions and final versions of reports.

Box Listing

The fifty cubic feet of Hayden records are included in seventy records cartons, as follows:

1. Personal and Miscellaneous Correspondence, 1960-1990

Box number:

1. Correspondence, 1960-1961.
2. Correspondence, 1962-1963.
3. Correspondence, 1964-1965.
4. Correspondence, 1966-1967.
5. Correspondence, 1968-1969.
6. Correspondence, 1970-1972.
7. Correspondence, 1973-1976.
8. Correspondence, 1977-1981.
9. Correspondence, 1982-1986.
10. Correspondence, 1987-1990.

[Box listings for Series 2 - 7 omitted from example to save space]

8. Records on Planning and Development of Auburn Arts Museum, 1970-1975

Box Number:

66. Flyers, brochures, and other information on arts museums in other cities, 1970-1971.
67. Correspondence regarding development of the Arts Museum, 1970-1973.

Inventory of Malcolm Hayden Records

68. Transcripts and notes on public meetings pertaining to Museum, 1974.
69. Correspondence regarding development of the Arts Museum, 1973-1975.
70. Reports of Citizens' Committee on planning Auburn Arts Museum, 1974-1975.

Bibliography

This bibliography attempts to include the most important periodicals and major publications on modern American archival affairs. It does not include each journal article used in the book; these are cited in the footnotes. Nor does it include booklets, brochures, finding aids, audiovisual productions, and other materials produced by individual programs, since these are too numerous to mention.

Periodicals

American Archivist. Society of American Archivists.
Archivaria: The Journal of the Association of Canadian Archivists. Association of Canadian Archivists.
Archivum. International Council on Archives.
ARMA Records Management Quarterly. Association of Records Managers and Administrators.
Midwestern Archivist. Midwest Archives Conference.
NAGARA Clearinghouse. Quarterly newsletter. National Association of Government Archives and Records Administrators.
Prologue: Journal of the National Archives and Records Administration. National Archives and Records Administration.
Provenance. (Formerly *Georgia Archive*). Society of Georgia Archivists.
Public Historian: A Journal of Public History. National Council on Public History.
SAA Newsletter. Quarterly newsletter. Society of American Archivists.

Books and Manuals

Archives and Records Programs and Historical Records Repositories in North Carolina: An Analysis of Present Problems and Future Needs. Raleigh: North Carolina Division of Archives and History, 1983.

Arizona State Historical Records Advisory Board. *Preserving Arizona's Historical Records: The Final Report of the Arizona Records Needs and Assessment Project.* Phoenix: Department of Library, Archives, and Public Records, 1983.

Barton, John P., et al. *An Ounce of Prevention: A Handbook on Disaster Contingency Planning for Archives, Libraries, and Record Centres.* Toronto: Toronto Area Archivists' Group, 1985.

Baumann, Roland, ed. *A Manual of Archival Techniques,* rev. ed. Harrisburg: Pennsylvania Historical and Museum Commission, 1982.

Bearman, David, ed. *Archives and Museum Informatics Technical Reports.* Pittsburgh: Archives and Museum Informatics, various dates.

Bellardo, Lynn Lady and Lewis Bellardo. *The Glossary of Archivists, Manuscript Curators, and Records Managers.* Chicago: Society of American Archivists, 1992.

Bennis, Warren and Burt Nanus. *Leaders: The Strategies for Taking Charge.* New York: Harper and Row, 1985.

Berner, Richard C. *Historical Theory and Practice in the United States: A Historical Analysis.* Seattle: University of Washington Press, 1983.

Boomgaarden, Wesley L., ed. *Preservation Planning Program Resource Notebook.* Washington: Association of Research Libraries, 1987.

Boorstin, Daniel. *Hidden History.* New York: Harper and Row, 1987.

Bordin, Ruth B. and Robert M. Warner. *The Modern Manuscript Library.* New York: Scarecrow Press, 1966.

Boyatzis, Richard E. *The Competent Manager: A Model for Effective Performance.* New York: John Wiley and Sons, 1982.

Bradsher, James G., ed. *Managing Archives and Archival Institutions.* Chicago: University of Chicago Press, 1989.

Brichford, Maynard. *Archives and Manuscripts: Appraisal and Accessioning.* Chicago: Society of American Archivists, 1977.

Brooks, Philip C. *Research in Archives: The Use of Unpublished Primary Sources.* Chicago: University of Chicago Press, 1969.

Bruemmer, Bruce and Sheldon Hochheiser. *The High-Tech Company: An Historical Research and Archival Guide.* Chicago: Charles Babbage Institute, 1989.

Calmes, Alan, Ralph Shafer, and Keith R. Eberhardt. *National Archives and Records Service Twenty-Year Preservation Plan.* Gaithersburg, Md.: National Bureau of Standards, 1985.

Casterline, Gail Farr. *Archives and Manuscripts: Exhibits.* Chicago: Society of American Archivists, 1980.

Caudle, Sharon L., Donald Marchand, et al. *Managing Information Resources: New Directions in State Government—A National Study of State Government Information Resources Management.* Syracuse: Syracuse University School of Information Studies, 1989.

Clark, Robert L. Jr., ed. *Archive–Library Relations.* New York: R.R. Bowker Company, 1976.

Cleveland, Harland. *The Knowledge Executive: Leadership in an Information Society.* New York: Truman Talley Books, 1985.

Commission on Preservation and Access. *Brittle Books: Report of the Committee on Preservation and Access*. Washington: Council on Library Resources, 1986.

Committee on the Records of Government. *Report*. Washington: Committee on the Records of Government, 1985.

Consultative Group on Canadian Archives. *Canadian Archives: Report to the Social Sciences and Humanities Research Council of Canada*. Ottawa: Social Sciences and Humanities Research Council of Canada, 1980.

Cook, Michael. *The Management of Information from Archives*. Brookfield, Vt.: Gower Publishing, 1988.

Cunha, George Martin and Dorothy Grant Cunha. *Library and Archives Conservation: 1980s and Beyond*, 2 vols. Metuchen, N.J.: Scarecrow Press, 1983.

Daniels, Maygene and Timothy Walch, eds. *A Modern Archives Reader: Basic Readings on Archival Theory and Practice*. Washington: National Archives Trust Fund Board, 1984.

Darling, Pamela W. and Duane E. Webster. *Preservation Planning Program: An Assisted Self-Study Manual for Libraries*. Washington: Association of Research Libraries, 1982.

Dearstyne, Bruce W. *The Management of Local Government Records: A Guide for Local Officials*. Nashville: American Association for State and Local History, 1988.

————, ed. *Archives and Public History: Issues, Problems, and Prospects*. Special Issue of *Public Historian* 8 (Summer 1986).

Deiss, William A. *Museum Archives: An Introduction*. Chicago: Society of American Archivists, 1983.

Drucker, Peter F. *Management: Tasks, Responsibilities, Practices*. New York: Harper and Row, 1974.

————. *Managing in Turbulent Times*. New York: Harper and Row, 1980.

Duckett, Kenneth W. *Modern Manuscripts: A Practical Manual for Their Management, Care, and Use*. Nashville: American Association for State and Local History, 1975.

Ehrenberg, Ralph H. *Archives and Manuscripts: Maps and Architectural Drawings*. Chicago: Society of American Archivists, 1982.

Elliott, Philip. *The Sociology of Professions*. New York: Herder and Herder, 1972.

Espy, Siri N. *Handbook of Strategic Planning for Nonprofit Organizations*. New York: Praeger, 1986.

Etzioni, Amitai. *The Semi-Professions and Their Organization: Teachers, Nurses, Social Workers*. New York: Free Press, 1969.

Evans, Max J. and Lisa B. Weber. *MARC for Archives and Manuscripts: A Compendium of Practice*. Chicago: Society of American Archivists, 1985.

Final Report of the California State Archives Assessment Project. Sacramento: Office of the Secretary of State, 1983.

Fleckner, John. *Archives and Manuscripts: Surveys*. Chicago: Society of American Archivists, 1977.

————. *Native American Archives: An Introduction*. Chicago: Society of American Archivists, 1984.

Geller, Sidney B. *Care and Handling of Computer Magnetic Storage Media*. Washington: National Bureau of Standards, 1983.

Gilliand, Anne J., ed. *Automating Intellectual Access to Archives*. Special Issue of *Library Trends*, Winter 1988.

Gracy, David B., II. *Archives and Manuscripts: Description*. Chicago: Society of American Archivists, 1977.

———. *An Introduction to Archives and Manuscripts*. New York: Special Libraries Association, 1981.

Gwinn, Nancy E., ed. *Preservation Microfilming: A Guide for Librarians and Archivists*. Chicago: American Library Association, 1987.

Haas, Joan K., Helen Wila Samuels, and Barbara Trippel Simmons. *Appraising the Records of Modern Science and Technology: A Guide*. Cambridge: Massachusetts Institute of Technology, 1985.

Ham, F. Gerald. *Selecting and Appraising Archives and Manuscripts*. Chicago: Society of American Archivists, forthcoming.

Hammond, Jay M., ed. *Utah Records Needs Assessment Project: A Report to the People on the Management of Historical Records*. Salt Lake City: Utah State Archives and Records Service, 1985.

Hedstrom, Margaret L. *Archives and Manuscripts: Machine-Readable Records*. Chicago: Society of American Archivists, 1984.

Hensen, Steven, comp. *Archives, Personal Papers, and Manuscripts: A Cataloging Manual for Archival Repositories, Historical Societies, and Manuscript Libraries*. Chicago: Society of American Archivists, 1989.

Hickerson, H. Thomas. *Archives and Manuscripts: An Introduction to Automated Access*. Chicago: Society of American Archivists, 1981.

Historical Records in Massachusetts: A Survey and Assessment. Boston: State Historical Records Advisory Board, 1983.

Historical Records in Minnesota. St. Paul: Minnesota State Historical Society, 1983.

Holbert, Sue E. *Archives and Manuscripts: Reference and Access*. Chicago: Society of American Archivists, 1977.

Jackson, Eugene B., ed. *Special Librarianship: A New Reader*. Metuchen, New Jersey: Scarecrow Press, 1980.

Jenkinson, Hiliary. *A Manual of Archival Administration,* rev. ed. London: Percy, Lund, Humphries and Co., 1965.

Joint Committee on Archives of Science and Technology. *Understanding Progress as Process: Documentation of the History Post-War Science and Technology in the United States*. Chicago: Society of American Archivists, 1983.

Jones, H. G. *Local Government Records: An Introduction to Their Management, Preservation, and Use*. Nashville: American Association for State and Local History, 1980.

Kanter, Rosabeth M. *The Change Masters: Innovation for Productivity in the American Corporation*. New York: Simon and Schuster, 1983.

Kesner, Richard. *Information Systems: A Strategic Approach to Planning and Implementation*. Chicago: American Library Association, 1988.

Kouzes, James M. and Barry Z. Posner. *The Leadership Challenge: How to Get Extraordinary Things Done in Organizations*. San Francisco: Jossey-Bass, 1987.

Kyvig, David E. and Myron E. Marty. *Nearby History*. Nashville: American Association for State and Local History, 1982.

Lynch, Beverly P., ed. *Management Strategies for Libraries: A Basic Reader*. New York: Neal-Schuman, 1985.

Lytle, Richard H, ed. *Management of Archives and Manuscripts Collections for Librarians*. Chicago: Society of American Archivists, 1980. Reprinted from *Drexel Library Quarterly* 11 (January 1975).

Marchand, Donald A. and F. Woody Horton. *Infotrends*. New York: John Wiley, 1986.

Maedke, Wilmer O., Mary F. Robek, and Gerald F. Brown. *Information and Records Management*. Encino, Calif.: Glencoe, 1981.

Matters, Marion, ed. *Automated Records and Techniques in Archives: A Resource Directory*. Chicago: Society of American Archivists, 1990.

McCarthy, Paul H., ed. *Archives Assessment and Planning Workbook*. Chicago: Society of American Archivists, 1989.

McCoy, Donald. *The National Archives: America's Ministry of Documents, 1934–1968*. Chapel Hill: University of North Carolina Press, 1978.

McCrank, Lawrence J., ed. *Archives and Library Administration: Divergent Traditions and Common Concerns*. New York: Haworth Press, 1986.

Metcalf, Fay D. and Matthew T. Downey. *Using Local History in the Classroom*. Nashville: American Association for State and Local History, 1982.

Miller, Frederic M. *Arranging and Describing Archives and Manuscripts*. Chicago: Society of American Archivists, 1991.

Mitchell, Thornton W., ed. *Norton on Archives: The Writings of Margaret Cross Norton on Archival and Records Management*. Carbondale, Ill.: Southern Illinois University Press, 1975.

Moss, William. *Oral History Program Manual*. New York: Praeger, 1974.

Muller, S., J. A. Feith, and R. Fruin. *Manual for the Arrangement and Description of Archives*. Translated by A. H. Leavitt. New York: H. W. Wilson, 1940.

Munden, Ken, ed. *Archives and the Public Interest: Selected Essays by Ernest Posner*. Washington: Public Affairs Press, 1967.

Naisbitt, John and Patricia Arburdene. *Megatrends 2000*. New York: William Morrow and Co., 1990.

National Academy of Public Administration. *The Effects of Electronic Recordkeeping on the Historical Record of the U.S. Government*. Washington: National Academy of Public Administration, 1989.

National Archives and Records Administration. *A Federal Records Management Glossary*. Washington: National Archives and Records Administration, 1989.

————. *Managing Electronic Records*. Washington: National Archives and Records Administration, 1990.

National Association of Government Archives and Records Administrators. *Guide and Resources for Archival Strategic Preservation Planning*.

Albany: National Association of Government Archives and Records Administrators, 1991.

———. *Preservation Needs in State Archives*. Albany: National Association of Government Archives and Records Administrators, 1986.

———. *Program Reporting Guidelines for Government Records Programs*. Lexington, Ky.: Council of State Governments, 1987.

National Coordinating Committee for the Promotion of History. *Developing a Premier National Institution: A Report from the User Community to the National Archives*. Washington: National Coordinating Committee for the Promotion of History, 1989.

National Historical Publications and Records Commission. *Directory of Archives and Manuscript Repositories in the United States,* 2nd ed. New York: Oryx Press, 1988.

———. *Electronic Records Issues: A Report to the Commission*. Washington: National Historical Publications and Records Commission, 1990.

National Research Council. *Preservation of Historical Records*. Washington: National Academy Press, 1986.

New York State Archives and Records Administration. *A Strategic Plan for Managing and Preserving Electronic Records in New York State Government: Final Report of the Special Media Records Project*. Albany: New York State Education Department, 1988.

———. *Strengthening New York's Historical Records Programs: A Self-Study Guide*. Albany: New York State Education Department, 1988.

New York State Historical Records Advisory Board. *Toward a Usable Past: Historical Records in the Empire State*. Albany: New York State Education Department, 1984.

O'Toole, James M. *Understanding Archives and Manuscripts*. Chicago: Society of American Archivists, 1991.

Peace, Nancy E. *Archival Choices: Managing the Historical Record in the Age of Abundance*. Lexington, Mass.: D.C. Heath and Company, 1984.

Pederson, Ann, ed. *Keeping Archives*. Sydney, Australia: Australian Society of Archivists, Inc., 1987.

——— and Gail Farr Casterline. *Archives and Manuscripts: Public Programs*. Chicago: Society of American Archivists, 1982.

Penn, Ira A., et al. *Records Management Handbook*. Brookfield, Vt.: Gower Publishing, 1989.

Peters, Tom. *Thriving on Chaos: Handbook for a Management Revolution*. New York: Alfred A. Knopf, 1987.

Peterson, Gary M. and Trudy Huskamp Peterson. *Archives and Manuscripts: Law*. Chicago: Society of American Archivists, 1984.

Public and Private Record Repositories in Virginia: A Needs Assessment Report. Richmond: Virginia State Library, 1983.

Pugh, Mary Jo. *Providing Reference Services for Archives and Manuscripts*. Chicago: Society of American Archivists, forthcoming.

Raelin, Joseph A. *The Clash of Cultures: Managers and Professionals*. Cambridge: Harvard University Business School Press, 1986.

Research Issues in Electronic Records. St. Paul, Minn.: Minnesota Historical Society for the National Historical Publications and Records Commission, 1991.

Ritzenthaler, Mary Lynn. *Archives and Manuscripts: Conservation*. Chicago: Society of American Archivists, 1983.

———. *Preserving Archives and Manuscripts*. Chicago: Society of American Archivists, forthcoming.

———, Gerald Munoff, and Margery S. Long. *Archives and Manuscripts: Administration of Photographic Collections*. Chicago: Society of American Archivists, 1984.

Roe, Kathleen. *Guidelines for Arrangement and Description of Archives and Manuscripts: A Manual for Historical Records Programs in New York State*. Albany: New York State Education Department, 1991.

———. *Teaching with Historical Records*. Albany: New York State Education Department, 1981.

Saffady, William. *Optical Disk Systems for Records Management*. Prairie Village, Kans.: Association of Records Managers and Administrators, Inc., 1988.

Sahli, Nancy. *MARC for Archives and Manuscripts: The AMC Format*. Chicago: Society of American Archivists, 1985. Updated periodically thereafter.

Schellenberg, Theodore R. *The Management of Archives*. New York: Columbia University Press, 1965.

———. *Modern Archives: Principles and Techniques*. Chicago: University of Chicago Press, 1956.

Social Research, Inc. *The Image of Archivists: Resource Allocators' Perceptions*. Chicago: Society of American Archivists, 1984.

Society of American Archivists, Task Force on Goals and Priorities. *Planning for the Archival Profession: A Report of the SAA Task Force on Goals and Priorities*. Chicago: Society of American Archivists, 1986.

———, Working Group on Standards for Archival Description. *Archival Descriptive Standards: Establishing a Process for Their Development and Implementation*. Chicago: Society of American Archivists, 1990.

Stielow, Frederick J. *The Management of Oral History and Sound Archives*. Westport, Conn.: Greenwood Press, 1986.

Stout, Leon J. *Historical Records in Pennsylvania: An Assessment Report for the State Historical Records Advisory Board*. Harrisburg: Pennsylvania Historical and Museum Commission, 1983.

Sung, Carolyn Hoover. *Archives and Manuscripts: Reprography*. Chicago: Society of American Archivists, 1982.

Thomas, Violet S., Dexter R. Schubert, and JoAnn Lee. *Records Management: Systems and Administration*. New York: Wiley and Sons, 1983.

Toffler, Alvin. *Power Shift: Knowledge, Wealth, and Violence at the Edge of the 21st Century*. New York: Bantam Books, 1990.

Treasury Board of Canada. *Management of Government Information Holdings*. Ottawa: Treasury Board of Canada, 1989.

Viola, Herman J. *The National Archives of the United States*. New York: Harry N. Abrams, 1984.

Vollmer, Howard M. and Donald L. Mills, eds. *Professionalization*. Engelwood Cliffs, N.J.: Prentice Hall, 1966.

Walch, Timothy. *Archives and Manuscripts: Security*. Chicago: Society of American Archivists, 1977.

Walch, Victoria Irons. *Information Resources for Archivists and Records Administrators: A Report and Recommendations*. Albany: National Association of Government Archives and Records Administrators, 1987.

Weber, Lisa, ed. *Documenting America: Assessing the Condition of Historical Records in the States*. Albany: National Association of State Archives and Records Administrators, 1984.

Whalen, Lucille, ed. *Reference Services in Archives*. New York: Haworth Press, 1986.

Wilsted, Thomas and William Nolte. *Managing Archival and Manuscript Repositories*. Chicago: Society of American Archivists, 1991.

Wisconsin State Historical Records Advisory Board. *Planning to Preserve Wisconsin's History: The Archival Perspective*. Madison: State Historical Society of Wisconsin, 1983.

Index

Bruce W. Dearstyne is director of External Programs at the New York State Archives and Records Administration and executive director of the National Association of Government Archives and Records Administrators. For many years he has directed programs to improve the care and management of historical records. A fellow of the Society of American Archivists and a Certified Archivist, he is a frequent speaker at professional meetings and has written extensively on archives and records management. Dearstyne has also taught a course in archives in the history department at the State University of New York at Albany.